MING SU

Ming Su

A DAUGHTER'S JOURNEY

Danel Lee

Kempriam Publishing

INTRODUCTION

After the middle of the 19th Century an influx of over 30,000 East Asian citizens from mainland China, Hong Kong, Macau, Singapore and Taiwan, along with other Chinese Diaspora immigrated to the San Francisco Bay area to escape their hardship, in search for their fortune in gold throughout the American North-Western Territories. Many fathers, sons and brothers convinced their families of a better way of life when they return to China. In desperation they sold off family heirlooms, livestock and other valuables to raise the money to pay for the long sea voyage across the Pacific. Never to be seen again.

However, those who did return not too long after the California Gold Rush did fulfill their promise to their families while others barely discovered enough gold to pay their way back home. California was not the only American North-Western Territory producing gold. There was also Washington, Nevada and Oregon. But most of all was the Idaho Territory. A new town about forty miles North of Boise had quickly become the site for professional and amateur gold prospectors from all over the world to flourish to. Bannock City, Idaho quickly became one of the largest gold producing territory of its time.

Needless to say, the great news traveled to China once again filling more hearts with dreams of becoming rich, or perhaps the opportunity to live beyond their accustomed poverty, attracting more Chinese immigrants to voyage to America. Nonetheless, the dreams that America held for the Chinese immigrants also created nightmares for the young wives and children who immigrated to America. To many, rumors became reality when they learned that over 80% of women and many children in San Francisco were turned out into a violent life of prostitution, abuse and usually an untimely death. America was no place for a young Chinese girl to be safe.

A NOTE TO READER

As the author or Ming Su, A Daughters' Journey, I tried to keep the story as real as possible to the Chinese culture, the American culture and the American Indian culture of the 19th Century.

I felt that Ming Su, A Daughter's Journey would be better understood if I wrote the three different languages in English. Realistically the three cultures did have their own languages.

However, I felt that it would be unrealistic to have written English in English, Chinese in Chinese and American Indian in American Indian. Simply because of the extensive research that I would have had to have done not to mention that I would have to anticipate every reader to know and understand all three languages. I hope that you enjoy Ming Su, A Daughter's Journey...

Thank you for your understanding... Danel Lee

1

The morning mist began to slowly burn off from the late spring sun climbing from the depths of the Eastern Chinese horizon to the open sky. Black silhouettes of the mighty trees found their colors of evergreen and brown as the dawn was quickly turning into day. Mountain tops looked as if they were floating on white fluffs of cotton. The forest came alive with the sounds of life. Birds of many species sang their morning songs and called out to one another as if they were sending morning greeting and welcoming others of their kind to the new day. Squirrels and other rodents scurried through the damp leaves, brush and grass in search for their first meal of the day. Occasionally warning one another of danger that may be lurking in the bushes, tall grass or even high above in the trees and the sky. Crickets rubbed their damp hind legs together to remove moister and dirt with the intent to improve their hearing. Little flying bugs gathered in groups, buzzing around frantically within the warmth of the sunbeams like thousands of little fighter planes in a midair dog fight. While the predators of the sky soar high above the treetops with their binocular vision, focusing in on an unfortunate rodent such as a mouse, squirrel or even little snake slithering along the ground. Their only motive is to swoop from high above, driving their talons into their unsuspected prey.

The morning dew that accumulated throughout the night dripped from the leaves of the mighty trees and the vegetation that covered the Earth's floor, forming puddles, nature's way of providing hydration for the indigenous wildlife.

The presence from an unfamiliar threat spooked a flock of birds, encouraging them to frantically vacate their perches and scurrying above the mountain fog. Unintentionally, signaling a herd of spooked deer sensing the threat deep within their hearts and bones and forcing the herd to run from potential danger.

Within moments the frightening presence of an unwelcomed guest secretly emerged from the deep Chinese forest.

A frightened Chinese girl about the age of ten ran along a trail with all her speed and might. Her gray dress hemmed slightly above the knees restricted the full pace as she ran to escape the pursuing predator. Her feet and ankles covered with mud as she splashed through the small shallow puddles formed from the mist, mountain dew and rain. Her ankles took a whipping with almost every step that slapped against the large fern leaves covering the edges of the trail and much of the forest floor. Leaving many small lacerations and the scent of blood for the pursuing creature's nose to follow as it pursued its morning meal.

Having never been that deep into the forest the girl unexpectedly ran directly into an enormous spider web covered with millions of water droplets that stretched between two trees and unexpectedly crossing the trail. With no time to think the girl began to scream uncontrollably while spinning and wrapping herself into a webbed balloon forcing the water droplets to drench the frighten prey. She forced herself to break away from the silk web and regain her strut away from the pursuing beast.

Quickly she began to tire. Her breathing became heavy and fast paced. Tears filled her eyes, forming muddy streams on both cheeks of built-up dirt and sweat. The frightening growls and pounding of the predator's feet became louder as the enormous cat gained ground on the frightened child. Her pace slowed as she approached a large, downed tree with a diameter over half her height. Quickly she climbed over the log and hid on the other side. Forming herself in the fetal position, she covered her ears with her hands and closed her eyes as the growls and grunts of the hungry predator got closer and closer. Suddenly she felt the weight of the animal as its foot landed on the log.

With fear and curiosity overtaking her heart and mind she opened her eyes to watch the heavy beast meet its demise as it plummeted down on a bed of carved wood spears protruding up from the black mud expending a loud roar of gravely pain.

The girl laid there sobbing as a moment passed, balled up watching the hunters' eyes slowly close as it took its last breath of life before her fear was interrupted by an older boy jumping from the brush, cheering, laughing and dancing to a non-existing musical beat. The young girl slapped her hand down in a puddle of gathered mist and rain, quickly jumping to her feet, running to the older boy, throwing her arms around his waist and resting her face against his belly. She sobbed in fear and relief as she looked at the dead animals' orange back with black stripes and red blood spreading out onto the forest floor. With a frustrated scream, she let go and pushed the boy away to scold him. "You are crazy to make me do that, I almost died. What would you have done then? You would have to go to America by yourself to find father." The boy shook his head with a big smile, bent down and picked the girl up, held her in his arms and began to dance around in joy. Then he said. "But you did it Su, you did it. I could have never done this without you, you should be so overly proud of yourself. This tiger will get us the money to go to America." The young girl still in a state of shock didn't know whether to laugh or cry as she held the boy tight.

The boy set Ming Su down then pulled an old curved hunting knife from its sheath fastened to his hip and stated. "I have to gut this thing before the meat spoils. Go fetch the cart from behind the bushes and help me load this beast onto it." Ming Su slowly walked around the defeated predator, keeping her teary eyes locked on it with hopes that it would not jump to life and devour her and the boy. She turned and watched the boy once she got in front of the head of the tiger as he pulled the wooden spikes from the muddy forest floor around the enormous cat. The boy looked at his frightened little sister. "Hurry, we don't have much time. We still have a long, long walk ahead of us and we want the meat to still be warm when we deliver it to the market to show that it is a fresh kill." Ming Su turned to retrieve the cart while the boy rolled the 340 pound cat with every bit of energy that he possessed within him to pull two impaired wooden spikes from its underside. When Ming Su returned, she witnessed the gruesome task of her brother removing the internal organs from the slit that he cut into the belly and chest of the tiger. She covered her nose with her hand, trying not to smell the stench coming from the beast. But the smell was too vile to ingest for Ming Su, she turned and began to choke up dry heaves from her empty stomach. The young duo fought and struggled with every bit of strength that they had to load the enormous tiger onto the two wheeled cart. Adjusting the tiger around was a challenge in itself so that the balance of the cart would be equal and easier to manage

The journey from the deep forest to the market had just begun as they struggled up and down the muddy trail. The day hadn't even turned to midday when Ming Su began to complain of her arms and legs aching. Hai noticed out of the corner of his eye a large shrub sprouting the sweet, tart tasting Bayberry. He cried out to Ming Su to stop for a break and to pick bayberries from the little branches.

The siblings sat on the damp ground enjoying the sweet and tart snack, leaving a pleasant taste in their mouths, an empty space filled in their bellies and some renewed energy that was probably a combination of the bayberries, rest and a sense of satisfaction. Nonetheless Hai was not willing to waste any more time to allow the tiger meat to spoil. Ming Su was left with no choice but to get up and push the cart with the heavy tiger once again.

The slow, strenuous journey seemed to last forever for the duo as they made their five mile march. Ming Su pushed on the back of the cart as the boy pulled from the front, along the muddy trail, through the slow-moving creek and the grassy field onto the dirt road and into the village. The sun had descended, and the bodies of the duo were exhausted by the time they reached the market. People gathered around in amazement as the cart came to a halt in front of a little building made of dried mud, rough stone and wood. A Chinese man who appeared to be in his early sixties, smoking a long wood pipe came from behind the structure. "I know you, you Fong Yeo kid, Hai. I hear that he go to America."

"I believe so Mr. Ping."

"But your mother had passed away I heard. Who is looking after you now?" Hai shook his head as he looked at Ming Su. "Nobody Mr. Ping, it's just my sister Su and I."

"Su, is that your name?" She replied. "My name is Ming Su but my brother just recently started calling me Su, I think he calls me that because he is getting lazy in his old age and I feel more mature in my younger age." Ping laughed as Hai butted in. "Mr. Ping if you don't mind, we would like to sell this tiger to you so we can have the money to sail on the junk to America in search for father and be a family again." Ping looked over the tiger lying in the cart, twisted and balled up with its tail dragging. He stated. "It has lots of hole on its belly, not too good for selling the fur." Ming Su replied sarcastically. "It only has two, but feel, it was killed today, real good meat and the holes are only on the belly of the tiger." The man took a puff from his pipe, looked over the tiger again and said. "Wow Hai, you have a feisty young sister there. Too bad Chinese women must keep their mouth shut, including her. But I will tell you what. I'll pay you market value and give the little girl a new dress and straw sandals since her bare feet are covered with mud and blood." Hai replied with a tone. "Yeah, it's well worth market value plus the dress and slippers considering what we went through to get this beast here." The old man laughed and said. "Okay, okay." Ming Su looked at Hai and then at the old man and said. "And two claws as trophies for us two, we killed it, we get trophies." The old man nodded with a grunt sound. Bickering as he walked back inside to fetch a big wooden box. "Little girl too smart for her own good, got to have two claws as trophies. She is breaking into my profit." When he returned he scurried through the toolbox that he set on the ground to find the right tool to properly remove the claws. He picked up the paw of the cat and pulled one claw, then a second right before he handed them both to Ming Su.

As the siblings walked away Ming Su was lost in amazement when she chuckled. "Wow! Did you hear Mr. Ping's worker? He said that deer and boar are way below market value. Why so much for the tiger?" Hai laughed. "You will learn my young sister, you will learn... Remember father was telling us about the tiger? Lots of wimps in our village that are too afraid to hunt a deadly beast." Ming Su snarled. "And we are the only dumb people to."

"But look at the money we made in just one day's work, but anyways Su. Father was explaining to us that with the rush to raise money to get to America, most of the local merchants no longer wanted deer or boar. Nobody was buying the meat. The price per pound was at an all-time low. The merchants may not want deer or boar, but father knew that they would want a mighty cat. Its claws can make jewelry, its pelt will make clothing and its meat will fill many bellies, the bones will be used to make much wine and medicine and if it is a male, the reproductive organ will sell for a great price to enhance the buyer's sexual performance."

"Sexual performance, what does that mean?"

"Ah, let's not worry about that right now. But father left that night and never returned but those thoughts stayed in my head and today it finally paid off."

"I cannot believe that he left for America without us. He has no right to call me his daughter anymore, he abandoned us."

"Don't fret my young sister, tonight is a time of celebration and then tomorrow we will board the ship to America." Ming Su and her brother stared at each other and smiled. Hai whispered. "We will find father but perhaps we will find gold too."

2

...Later Ming Su sat crunched up in a wood half barrel that once whole contained an intoxicating beverage as it aged to the proper fermentation. The room temperature water quickly became tinted with mud, blood and sweat to a brown dark whiskey color as she scooped it up with her hands and splashed it onto her young flawless face to rinse of the soap and filth. Brother sat on the other side of a petition made of wood, bamboo and twine to give privacy to his sister as they shared in conversation and reflected on the exhausting day while a single candle gave illumination to the small one room square home that was constructed of dried mud, rough stones, and wood. The thatch roof was made of straw and reed bundles supported by wooden poles. The only door constructed of wood. Around the back side of the house was a small empty corral constructed of wooden poles with a gate hinged with rope as it was secured as well. Dirt and mud surrounded the little home while a nearby stream provided water for consumption, cleaning and bathing.

Ming Su asked her brother in a soft tender innocent voice. "Do you think that we will find father when we get to America?" Hai let a breath out through his nose. "I really don't know Su. He left so abruptly and showed very little compassion when he did that, I am not so sure that he wants us to find him."

"What is compassion mean?"

"Care, it means "care" Su. Father showed very little care ever since mother died from her sickness and I don't think that he cares for us now Su, I'm sorry." Ming Su sat silently in her water of mud, blood and sweat as tears ran down her cheeks. A moment of joy filled her memory, encouraging her to smile as her mind wandered.

...Ming Su sat on a rickety wooden produce crate as a Chinese woman knelt behind her in the flickering candlelight with a brush clinched in her right hand, brushing the long ebony hair of her young daughter. She set the brush down and removed a thin silver chained necklace from her own neck that a star pendant of sparkling silver hung from. Mother lowered the pendant in front of Ming Su's face as her eyes opened wide, knowing exactly what it was. Mother pulled the silver chain over her daughters' head and lifted her freshly brushed ebony hair over it, hiding the chain between her hair and her neck...

Ming Su turned her head to her right where her dirty, bloody dress laid on the floor and the silver chain and pendant sat absorbing and reflecting the candlelight that turned them into sparkles. She reached for a cloth lying beside it on the floor to cover herself as she stood from the filthy water. She tucked the end of the cloth within itself to keep it from falling to the floor then bent down and picked up the necklace to hold it up as the star reflected in her eye. Slowly and carefully, she slid it over her head as she sniffled and said. "I miss you mother."

Brother remained sitting on the short three-legged stool made of Asian pine. He extended his arm out for Ming Su to see the new dress hanging from his finger. Ming Su's face lit up at the sight of the lavender colored dress. She stepped over to it to take it from her brother's hand as she whispered. "I can't believe this is for me Hai, it is so pretty." Hai sat smiling with pride as he whispered back. "You are the one who will make that dress look pretty." Ming Su stood in front of the cracked looking glass, holding the dress against her with a smile glowing on her face.

Hai allowed his little sister to enjoy the moment as he sat and listened to her giggle with joy. Then he said to her. "Save the pretty dress for tomorrow and slip into your sleep clothes. I will go prepare supper after I put medicine on the cuts that are all over your feet and legs. We don't want them to get infected"

"You should really bathe yourself first."

"No, I will be fine Su. I still have many chores and you must eat. You had such a long hard day, and your energy is down. I will empty the tub shortly; I do it much faster than you."

Ming Su sat on a mat playing with a small wooden horse carved from wood. Reflecting on the stories she heard from her father about the wild horses that ran free in America. She made the wood horse gallop across the mat within the loose grasp of her tiny fingers. Brother called to her. "I have supper ready for us." He set two bowls made of pottery on to a table that sat close to the floor and sat on one side as Ming Su sat on the other. Hai watched his little sister consume the rice and vegetables like she had never eaten before. He said to her with a grin. "You should slow down a little; I don't want you to upset your stomach." Ming Su's chewing slowed as she looked into her brother's eye before setting the chopsticks down on the top of her bowl to ask in a soft voice. "How long will it take to get to America?" Brother shook his head and replied. "I don't really know Su; I don't even know if Father made it there yet either."

"Will there be a lot of people on the big boat?"

"It is called a junk, Su. There will be very many but stay right by my side and hold my hand anytime that you feel scared or uncomfortable. I will always be there for you. Now finish your food. We have a long walk to the dock in the morning. I will help you pack before we leave but we must take only what we need so we can travel light. We will get prepared food on the junk to eat as we travel across the ocean but I have heard as the days go by, the smell of other people, rotting food and people waste is going to leave a terrible odor on the big boat and I don't know how long that will be until we get to America, but most of all, always stay by me."

"Will we be able to bathe?"

"Probably not, we will have to wait until we get to America. Now, that's enough with the questions. Finish eating your food and get some sleep. I will wake you in the early morning when it is time." Ming Su looked deep into her brother's eyes and asked. "You would not leave me like father did?" Hai scooted himself around the table on his hands while shuffling his legs, he wrapped his arms around his sister, shook his head and replied. "Not a chance."

Hai stood 5' 9" for a sixteen year old Chinese boy. He was thin and probably weighed about 140 pounds with long thin arms and legs

It was before daylight when the siblings were ready to leave. Hai looked around at the one room home before letting out a deep breath through his nose. "Su, look around one last time before I blow out the candle. This moment will be the last time that we will ever see this place as our home." Ming Su looked around slowly as small things caught her eye like her mother's handmade blanket stretched neatly over the bed, the built up candle wax that hid the Chinese wine bottle from years of melting and dripping and the half barrel where she took her many baths. Hai took notice as tears ran from his little sisters eyes. "What's wrong?" He whispered. Ming Su sniffled a couple times. "I hope that I don't forget mother. I miss her so much and now we are leaving the only place that I remember her best."

"Did you remember to bring her hair brush?" Ming Su gasped as her eyes opened wide. "Thank You Hai, I almost forgot." She hustled to a wooden produce crate sitting in the corner of the room and retrieved an old hair brush from it. "Okay, I am ready to go." Hai knelt on one knee and shook his head as he looked Ming Su deep in her eyes. "Just remember that necklace that you have around your neck. Mother knew that she wouldn't be here too much longer when she gave the necklace to you. Every time that you see the North Star you will be reminded of mother. I promise that you will never forget her."

"But I don't know where the North Star is." Hai chuckled. "I will show you my young sister. Hai watched Ming Su step out before him and shut the door behind them.

Ming Su and Hai made their way along the cart road in route to the dock where the junk would be waiting to sail to America was awaiting. Hai was dressed in dark blue pants and shirt with straw sandals on his feet. He carried a gray sack over his right shoulder containing his belongings and other things from his parents' home to sell or trade to help the brother and sister when they arrive in America. A smaller sack in his right-hand containing Ming Su's belongings as she kept her wood horse grasped in her little hand, proudly skipping along in her new lavender dress with straw sandals on her feet. The hike to where the ship was set to sail was about three miles. The dark had not quite turned to day as Ming Su and Hai traveled down a muddy dirt road with rocks to step around and holes that were full of muddy water appearing to be impossible to know the depths. Tall grass grew in clumps on both sides of the dirt road and sometimes in the middle. Travel on that particular dirt road was scarce but it was a short cut. The popular route was about four and a half miles and that extra mile and a half was a long way to hike with the heavy sacks that had to be carried and for Ming Su's feet only being protected by straw sandals that would have hurt her even more. Along the way the siblings kept conversation going to help keep their minds off the thought of the long walk ahead of them. Hai told Ming Su about a tale that their father had once told him. "Do you know what porpoises are Su?" Ming Su shook her head and looked a little confused. "Porpoises are like dolphins. Do you know what dolphins are?" Ming Su shook her head even more while expressing a more confused look. "Porpoises and dolphins are like big long fish but they don't have gills like fish they breathe air through their nostril on the top of their head like a whale."

"Oh, I know what you mean."

"Okay, well! Father told me about how the porpoises swim as fast as the junk. They leap out of the water at the bow.' Ming Su looked even more confused. "They bow like we do?" Hai chuckled. "No Su, the bow is what they call the front of the junk and the stern is the rear of the junk."

"Oh, I see, so they leap out of the water at the front of the junk. Why don't they get out of the way? Does the ship ever hit them and hurt them? I hope that the junk doesn't kill them." Hai shook his head chuckling. "You are always so caring and selfless Su but I don't think that the porpoises get killed or even hurt, they swim and leap at the bow for their entertainment and fun."

"Do the dolphins do that too?"

"They might, but I don't think so. Dolphins and porpoises are like wolves and dogs. They are a lot alike but are different too."

"I think I understand."

"We don't have much further to go, but I will show you the porpoises when we get way out in the deep ocean."

The crowd standing on the dock took Ming Su by surprise, never imagining there would be so many people trying to board the junk to get to America and most of them were men. The junk was long, high-sterned with a projecting bow and five masts with square sails made of panels of linen. Ming Su took her bag from Hai once they stopped. She placed her wood horse inside it before wrapping her arm around the bag and tightly gripped her brother's hand. The look on her face showed fear and concern potentially catching the eye of the criminal element that would be joining the long see voyage. Hai looked down at his sister and stopped before squatting down and whispering in her ear. "You are safe with me, but you must smile. We are going to America, and we need to look proud and confident." Ming Su nodded her head many times and presented a fake smile to show that she was happy and carried much confidence while lightening the grip on her brother's hand as they stood in line.

Further up in the line an older man turned around and noticed Hai. He called out. "Hai, are you and Ming Su going to America too?" Hai nodded his head many times quickly with excitement, Ming Su let go of her brother's hand and waved with excitement as well. The man smiled and yelled. "I will see you on board." Hai nodded and waved.

A few moments later the man at the gate taking boarding tickets stopped Hai and Ming Su. He asked Hai. "How old are you." Hai replied. "Sixteen." The man stated. "I don't believe you. Suddenly the older man that was now on board the ship yelled. "Hai, come on, I am waiting for you." The man instantly caught the attention of the man taking boarding tickets. Hai said. "We are with him." The man taking the tickets quickly smiled and nodded his head. "Oh, you are with Ben Kin? Have good trip." The brother and sister hustled up the wooden ramp on to the massive junk with sails. Ben Kin walked up to Hai and said. "I could see that he was giving you trouble. He is my sister's husband, he knows that I have many children but have never met them all, he must have just assumed... Where is your father?" Hai shook his head and replied. "Already in America."

"Oh, I see. I need to have a word with him for leaving his children behind. But you must be careful on this journey, many bad men, protect your sister well. If you have any problems then you let me know. I know the captain too. I travel back and forth quite frequently and understand that not all men who leave China arrive in America." Ben Kin nodded with a smile and walked off.

3

The sun was climbing higher in the sky when the crew of the junk set the sails for the open sea. Seagulls flocked around the ship as some of the passengers threw small bite size pieces of bread in the air to encourage the gulls to swoop down and grab their meal in midair with their beaks. Ming Su stood on a wood crate, leaning against the rail as Hai stood behind her with his arm around her to prevent her from falling into the frigid salt water. She smiled and giggled at the gulls precision and determination to capture the midair morsels. The flocks of gulls were overwhelming to her young eyes and mind as she continuously tried to watch as many pieces of bread would get attacked by the gulls.

The wind blew hard, forcing the junk to move at what seemed to Ming Su, a very fast speed but before she knew it the land was nowhere in sight, causing her to panic with the rocking of the junk as the swells and waves slapped against the wooden hull. She had no idea that the sea voyage would be uncomfortable or even painful to her stomach. She hung her head over the side, alongside her brother to vomit her breakfast into the sea to be left as food for the fish below.

The heat on the open sea spent no time drying out the throats of the passengers but water was limited and had to be rationed accordingly. Ming Su and Hai were left with a foul taste in their mouths for a couple more hours. To Ming Su's surprise Hai had some oranges that he tucked away in his bag. Her face lit up with the thought of the citrus juice running down her throat covering up the foul taste and taking away her thirst. Hai said to Ming Su. "I have two more oranges left and a small sack of Bayberries too. We need to do our best to conserve what we can over the next week or so. After that the fruit will not be any good." Ming Su replied. "I want to make sure that we eat them and not let them get wasted." Hai shook his head. "They will not go to waste Su." He peeled the round citrus fruit, tossing the small shards of skin into the sea. Ming Su watched the peels disappear into the white splashes of sea created by the ship with confusion. She wondered why the seagulls had no interest in the orange peels but targeted the bread. However she felt that she would keep the thought to herself so she would not seem so ignorant.

A man walked up behind Ming Su and placed his hand on her shoulder. "Are you going to be okay little girl? You look a little lost" Ming Su jerked away. Hai heard the gesture and noticed the strangers' hand reaching for his sister's shoulder. He slapped the stranger's hand away and snarled. "She will be fine; she does not need your help. I am her brother and I will look out for her. The stranger put both his hands in the air as he backed away with a deviant laugh. Hai looked at his sister. "We must be very careful Su. You must always stay close to me and be very cautious and observant, especially when we sleep. You must sleep very close to me. In fact I shall find a piece of rope to tie to both of our arms as we sleep so we are connected to one another. If someone tries anything then I will be a woken." He finished peeling the orange and ripped it in half before handing half to his sister. Ming Su felt a little baffled she said to Hai. "But if somebody takes me on the ship then where would they go with me? I don't think that they are going to swim to America with me on their back." Hai rolled his eyes as he sighed. "Su, sometimes you are too smart for your own good but you also have the capacity of being very ignorant."

"What do you mean?"

"Su, the bad men could take you someplace else on the junk and do bad things to you and then even throw you overboard." Her eyes opened wide as she gasped in fear. "Don't let that happen to me Hai."

"I won't Su, just stay tied to me every night and stay close to me during the day and you will be fine. I will always protect you."

Ming Su tore a sliver from her half of the fruit to stick in her mouth. Juice oozed from her smile, down to her chin as Hai smiled back at her with a slice of orange wedged between his teeth encouraging Ming Su to laugh at his silliness. They took their time eating the orange as the citrus tingled their tongues and throats. Their thirst disappeared as they enjoyed the sweet citrus flavor. Suddenly Ming Su heard a man's voice from a few steps away. "Hey little girl if you get hungry I have much fruit to fill your belly." She looked up at her brother with a frightened look on her face. Hai stood up and set his hand on the handle of his knife that hung from his belt. The man laughed as he turned around and walked off. "I am afraid of the strange men on the junk. I know that they are going to hurt me and do bad things to me. I want to go home."

"Su we cannot go home now. We have no choice but to finish the voyage to America. I will keep you safe and not let anything happen to you." Ming Su wrapped her arms around her brother's neck as he knelt in front of her. A chill ran through her as she noticed the strange man staring at her with a devilish grin. Hai returned a cold stare. But neither of the three had any idea that the stare down was being watched until a familiar face charged up to the strange man and shoved his grip into the man's neck, slamming him against the rail, bending him backwards as the water splashed up on him. The fear on the strangers face struck fear and relief in Ming Su's heart and mind as she and Hai watched in amazement at how Ben Kin took charge of the situation and showed very little mercy to protect Ming Su.

Many of the other passengers quickly got the message as well as they watched on and knew the reputation of Ben Kin and his sincerity. Ming Su looked around and knew that she would be safe on the journey to America but was also aware that her fear would not subside that easily.

Ben Kin was a tall stalky man from a well off family, but not necessarily rich. It was his stature and his confidence that made him who he was. He stood about 6 feet tall. That was very uncommonly tall for a Chinese man. He was a well-known business man from the classier side of town and was always dressed in the best of suits with jet black hair neatly cut and parted to the side, a mustache and goatee, he was intimidating to any other man.

The many days on the junk to America were long and exhausting. Ming Su and Hai would pass time by playing simple card games during the hot voyage but in the early evening before the sun began to sink into the ocean, Hai would watch Ming Su feed a strong thin needle and thread through little beads made of wood, rock, sea shell, coral and other materials to create jewelry. Therefore taking the two tiger claws and making two separate decorative necklaces, one for herself and the other for her brother Hai.

Most nights Ming Su slept very close to her brother as he instructed and was tied to him with a short length of rope joining them at the wrists with triple knots. The other passengers avoided sleeping too close to the brother and sister in fear that they would inflict further fear into Ming Su and be the one that does end up in the deep sea to drown and be devoured by the hunters of the deep as tales were told about Ben Kin.

One morning a crowd gathered at the bow of the ship catching Hai's attention. He chuckled. "Get up Su, Come on, you are going to love this." Ming Su hustled to the bow behind her brother and looked down into the water to watch the porpoises first hand as they leaped from the ocean and swam with the speed of the ship. Hai chuckled. "See I told you Su." Ming Su laughed as she watched the porpoises race the junk.

Many weeks into the voyage a blanket of dark clouds covered the sky ahead of the junk as the swells gained height and strength. The wind became powerful as the junk rocked side to side. The bow raised high into the air and slammed down into the violent sea. The deck of the junk filled with rain water from the sky and salt water from the ocean. Provisions and supplies had to be stowed away securely by the crew to minimize any injury to the passengers. Ming Su sat huddled up in the corner with Hai alongside her watching in fear as the water dripped from the deck above and ran down the inside of the hull. The sleeping quarters wreaked the odor of vomit from the passengers who could not handle the irregular movements of the thriving vessel. But what was really stomach turning was the vomit that was sloshing around on the floor in the water that was slowly gaining depth and soaking the passengers as they sat and lay on the wooden floor. Flashes of light lit us the sleeping quarters as the lighting split the storming sky and glowed through the uncovered bulk head that lead to the deck above the ladder.

After what seemed like days, but was only the late afternoon, the night and the next early morning the junk smoothed out. The sleeping quarters glowed from the bright sun that quickly warmed up the room and intensified the stench to the point where it was almost unbearable.

Hai stood up and removed his big sack and Ming Su's smaller sack from a clasp above his head. He took Ming Su by the hand and headed up the ladder to the bright sun. The look on Ming Su's face was lost in disgust from the smell of her clothes and the passenger's vomit clinging to her. Right away Hai spotted a wooden bucket full of rain water that somehow kept its balance through the rigorous storm. He told Ming Su to grab it by the handle and follow him. They hustled to the back of the vessel and stood behind a bulkhead. Hai instructed Ming Su to take a drink now as he did the same. Then he told her to take her clothes off as he handed her a worn down bar of soap and a cloth from his sack. "Dunk the cloth in the bucket of rain water Su and clean the vomit off your skin." Hai stood saddened as he watched Ming Su sit on the deck of the junk in her under garment after removing her lavender dress that she wore since the day they left about five weeks ago. He said to her as tears filled her eyes. "You have no choice but to wear one of your old dresses." He looked around and kept watch to keep privacy upon his sister. Ming Su took the clean dress from Hai as she sat on the deck, staring at the ugly faded gray. She broke down and began to sob while clinging to her old dress. Ming Su looked at Hai as she rose to her feet and slid the dress over her head. "I hate father for putting us through this." She pulled her right wrist back over her right eye and her left wrist back over her left eye to wipe away the tears before letting out a quick frustrated breath... Her eyes slowly closed as she took in a slow but deep breath. "I smell flowers." Hai smiled knowing that he did well packing Ming Su's clothes in dry flowers to transfer the scent to her wardrobe. Ming Su smiled back at her brother, realizing how pleasing it was compared to what she had just removed. Hai looked on with pain on his face as he watched Ming Su toss the pretty lavender dress overboard into the depths of the ocean. "I promise that we will get you another one Su." Ming Su didn't say a word. She just nodded her head in response of acceptance. Deep in her heart she knew that Hai would not let her down and she could be covered in a pretty dress once again.

The junk came alive with passengers' scurrying to get cleaned up the best that they could. Cleaning the vomit off their bodies and leaving a dry sticky film on their skin from using salt water that they gathered from throwing wooden buckets overboard attached to ropes and pulling it back in. Many passengers had to leave their dirty clothes on while others were changing into clean clothes that they saved for their arrival in America. Hai and Ming Su were overcome with excitement when America had come to dominate the horizon.

Little by little the wind died down to almost a mouse's breath, leaving the junk to drift opposed to sail toward land. The vessel's crew took the opportunity to begin cleaning the deck of the dried up human foulness. Human regurgitated dried rice and vegetables were hard to remove from the wooden deck and gunwales using brooms. The captain instructed the crew to use sea water, soap and scrub brushes to clean the deck and gunwales thoroughly. The crew dry swept what they could then dumped it overboard. The cook and his assistants began throwing the rotted meat, fish and vegetables overboard. But to Ming Su's amazement, fast aggressive fish with pointy fins and tail ripped their teeth into the foul food, devouring it almost instantly. She looked at a crew member with fear in her eyes. "They don't look like porpoises or dolphins'. The crew member looked back at Ming Su and chuckled at the expression of fear on her face. Hai returned a dirty look at him and told his sister. "They are sharks, they are like sea tigers. They will kill and eat you until there is nothing left." At that moment an enormous dark gray shark arose from the depths at great speed, clamping its jaws of sharp white teeth into a feeding shark. It rolled over showing off its white belly as the sea water turned red. Ming Su stepped back a few feet in fear, wrapping her arm around a rope attached to the rigging.

As the ship drifted closer to land the passengers scurried to gather up their belonging and wait to dock in the new country. The last few miles as the land got closer seemed to be the longest on the journey for Ming Su but her excitement never failed.

The smell of fish filled the air as the ship entered the San Francisco Bay and eventually docked on the South side, Seagulls filled the sky and the surface of the bay waiting for the fishermen to throw the wasted part of slaughtered fish. They fought among themselves to fill their bellies and to prove position. The sun was high and the air was humid. Ming Su was beyond exhausted from the thirty-nine days of sea travel.

Despite the safety concerns the passengers disembarking the ship pushed and shoved each other to be the first to walk down the gangway and onto American soil. Ben Kin grabbed Hai by the arm and instructed him and Ming Su to wait a few more minutes to disembark to prevent from being trampled by the anxious passengers. Ming Su watched in disbelief at the violence that occurred between the other passengers and even the crew. Tightly she clung onto Hai's forearm as he held her bag in his hand and set his at his feet. The siblings were of the very few that remained calm.

4

Brother and sister stepped off the wood dock, onto the dusty dirt road. Hai stopped and looked down at his sister and said. "Let's go sit down I want to talk to you." Hai sat down on a wood crate that was on the edge of the dock. He tapped his knee to signal Ming Su to sit on it. He had to raise his voice for Ming Su to hear her brother over the crowd. He said to her. "Su, we are in America." She smiled at him but her smile quickly faded when he said. "China is no longer our home, we will never go back. America is now our home. We will have to learn their language and their customs while still honoring the Chinese culture. You will need to prepare yourself well little sister, we still have a long journey to a place called Idaho, to Bannock Village. Perhaps we will see father there, if he didn't go someplace else."

"I don't want to see him Hai, he left us."

"I know Su, but he is still our father."

"You are my big brother and you are all I need, you will always protect me." Hai grinned and nodded his head. "You're right Su. I will always be there for you and we will find our gold, but for now let's go fill our bellies with some real food." Ming Su looked up at her brother with a big smile and excitement. "Real food, yeah!" Hai looked left and right to try and spot a Chinese restaurant but what he did see was not what he was used to. Many travelers stood outside the restaurants with horses, mules and other live stock. The odor of the animal waste combined with the unbathed travelers and the rotting fish from the ocean was stomach turning. Hai put his hand out for Ming Su to take hold of and he began to walk along the walkway. Many people of many races looked at the young siblings, laughing, pointing and mocking the lost duo. One Chinese prostitute made an attempt to proposition Hai, but Hai showed no interest. An American man selling black puppies tried to entice Ming Su but brother lightly tugged on her arm and shook his head. Unfamiliar music from stringed instruments made a large gathering place for American faces. The strong smell of whiskey and beer tickled their noses as they walked slowly past. Ming Su released the grip from Hai's hand as she came to a stop. Hai stopped and turned around to find his young sister focused on an American man dancing on the porch of the saloon playing an instrument that rested on his shoulder. He held on to the instrument with one hand and a long skinny stick that he dragged across the strings of the instrument. The music that the man was producing with the instrument was very pleasing to her ears. It was fast paced, all the notes seemed to come together causing some of his audience to dance to the music. The women with long dressed hopped around, flapping their dresses in the air while kicking out their feet and twisting them. The men did the same thing but were not wearing dresses but instead hung on to their straps that went over their shoulders to hold up their pants. Ming Su could not help herself as she began to mimic the dancing Americans. Hai took a couple steps back to give Ming Su some room as he watched her with a smile across his face. Unfortunately Hai knew that the sun had traveled across the sky leaving the first half of the day behind. He stepped towards Ming Su and touched her on the shoulder. "We must go Su." Her dance quickly halted. She stared at Hai and asked. "Just a little longer?" Hai put out his hand and shook his head.

 As the music began to fade with distance an older Chinese man, very frail with no hair on top of his head and a long beard and mustache caught the eyes of Hai and Ming Su. He smiled a toothless smile at them and nodded in a friendly gesture. Ming Su spotted the bushel of oranges that the man was selling. She asked Hai with excitement. "Can we get some oranges?" Hai smiled politely at the old man and asked. "Where can we get some real food to eat?" The old man turned and pointed to a building that had a sign with American lettering. Hai put up four fingers and pointed to the oranges. The old man smiled a big toothless smile and grabbed four oranges from the bushel to hand to Hai. When Hai took the oranges, the old man rubbed his fingers while holding his hand out. After slipping the oranges into his sack, Hai reached into his pocket to retrieve a Chinese coin and placed it into the man's open hand.

Ming Su began to feel a little uncomfortable as they approached the steps of a weather beaten wood building. Side by side she walked with her brother up two steps and onto a large patio with matching weather beaten planks for the floor. Her eye stayed glued to a creepy looking tall Chinese man dressed in a gray coat down to his knees, an off white button down shirt that was probably once pure white but has lost its brilliance with wear, dirty tan trousers tucked into dusty black boots with shiny metal spurs over both heels. His dark beard and mustache was not neat at all but very scruffy and ungroomed. His hat was black and round as a melon on top with a small brim that sat slanted on his head. He smiled at Ming Su as she stared with an emotionless expression while Hai reached to open the door and pull it outward. The man asked. "If you are lost, I can help you out. I have traveled all over this part of the country. I can help you to get to where you want to go." Ming Su hustled inside as Hai shook his head and waved his hand in a negative gesture. The man's laugh was long and eerie and could be heard inside the restaurant.

The pine tables were not what Hai and Ming Su were accustomed to even though they were surrounded by American's and Chinese. Hai looked at Ming Su and said. I suppose that Americans do not sit on the floor to eat like we do in China, the tables were almost as tall as Ming Su and the backs of the chairs were actually taller than her. A variety of unfamiliar food filled the plates of the patrons sitting at the tall tables in the tall chairs. Hai began to look around as the sibling sat quickly coming to realize that all the lettering on the walls were not Chinese but American. It was only a moment when a Chinese man approached the table and asked what Hai and Ming Su would like to eat. "Hai replied. "Something fresh from home and some tea." The man began to laugh as he walked away, slapping a white hand towel over his shoulder.

They sat quietly waiting for the meal. Ming Su noticed the creepy man staring at her from outside the glass pane. She tried not to let the creepy man know that she knew he was watching so she made a point to look around the room at the decor on the wood shelves and walls consisting drawings and paintings of different people from America and China. Big dead fish with bright colors stuck to the wall with fishing nets, boat oars and other fishing gear from China and America.

As a short time passed, their food arrived on a large platter. The man set it down on the edge of the table and transferred plates of food from it and positioned them in front of the two hungry travelers. Their innocent grins disappeared as their eyes opened wide and their hungry mouths fell open in an amazed disappointment. Ming Su looked at the man and said. "It looks like dog vomit." The man chuckled and replied. "American stew with beef and vegetables poured over white rice. You are in America now, America is your new home and this is made today, very fresh." He then transferred two large drinking cups from the platter onto the table in front of Ming Su and Hai then set a metal pot onto the table. Hai looked at the man and stated. "That does not look like Chinese tea from home.' The man replied "It's not. It is American tea from England." The man walked away. Ming Su slowly pushed the plate away and stated. "I'm not eating dog vomit and I am not drinking tea from England." Hai smiled at his young sister. "Come on Su, just eat it, we have to get used to America food."

"Is there not Chinese cooking where we are going?"

"I really don't know Su, but if there isn't. You have to get used to American food, so you should get started now." Ming Su leaned forward and took in the aromas of the food forcing her face to crunch up in sickening disgust. Hai reached onto his plate with is fingers and grabbed a piece of beef, then placed it between his hungry lips. "Mmmm! That is good he said." Ming Su then took a piece of beef from her plate with her tiny fingers and placed it into her mouth. When the morsel touched her taste buds she instantly spit it out onto the dusty wood floor and stated. "I am not eating dog vomit. It even tastes like dog vomit." Hai chuckled and asked. "I didn't know you knew what dog vomit tastes like." She grouched back. "I didn't but I do now." Hai picked up a silver utensil from the table and whispered. "I suppose this is what we use in America to scoop food into our mouths." Ming Su gagged when she watched her brother shovel a big scoop of white rice and American stew into his mouth. Forgetting his manners Hai began to speak with his mouth full. "Su, do you know how many people back in China would love to eat what you have sitting in front of you?"

"If they want it so bad, why don't you send it on the ship back to them? Cause I am not eating it." Suddenly Hai quickly became irritated, not at Ming Su but at the strange man standing outside the door of the restaurant watching Ming Su like a cat would watch its prey before the big attack. Hai dropped his fork, sprung off his chair and charged toward the door. The strange man saw Hai quickly heading his way with an angry look on his face and ran off like a cat being chased by a dog. Hai was not going to let it pass, he ran after the stranger, leaving Ming Su alone at the high wooden table and a plate of rice and stew that looked like dog vomit. As Ming Su sat with her arms crossed and a disgusted look on her face, she noticed a young American boy outside the window looking in at her. Ming Su smiled and waved at the lonely boy. When the boy waved back Ming Su waved her hand in a gesture to invite him to come to her. Suddenly his little head disappeared from the window and a moment later a boy about eight years old came walking through the door. Ming Su tapped on the back of the chair for the little boy to sit. The boy climbed up into the chair and could barely reach the top of the table. All one could see is a head and a pair of shoulders. Ming Su patted on her chest and said. "Su." The boy looked a little confused so Ming Su once again patted on her chest with her hand and repeated. "Su." The boy quickly smiled and patted his chest and replied. "Thomas, Thomas." Ming Su smiled and repeated. "Thomas." Thomas leaned towards Ming Su and sucked a breath in through his nose and smiled. He said. "You smell like pretty flowers." Ming Su had no idea what he had said but somehow knew it was a compliment about her dress that Hai had packed in dry flowers. She put her finger up as a gesture meaning. "Just a moment." She climbed down off the tall chair and skipped with joy to the door to see if her brother was coming, sticking her head out the door, looking both ways before turning around with a deviant smile on her face. She skipped back to the table, climbed back up into the tall chair. With both hands she slowly pushed the plate of white rice and American stew in front of the little boy and handed him her fork. The boy wasted no time devouring the plate of food. By the time Hai had returned the plate was almost empty. Hai looked at his sister and then at the little boy and began to giggle while shaking his head. He knew the good heart that his young sister possessed but also knew that she didn't want to eat the food that looked like dog vomit and was somewhat proud of her for feeding a hungry boy and decided that it wasn't a big deal that Ming Su didn't want to eat the white rice and American stew. He waived his hand to the waiter and asked. "Could you bring a bowl of rice and vegetables for my sister please?" The man nodded and a few moments later Ming Su had a familiar meal sitting in front of her.

Bellies were full and the sun was falling. Hai told Ming Su that it was time to go. She asked. "What about Thomas?" Hai looked confused and stated. "I don't know we can't take him with us."

"Why not?"

"Su try to understand that we have a very long journey awaiting us. I am going to try and get us a packing mule for our supplies and there may be a little room for you to ride it when you are tired but Thomas is so little and young that he won't be able to keep up."

"He can ride on the mule too, can't he?"

"Su if I take responsibility for Thomas I have to make sure that he eats. He has clothing and shelter too. And it is such a long way to Bannock Village and I know that we will run into snow, and rain and it will get very cold and may be real hot too. And if he gets sick then I will have to make sure that he gets well and that will slow us down."

"It won't be that bad Hai. He won't be that much trouble. He has no place to go. Please Hai? He can be the little brother that I always wanted." Hai looked away and noticed that the waiter was eavesdropping. Hai grouched at the waiter with an attitude. "I already paid you, is there something else that you need from me?" He waived both his hands with a smile and called him closer. Hai took a few steps toward the man. The server stated. "Thomas is a good boy. He has no family, His father drowned on fishing trip in the big water. He was eaten by a big fish with a white belly. Thomas does not know about the big fish with the white belly, don't ever tell him. I don't think that he has a mother either. He can be a little bit of a nuisance here because he is hungry and we look after him a little and let him bother the customers to get something to eat but we cannot keep doing that, it is not good for business."

"I am sorry to hear all that but it is not my problem. He will just slow us down."

"Okay, I got an idea. If you meet me around the back door later when you get your packing mule I can give you two sides of bacon, sack of rice and some jerky and a warm blanket for Thomas." Hai looked at the floor shaking his head and let out a long sigh. He looked over at the table to witness Ming Su and Thomas smiling and laughing, then let out a short sigh and said. "Okay, I will meet you at the back door later. Don't disappoint me and don't disappoint Thomas either."

"Ming Su was so excited to hear the news about Thomas joining the expedition. She threw her arms around Hai's waist and held her cheek against his belly. When she finally let go, Hai said to her. "This will definitely be an adventure. He can't understand us and we can't understand him." Ming Su laughed and stated. "We will learn."

5

Hai stepped off the porch of the restaurant and onto the dusty street, closely following was the two new friends holding hands and laughing, Hai heard a familiar voice calling out to him. He looked down the street and noticed who it was. "Ben Kin." He nodded and replied. "Hai, I have been looking for you."

"America is crazy, not like China."

"America is nothing like our home of China, People here are selfish, self-centered and very cruel to the Chinese. Do not trust them. Do you know where you are going and how you are going to get there?" Suddenly he noticed Thomas. "Who is this American boy, don't tell me that he is traveling with you."

"Yes, His name is Thomas, he has no family and I will be responsible for him." Ben Kin shook his head quickly and asked. "Do you know what you are doing? Do you know where you are going?"

"Yes, I know where we are going, it is North East from here and travel will be long and great."

"You must be going to Idaho?"

"Yes, that is where our father said he would find gold and that is where he should be."

"There is much gold here in America, much more danger through the forest and the mountains too, perhaps you should travel south with me to seek gold."

"Much appreciated but we cannot, do you have any advice for our journey?"

"Such as?"

"Where I can get a mule and supplies?"

"You really don't know what you are doing, do you?"

"I am a good hunter and fisherman, father taught me well. Food will not be a problem. I just do not have ammunition or rifle."

"Do you know how to load and use a rifle?"

"Yes, father taught me well."

"I will help you because your father is my friend and I want you to succeed on your endeavor. Follow me. I will buy you a rifle, ammunition and other supplies."

"I have some money left over from China."

"I heard about the tiger, very brave and very wise decision. But keep your money, you will need it but we must change it to American currency and Ming Su must cut her hair and wear boy clothes so bad men will think that she is a boy."

"What do you mean bad men?"

"The bad men are abductors of children, mainly girls. They watch for young Chinese girls when they get off the ships and travel. The abductors are like the great birds of the sky scooping in and grabbing the young girls and disappear before you know it. They stalk or hunt them. Make no mistake. If Ming Su is taken then she would eventually be used to make money as sex slaves and prostitutes then probably killed once she is no use to them anymore."

"Oh, like the men on the ship."

"Exactly what I am talking about Hai. Ming Su must look like a boy. Trust me."

"But Ming Su is only ten, and she is very small for her age. Why would they want her?"

"They would make her in to a slave to clean and learn to cook among other things that you and I would not approve of. Then when she became of age they would turn her over to prostitution. When a Chinese girl is a young virgin, she will bring in a lot of money for the right man who is into that kind of thing." Hai let out a sigh of disgust and said. "When we were at the restaurant there was an older Chinese man who was watching Ming Su, but I chased him off. I could not catch him but I assumed that he was there to cause trouble. It all makes sense now. I agree with you, she must look like a boy to make this long journey to Bannock Village. I will do everything that I can and will protect her, she is my sister."

"I understand and have great faith in you but you must take my advice." Hai looked at Ming Su and she nodded her head in acceptance." Ben Kin said. "Come with me." Ming Su looked up and down the street with fear running through her heart. Ben Kin noticed Ming Su and Thomas' hands within each other and snarled. "Don't hold hand, get into the habit. Boys don't hold hands in America." They looked at each other and let go.

They came upon a wood building with much supplies and livestock outside. Ben Kin entered first as Ming Su, Thomas and Hai followed. Ben Kin said to the man at the counter. "Cheng?" The man pointed to the back and the trio followed Ben Kin. Ming Su looked around at all the merchandise on the floor, walls and even hanging from the ceiling. She was quickly overtaken with fear when she recognized an enormous jaw with large serrated teeth. She knew it to be from the big shark with the white belly.

A Chinese man sitting at a table showed great excitement at the sight of Ben Kin before his face frowned when he noticed Hai and Ming Su and then the familiar little boy that he had seen on the streets many times. He looked back at Ben Kin. "What can I do for you my friend?"

"I need a great favor."

"You always need a favor Ben Kin."

"Yeah but I always make sure that good things go your way, besides this one is important. These children belong to a longtime friend of mine from China, they are on a quest to find their father but girls do not travel well with bad men on the prowl."

"What about the American boy?"

"He will be traveling with them."

"Oh, I see, so what is it that you want from me?"

"Ask your wife Sing to cut the girls hair to look like a boy and provide her with boy's clothing."

"Oh yeah, she is about my youngest son size, I will give her some of his old clothes. Perhaps change her name to Chen and I may have some clothes left over from when he was younger for the boy too."

"Good idea." Ming Su looked at Hai, and then at the two men smiling with a disappointed expression of disgust on her face and asked. "So I will be a boy now?" Hai squatted down and looked at his unhappy sister and said. "Only while we journey, it is for your own safety and I will teach you and Thomas to hunt, fish and you to act like a boy. I am sorry but it must be done."

"Okay. I trust you and only you. I don't like the bad men."

Cheng yelled out to his wife. "Sing, Sing." When she entered the room he got real close to her and whispered in her ear. "Take the little girl and cut her hair to look like boy, put some of Bolo's clothes on her so she is mistaken for a boy and fetch some old clothes for the little American boy." Sing bowed quickly to her husband then took Ming Su by the hand to lead her out of the room with her. Cheng handed Ben Kin a pottery cup containing an American whiskey. They held the cups up in the air, bowed their heads to each other before drinking the intoxicating beverage.

Later Hai, Ming Su, Thomas and Ben Lin came from the back room of the mercantile. The man at the counter did a quick double take, not expecting three boys but two boys and a girl. Cheng looked at him and grouched. "Not a word to anyone." He nodded his head quickly and responded. "I understand." Hai was dressed in an American light gray button down shirt, dark gray pants tucked into his black boots that went almost to his knees and a tan brim hat. His make believe brother was dress in similar clothing but with worn boots tucked under the pant legs. However Ming Su was heartbroken that she had to travel looking like a boy and could not be the feminine young lady that she was growing to be. She was proud of the Lavender dress and slippers that her brother bargained to get for her and hated that she had to toss the dress overboard. Ming Su began to sob as she ran to Hai. Hai squatted down to embrace his little sister and noticed a light blue dress about the same size that would fit Ming Su. He let go of his sister and slowly stood up as he stared at the dress hanging on the wall and asked "How much for dress?" Ming Su turned around to see the dress that had her name invisibly printed on it. Her deep brown eyes opened wide as her mouth dropped open. Cheng saw the excitedly amazed look on the little girl and smiled. "Ah! What a pretty dress." Cheng chuckled. "My gift to the little lady for making such a long journey to America." Cheng took it down off the wall and handed it to Ming Su. She wrapped her arms around Cheng as he returned a pat on the back of her head. "Okay, okay, okay." Ming Su exchanged big smiles with her brother and Ben Kin before she place the dress deep into the bottom of her bag.

Thomas didn't need much except for a hat and a new pair or used boots. The trio stood on the edge of the street with Ming Su keeping the attention of the other two because of the way she looked. Suddenly Ming Su began to break down sobbing. Thomas felt her pain deep within his little heart and stepped over to her, wrapping his arms around her. Hai knelt down beside them and wrapped his arms around them both. He whispered in Ming Su's ear. "Everything is going to be fine. You are a princess and always will be a princess. Those ugly clothes that you are wearing will never change that." The trio broke apart and Ming Su wiped her eyes with the arms of the shirt, presented a fake smile and said. "I am glad that you are my brother."

Moments later Ben Kin and Cheng came from around the musty wood building. Cheng, leading a mule by a rope with supplies saddled in the arch of its back. Ben Kin handed Hai a rifle, leather pouch containing gun powder, round lead balls and other supplies to maintain the rifle and to hunt. He then reached into his coat pocket and handed Hai a new knife and sheath. Slowly Hai took the knife from him looked at it and handed it back with a smile and stated. "Thank you Ben Kin, but I have the knife that father left for me. I will always carry it." Ben Kin smiled and looked at Ming Su and asked. "Would it be okay if I gave it to Chen?" Hai's expression looked confused when he asked. "Who?" Ben Kin grunted. Ming Su is now Chen, don't mess that up."

"Oh yeah, Chen, he can have the knife, I mean she can have the knife, I mean, Yeah just give the knife to Ming Su, I mean Chen."

Ming Su grinned as she looked at her brother shaking her head. His smile quickly faded as she took the knife from Ben Kin's grasp. Cheng stepped forward as he reached into his pant pocket, retrieving a folding knife with genuine ivory inlays and a sharp carbon steel blade. Kneeling down on one knee in front of Thomas and handed him the folding knife. The boy held it in both hands as his face lit up. Cheng took Thomas by the chin and said to him in what little American English he could speak. "Thomas. This was your father's. He needed money to feed and care for you and sold me this knife. This is not a toy, this is a serious tool, it could hurt one and it could kill one, so be very careful with it. Hai will teach you to use it properly but until then do not take it out of your pocket, not even to show anyone. This is my gift from me to you. I know that your father would want you to have it because I know it broke his heart to have to sell it." The young boy began to sob as he clinched the knife in his left hand and threw his arms around Cheng and stated. "I remember this knife. Pa used it all the time. He carved wood with it, cut rope and skinned rabbit with it. Every Sunday evening he would sharpen the blade on a piece of leather. I just could never figure out how an animal skin could make a knife blade sharp again. I guess it doesn't matter, I will keep it always because it was my Pa's and it is all I will have to remember him." Cheng stood up wiping a tear from the right side of his face with his left hand. He quickly sniffled and said in Chinese as he looked at Hai. "This is one of my workers." He waved a Chinese man in his early twenties over. "He will escort you to the road leading to Idaho. Don't trust anybody. They are all looking for the same thing as you. They will hurt you or even kill you if they feel threatened by you. Keep a low profile. Travel from dawn to dusk. Make one good meal a day and that is at dusk before you sleep. Any meat that you make from hunting make extra to eat throughout the next day while traveling. Be careful of little bugs called ticks, they look like spiders with short legs. They suck your blood and can cause sickness or death. Get water every chance that you get, the rivers lakes and ponds are clean for drinking, cooking and bathing and always keep your rifle loaded and ready to shoot. Maybe one day you will find your gold and then you can pay me back but until then, you owe me nothing." Hai bowed to give thanks and respect to the elder then did the same to Ben Kin. He took the mule by the lead and began following his escort with Ming Su and Thomas close by.

Hai said to the escort. "My name is Hai." The escort turned and looked at him. "My name is Wong Li. We will travel to the outside of the city and make camp, it's too late in the day to travel beyond and I will turn back and leave you dawn after next."

"I understand Wong Li but we must stop at the back door of the restaurant down the road. I have more supplies to pick up."

"Two sides of bacon, sack of white rice, jerky and a blanket for the little boy."

"Yeah, how do you know?"

"Already packed on the mule. News travels fast when involves Cheng. We will go through all your supplies when at camp later."

It was about a four mile walk for the expedition as much of it was up hill and exhausting before coming to a place to set up camp. A small spring provided cold water for their drinking to refresh and hydrate, even the mule took a drink.

Hai and Wong Li unpacked the mule that they named Loco, short for locomotive. The two went through all the supplies while water was heating to prepare the rice on the trail. Ming Su and Thomas rested by napping. Wong Li stood in the brook of cold water coming from the spring and demonstrated how to use a tin pan in a slow rotary motion to pan for gold. To Wong Li and Hai's amazement, Hai discovered a small nugget of gold about the size of a pea as he panned for the first time. He looked real close at the nugget for a moment then handed it to his teacher and said. "Keep it, I will find a whole lot more when I get to Idaho. Wong Li didn't know what to say. He had escorted many prospects to the road to Idaho but never did anyone ever offer him a gift. About that time the water was at a boil and ready for the rice. Hai sat on the ground listening to the water boil as he stared at Ming Su and Thomas. A smile grew on his face as he thought about how happy they make each other feel. Thomas had someone who wanted him around to love and Ming Su had a younger counter part that she could be a big sister too and feel responsible for.

It wasn't too much longer when the aromas of the opened fire and cooked pork tickled the noses of the sleeping youngsters. Ming Su sat up stretching her arms and sucking fresh mountain air into her lungs as she yarned. Thomas remained laying on the blanket as he slowly moved his head and eyes around, panning at the surrounding landscape. Hai said to the youngsters. Go over to the brook and get cleaned up for supper." Ming Su turned and looked down at Thomas with a smile and waved in a motion for him to follow her. Quickly he bounced up and followed her to the brook. Thomas quickly got the idea when Ming Su began washing her hands with the cold water and began to follow suit.

The four travelers sat around the camp fire of ember coals, eating their supper as the sun descended and began to touch the ocean's surface. Ming Su watched the sun as it sank deep into the distance water and asked her brother. "Is that why it gets dark every day?" Hai smiled and shook his head as if he didn't understand the question. Ming Su seemed a little irritated and asked. "Does it get dark every day because the sun gets put out in the sea every night?" Hai smiled and thought cleverly to entertain his young sister. "Every night the sun falls into the sea but it does not burn out because it is so hot that it keeps burning under water and then it rolls over the bottom of the ocean around the world and comes up out of the sea the next morning and makes its way across the sky once again before sinking into the sea again the next night." Ming Su's eyes were opened wide with amazement and understanding. She and her counterpart stood up after they finished their supper. They walked toward the sun a few steps and watched the last quarter of the fiery ball sink into the distance sea. At that point Wong Li placed a lit wooden match to the wick of the lantern to replace the darkness with light. Ming Su took Thomas by the hand and then let go quickly as she remembers that boys in America do not hold hands. Then she waved for him to follow once again. With the language barrier between them, Ming Su was able to get Thomas to understand that even though they are young, they must still help out and carry their own weight as she showed Thomas how to clean off and wash the supper plates and utensils.

Wong Li took a long thin rope, tied one end to a stick about two inches thick and a foot or so long before throwing it high over a tree branch. Hai tied a cloth bag containing the left over pork to the end of the rope that fell from the tree branch. Wong Li pulled the other end of the rope, raising the bag of left over pork up into the air before tying the end near the base of the tree. Thomas looked at the bag hanging about twenty feet high and then at Wong Li with a curious look on his young face. Wong Li smiled and knelt down beside Thomas and spoke to him with what little English he knew to get the young American boy to understand. He pointed at the bag and put his hand in front of his mouth and pretended to chew as he said "food." Then he rubbed his belly and said. "Tomorrow," As he walked his fingers like a person's legs. Thomas smiled and nodded his head and said. "Food while we are walking tomorrow?" Wong Li got a strong feeling that Thomas understood and nodded his head quickly and replied with a smile. "Food while we are walking tomorrow." Ming Su and Hai smiled at the language barrier breakthrough between the two strangers. Ming Su slowly walked over to Thomas and put her hands together, closed her eyes and laid her head on her hands and said. "Sleep," Before yarning. Thomas replied. "Sleep," And followed Ming Su to his blanket that was still lying on the green grass. Thomas lied down on his blanket while Ming Su lied down on hers. They pulled the ends of their blanket over themselves and quickly scooted toward each other to be close, to feel safe, to be warm and perhaps to feel one another's love. Hai whispered to Wong Li sitting beside him by the fading embers. "Looks like I have been replaced." Wong Li shook his head and replied. "I don't think so. They both need you too. They have a new relationship between the two of them and we should let them enjoy that as it gives extra comfort to them both." Hai smiled and nodded before laying back and using his bed roll as a pillow, staring up at the millions of stars as he faded off to sleep.

Ming Su and Thomas were woken by the sounds of Hai and Wong Li exchanging simple conversation as the sun was rising to a new day. The youngsters quickly got up and hustled in different directions to find a bush or a tree to empty their tiny morning bladders. Moments later Ming Su returned and wrapped her arms around her brother. Hai knelt on one knee and returned the morning gesture. Ming Su said to her brother. "I think that we should start using the boy name for me now, but I don't like Chen." Hai and Wong Li chuckled. Ming Su said. "I like Hon." Hai smiled and nodded as he replied. "Then Hon it will be."

Thomas returned from the bushes and began rolling up his bed roll immediately. Ming Su hustled over to her bed roll and began rolling hers up as well. Moments later Wong Li took the rolls from the two youngsters. Ming Su patted on her heart and said to Thomas. "Hon, Hon." Thomas looked at Wong Li with the familiar look of confusion or curiosity. Wong Li shook his head and said. "No more Ming Su. Now her name is Hon." Thomas looked at Hon and then at Hai and back at Wong Li and asked. "Why?" Wong Li shook his head and explained to the young explorer. "Bad men may try to take Ming Su if they think she is a girl, but will not if they think Hon is a boy." Thomas slowly shook his head and asked. "They will not try to take me?" Wong Li shook his head and replied. "No, Because you are a boy. So for now on Hon is a boy."

"No more Ming Su as a girl?"

"No more Ming Su as girl, now Hon the boy." Thomas thought for a moment and then asked. "Can I be Tommy?" Wong Li smiled and nodded. "Yes you can now be Tommy." Wong Li turned to Hai and Hon then stated. "Thomas is now to be called Tommy." Hai and Hon smiled and began chanting. "Tommy, Tommy, Tommy." Wong Li chuckled and said. "We better get on. it's going to be hot today."

6

Wong Li took Loco by the lead, followed by Hon, Tommy and Hai bringing up rear, heading North with the rising sun to their right and the Pacific Ocean to their left. Seagulls filled the morning sky as they searched for remnants of food left by travelers as well as little lizards, toads and snakes. Two parallel trails were barely wide enough to accommodate a wagon drawn by a team of two horses or even one if that was all the prospectors could afford. Wong Li knew that travel would be easier if he lead the mule on the packed down soil made by the many wagon wheels and foot travelers. The grown over center between the parallel trails were covered with ankle high grass and larger stones that would make it complicated for a wagon wheels to safely and comfortable roll over. Limbs of bushes and saplings protruded over the duel trails, scratching ones leg while passing and whipping back to slap the next person who may be walking too close.

Along the way they travelers noticed empty supply crates, broken tool handles, punctured water barrels, pots, pans and an occasional stripped down wagon collected dust while rotting under the elements. It became apparent to them that not even the horses, mules or steer were immune to the treacherous travel on the trail to Idaho as rotted, animal scavenged carcasses occasionally lied alongside the trail.

About half way through the days walk a young Chinese man was sighted walking toward the travelers. Hai asked Wong Li. "Do you think that he turned back or got lost?"

"I don't think so. He seems to be traveling with light equipment and a rifle as I. I believe that he is an escort as well." A moment passed as the man gained a little bit more ground. Wong Li quickly became to realize that he recognized the man. "That is Ho, he is an escort too. He can tell us how travel will be for the rest of the day."

"Will we have to worry about him recognizing Hon as a girl?"

"No way, he is not a bad man and has good reputation and has his own family as well."

As Ho got closer to the traveling party he suddenly recognized Wong Li. He slapped his hands together a couple times with a big smile and shouted. "Wong Li, Wong Li, good day for travel today but many travelers a half day ahead of you." The two friends approached each other and bowed to greet one another. Ho looked at Hai, Hon then smiled at Tommy. He shouted. "Thomas has family again?" Wong Li smiled and replied. "Yes, he is traveling with Hai and his brother Hon." Ho looked at Hai. "Wait a minute, I know a Hai. Are you going to Idaho?" Hai nodded his head. Ho got excited. "Yeah, is your father Fong Yeo?" Hai's and Ming Su's eyes opened wide. Hai replied. "Yes, he is our father. Is he okay?" Ho looked at Hon and said. "He is fine but Fong Yeo said he had a daughter." Instantly Wong Li lunged forward and snarled. "You do not tell anyone. You know as well that it is dangerous for young Chinese girl to travel." Ho looked at Hon and then at Hai and stated. "Your secret is safe with me. I will tell nobody. But Fong Yeo is about a week or so ahead of you. He is traveling with people who are not very nice. Mr. Esposito is well known in San Francisco and hates everyone. He and his friends drink a lot of whiskey and very careless with their rifles. Kill deer and other animals for no food but for fun. Be very careful." Hon ran to Hai and threw her arms around him. Hai rubbed the back of his sister's head to comfort her and said to her. "It will be okay." Then he looked at Ho and said. "Are you sure that it was him? I mean he left China two months before us and he is only a week or so ahead of us now? How can that be possible?" Ho shook his head and replied." I am sorry. I understand your concern but when he got here to America he lost all his money." Hai asked. "How?"

"I heard that he was robbed, I also heard that he was gambling and he owed Mr. Esposito a lot of money and is traveling with him and some other men to help them so he can pay back his debts. I really don't know what the truth would be. I am just telling you what I heard." Hai quickly became agitated. Turned and began to kick the tall grass to express his anger. He snarled. "My father would not have stooped so low to lose everything on gambling. He doesn't gamble. Now he has nothing and he has to work a lot harder to get to Bannock Village. My father is a smart man who makes stupid decisions sometimes." Ming Su nodded her head and said. "He isn't kidding." Ho chuckled and replied. You will never catch up to him unless they stop for about a week and you just happen to be on the same path that he and the American's took." Hai, snarled. "We didn't come to America for him, we came to seek our own futures we don't need him. Let's get going." Hai picked Tommy up and set him on the mule with the gear, then picked up his sister and set her on his shoulders before storming away clenching the lead to Loco so he would follow. Wong Li quickly bowed to Ho and said. "I will see you soon." He then followed Hai.

As the morning became mid-day and the afternoon began there was little words spoken between the travelers, Hai was quickly becoming tired with the extra weight of his sister on his shoulders. He turned to Wong Li and handed him Loco's lead and said. "I am sorry. My father has disappointed Ming Su and I very much. He took all the money that he and I worked for to bring all three of us to America. He abandoned us and left us with nothing, not even a coin or anything of value to trade for food or anything. Ming Su is my sister and I have suddenly become her father and her teacher. I love her dearly, I will die for her if I have to, but if I ever see my father again I may just want to... Never mind."

"I understand your grief Hai. I was brought to America with my father and mother five years ago, I woke up one morning and my parents were gone. I don't know where they went, I don't know if they are alive or dead, I don't know if they returned to China and left me here. But I live on, I take care of myself, I was a young man like you when I arrived here on the coast so I am sure that you can Imagine that I did what I had to do to survive and to make some kind of a life for me. My gold is waiting for me and one day perhaps I will seek it out and find it but for now I know the right thing to do is to help you and Ming Su, well! Hon find your gold for now." Hai stopped and put his hand on Wong Li's shoulder and said. "Thank you, I never realized that we were not alone." Wong Li nodded his head with a smile and said. There is a stream not to far ahead, we should stop and take a break for a short time and maybe give the children some left over pork from last night's meal for energy."

"That's a good idea."

7

The sun was high and hot when they travelers moved on from the cold stream and filling their bellies with the left over pork from the night before. Wong Li began sniffing the mountain air as they walked through the red wood forest. Hai Looked at him with concern and asked. "What is it?" Suddenly Hai said. "It smells like a rotting animal. Wong Li took the rifle that was slung over his shoulder and got it ready to fire. Hon and Tommy stopped walking and hid on the side of Loco as Hai removed his rifle from the case on Loco's side. Hai's focus quickly became directed at the sound of crows squawking and scurrying around on the other side of some lowly grown brush. Hai and Wong Li slowly walked around the bush with their rifles ready. Taking aim in the direction of the potential threat. Wong Li who was leading quickly stopped and turned his head as he let out a cough and covered his nose and mouth with his hand. Hai hustled around him and came upon an old American man that looked to have been rotting and consumed by the wild birds and insects for about a week or so. Hai ran over and began kicking the birds away. He knelt down and noticed the man's neck was slit with a knife or some kind of a sharp utensil. Quickly he stood up, raising his rifle as he twisted around, ready to fire at anything that presented to be a threat. Without warning he heard a high pitch whine coming from the bushes. He knelt down and noticed a long haired black and white dog hiding in the bushes. Carefully holding out his hand he whispered to it. Slowly the pooch crawled out from under the bush to smell the scent of Hai's hand. Quickly the pooch backed away, its top lip rose, bearing its teeth as a warning that it was uncomfortable with the stranger's presence. Curiosity overcame the youngster. They slowly made their way.

Hai tried to stroke the fur on the top of the dogs head but the dog showed its teeth and began to growl. Hai stood up and said to Wong Li. "We need to bury the old man so the animals can't eat it and we will take the dog with us." When Hon and Tommy heard the word dog, they instantly became excited and moved in for a closer look. Hai told the youngsters to stay back because the dog is scared and could be vicious. However, Tommy smiled when he saw the dog and noticed the old man lying on the ground dead. "Tommy said. That is Mr. Stafford." Wong Li didn't know what the young boy said but understood the excitement in his tone. Tommy smiled and said. "He was a friend of my father's; his dog's name is Gordy. He won't bite you, he just don't know you so he is scared." Hai said. "He must know the old man and Gordy too." Tommy giggled while calling. "Gordy, come on Gordy." The floppy ears of the pooch heard a familiar voice calling its name and slowly crawled out from under the bush. Tommy knelt down beside him and wrapped his arms around the scared and lonely dog, pulling Gordy's head closer to his to feel his fur against his own cheek. He asked. "Can we take him with us?" But nobody understood his question." Hai replied. The dog will be another mouth for us to feed."

"Will you be prepared for that?" Wong Li asked.

"Yes, I suppose. He will eat much of our wasted food and will help to protect the children. But for now let's grab the shovel off of Loco and bury the old man." Wong Li nodded his head and said. "We will bury the old man then we must get going, we still have many hours of travel today.

"It was almost dusk when the expedition began to set up camp in a clearing within the forest of redwood trees. Hon and Tommy were worn out from the long walk on the second full day of travel. They both took their bed rolls from the cargo on Loco's back and lied down on a small patch of grass with Gordy between them. Hai began to gather wood to start a fire for cooking the white rice and rabbit that Wong Li shot earlier in the day. Gordy picked up on the scent of blood as Wong Li cleaned the rabbit and prepared it to cook slowly over a make shift rotisserie. He followed Wong Li around like a young puppy staying close to its master with possible hopes that he may get a scrap or two from the carcass to fill a little bit of the void in his stomach.

Darkness fell upon them as the aroma of the freshly roasted rabbit filled the air and tickled the noses of the sleeping children. Wong Li sat on the ground with his back against a fallen log, cleaning his rifle and sipping on a cup of Chinese tea. Hai noticed Hon and Tommy getting up and took the initiative to fix their dinner on two metal plates. Hon wanted to try and act a little bit more like and American so she placed the chopsticks back into the woven basket and retrieved a metal fork. She fumbled with the metal utensil for couple moments before finding a comfortable grip on it and feeling proud that she had learned how to hold it properly by watching her sidekick Tommy.

Hai finished his meal, wiped his mouth on the wrist of his shirt then made his way over to sit on the ground beside Wong Li, who was laying back, resting his upper shoulders against the log, staring up at all the white stars that seemed like a billion miles away. Hai asked Wong Li. "Do you have to leave us tomorrow morning." Wong Li nodded his head and replied. "Yes I do. But I will travel all the way back until I am home." Hon looked at the two friends with confusion and asked. "All the way back to San Francisco without stopping for the night?" Wong Li smiled as he nodded his head at Hon. "Yes, it is a long walk but I will walk much faster by myself and gain more ground." Hai looked at Wong Li, slowly he nodded his head. "I wish that you were coming with us Wong Li. I haven't known you very long but I consider you a friend, especially in this strange land of crazy Americans." Wong Li chuckled and replied. I understand but this is where I must turn back. There will more than likely be other travelers needing a guide. But listen to me and listen to me very well my friend. Be careful out here and have your rifle ready as you get deeper into the forest. There are bear here, bigger and meaner than the black bears in China. They would devour Hon or Tommy and kill you just for standing in its path.

There are also big tan cats called mountain lions. They will attack anyone who they feel threatened by. Traveling with the dog is good for warning and protection but a dog will also attract predators so at night try to keep him from barking or whining. Learn to know the difference in Gordy's barks. Some barks are playful, some are alerting you and some are fear or aggression. Gordy knows your scent if he runs after prey or a threat. Do not follow him. He will find you by following his nose." Hai nodded and said. "I understand. I still wish that you were coming with us." Wong Li looked up at the bright moon lighting up the edges of the clouds and said. "It's going to be a full moon tomorrow night but from the feel of the wind and the heavy clouds moving in this night, we may have some rain too. So be prepared." Hai grunted from the aches of his young muscles and bones as he stood up, rested his hand for a quick moment on Wong Li's shoulder then headed over to clean the dinner dishes and pack them away for tomorrow's journey. Hon noticed her brother being worn out and motioned to Tommy to follow her. She said to Hai. "Go rest Hai, Tommy and me will clean the dishes and pack them in the basket." Hai was over taken by the gesture of his young but maturing sister. He knelt down on one knee and took Ming Su into his arms and held her tight. Tommy stepped over and wrapped his short little arms around the siblings. Wong Li who found great comfort leaning against the young red wood log smiled as a tear filled his eyes. Slowly his tear filled eyes got heavy and he faded off into a dream... A man who appeared to be Wong Li's father shook Wong Li's shoulder to wake him up. "Father what is it? Is mother okay?"

"Your mother is fine my son. Today you had come of age, you are now sixteen and I consider you a man. We all leave China in five days to journey to America." Wong Li stretched as he sat up, leaning his weight onto one hand he scratched under his neck with the other. "Father I don't want to go to America, China is our home."

"But my son, there is great opportunity in America, lots of treasures, lots of gold that only leads to great fortune but for now I have a gift for you."

"A gift for me father?"

"A gift for coming of age and because I love you my son." The father reached down along his side as he remained squatted beside Wong Li. He retrieved a long, thin rolled up blanket from the floor then handed it to his son."

"This is a rifle for me, isn't it father?"

"It is my son. I know that you will make great use of it in America, you are a great outdoorsmen like your father taught you and my father taught me. I know that I will remain proud of you."

"Thank you father, I won't let you down...

8

Wong Li was nowhere in sight when Hai was a woken by drops of rain exploding on his face. He wasted no time waking up the children and packing up Loco for an anticipated miserable day awaiting them. The rain invaded slowly but began to fall hard in less than an hour into the morning travel. Tommy tried to find comfort by staying as dry as possible by draping his coat over his head. Hon thought it to be a good idea and followed suit.

It didn't take much longer for the rain to be falling so heavy that Hai couldn't see more than thirty feet in front of him. The cold wetness began to seep into the clothing of the travelers and make them uncomfortable and irritable. Hon looked down at the border collie that joined the journey the day before and began to laugh at Gordy for looking like an over sized rat as he was soaked to the bone.

Hai's pace began to speed up. Hon and Tommy looked at each other and their walk evolved to a hustle to try and keep up with Hai. But to their surprise, Hai spotted an abandoned wagon with two broken wheels on the front. The cover was weathered and torn but would provide adequate shelter from the cold rain. Hai tied Loco's lead to the wagon and unloaded the gear from the mule, placing it under the broken down wagon as Hon and Tommy crawled up into the bed of the wagon that was wet but still much dryer than the environment outside. Tommy called Gordy but Gordy could not jump into the wagon. Hai walked up behind the drenched dog and picked him up, placing him into the wagon bed. With Gordy looking for comfort, his first instinct was to shake off the rain, instantly showering Hon and Tommy.

Hai unpacked the blankets and bed rolls from the mule pack. The edges were wet but for the most part, the bed rolls were dry enough to cover up with to bring warmth and increase the body temperature of the trio. Hai stripped down to his under garments and hung his wet clothes over a strand of rope that was stretched along the inside of the wagon. He commanded his sister to do the same and following suit was Tommy. Their wet clothes hung dripping as they tried to dry in the cold and wet climate. Hai leaned back against the weathered wood side of the wagon, wrapped up in is bed roll. Ming Su snuggled close to Hai with Tommy snuggled to her as they struggled to warm up from the cold wetness.

The day passed by as the rain continued to plummet the top of the canvas cover and the trio faded off to sleep with Gordy's head resting on Tommy's lap.

Hai was later a woken by Loco acting as if he was spooked. The rain was no longer falling and the sounds of the forest echoed as the spent rain drops continued to drip from the trees. He crawled out of the wagon to take a look around. After a couple moments of peering around he was convinced that Loco was just reminding the others that he was still with them. Hai decided that he would look over the wagon to see if it was repairable. His imagination created illusions of Loco pulling the heavy wagon on his own but when Hai's mind cleared up and reality set in he concluded that he would need another mule and decided to just retrieve the brush from the mule pack and he proceeded to brush the rain from Loco's coat. Suddenly the clouds began to break apart allowing the afternoon sun to glow and raise the temperature. Hai took everyone's clothes and strung the rope between two small trees before hanging the wet clothing to dry in the hot sun. Looking at the location of the fireball in the sky he decided that they would spend the rest of the day and the night there. Hai unpacked the mule pack and started a fire to cook for him and the sleeping duo.

Ming Su was sleeping on her back with the back of her head pushed against the side of the wagon when she was a woken by the aroma of rabbit and rice cooking on the open fire. As she opened her eyes she became instantly shocked, looking down at her chest. Gasping she pulled back and then smiled. She didn't realize that she had made a new friend while she was sleeping. Slowly she extended her hand, placing her tiny finger on the top of the bullfrogs head that found comfort, perched on her chest, staring back at her. She giggled as its little body expanded and contracted as if it took a breath of air. The amused little lady continued to giggle as she pat her new friend unexpectedly waking of Tommy. Tommy, who was sleeping with his back toward Ming Su, slowly rolled over grunting as his little bones and muscles ached with traveling pain from sleeping on the hard wooden floor of the abandoned wagon. His eyes widened when he saw what Ming Su was giggling about. He extended his arm and began to stroke the little amphibian with his finger. The giggling and laughing of the two caught Hai's attention and he quickly made his way to the back of the wagon.

Peering in, the kids did not know that he was watching. Hai smiled and startled the two when he said. "Frog legs, good eating what I hear. I wonder if there are any more around." Ming Su's eyes opened wide in a slight state of fear, she quickly shook her head. Hai chuckle as he walked away.

Before long Ming Su and Tommy had made their way out from the wagon into the wet mountain air. Their blankets wrapped around them to keep them warm as their clothes remained hanging in the sun. Hai began to prepare plates for the two as the sun was on its late afternoon descent.

There was not too much conversation between the sister and brother and with the language barrier. Tommy didn't have too much to say either as the day faded to night, leaving the only light to be from the camp fire. Hai said to his young sister. "We should get some sleep soon. It will be a long day tomorrow." But Ming Su replied. "We slept most of the day, we are not tired." Hai shook his head and said. "It doesn't matter we must stay on a regular sleep schedule and sleep at night so we have the strength and energy to travel during the day." Ming Su quickly became disappointed and snapped back at her big brother. "No! I am not ready for sleep, and Tommy is not either." She placed her metal plate on the ground and stood up, before she stormed off toward the full moon that made its appearance from behind the mountains. She didn't walk far in fear of the dangers of the night and what may be waiting in the shadows. She sat down on a small boulder and looked up at the full moon that was staring down at her. Softly she said as she looked deep into the white of the moon. "Father why is it that you left us? I Know America is so beautiful but it is full of mean and ugly people. I miss you father and I know that Hai misses you too even though he will not say it. You abandoned us like the people abandoned the wagon because it was broken." Tears filled her eyes and she began to sniffle." Father I am so sorry that I am broken and you left me behind. You left me an orphan like so many other children in China. You left Hai and me with no money, very little food. Wherever you are Father I hope that you are remembering me and that you are okay. Maybe one day I will no longer be broken and you will hold me again like you did before mother died." She rested her face in the palms of her hands and continued to sob.

On The other side of the mountains where the full moon rose from, a Chinese man dressed like an American gold prospect woke from a deep sleep. As his eyes opened they focused on the full moon high in the sky. His heart began to race from a pain of loneliness that was all too familiar to him. He sat up and looked around at all the other men sleeping under their bed rolls with whiskey bottles, some empty, some still with the brown intoxicating poison scattered around the camp. The camp fire burned down to orange embers, but still producing heat. The man stood up and slowly maneuvered around the half-drunk sleeping Americans. He noticed a boulder highlighted from the white glow of the moon and sat upon it. Staring up at the full moon he began to sob. "Ming Su, such a beautiful young girl with her mother's heart. Don't know how I came to travel with men who have no honor, no respect, no love for anyone. I was a fool to leave you and my wonderful son Hai. I am so sorry my young daughter who needed her father but he was too broken and lost in sorrow from the death of the woman that he loved so. If you are out there and you can hear my heart, please forgive me for leaving you and not bringing you and Hai with me to seek a fortune in gold as a family. I was selfish and I am a fool, I am also heartbroken to know that I may never see you again to hold you high into the sky as you laugh. Be safe my princess." His head fell, leaving his face to settle in the palms of his hands as his elbows rested on his knees.

Moments later he heard a voice from behind him speaking Chinese but with an American accent. "Who are you talking to Fong Yeo?" He quickly turned around, noticing it to be Benny, a man from China but also able to speak English to translate for the Americans. Fong Yeo shook his head. "I think I made a very bad mistake coming to America." Benny chuckled. "Nothing that you can do about it now, you have no money to get back to China and any gold that you find with these men will be taken from you. They will give you some money for it but not enough to go home with."

"But I left my son and my daughter behind, my daughter is only ten."

"The best thing that you could do is forget that they were ever born because the chances are, you will never lay eyes on them again." Fong Yeo shook his head and said. "I will see my children again. You can bet on that."

"Yeah I'm sure that you will." Benny replied with a sarcastic tone.

"Let me ask you something Benny."

"What is it?"

"Are you friends with these American men."

"I have no friends here in America. I do not trust Americans even though I am one. You and I are strangers in this crazy world from other places to find gold in this land. They will kill us if we show any threat. They want our help only as mules and slaves to work for almost nothing. When your debt to them is paid, be on your way."

"What if I leave before my debt is paid?"

"Not a good idea. You owe them. They will take your life as payment if they must. Besides where will you go?"

"Home to my family."

"But you have no money."

"I have some, just not enough. So I would make it to Bannock village on my own and work until I did and surprise Ming Su and Hai when I get back to China."

"You're dreaming Fong Yeo."

"Can I trust you to keep all this a secret between you and I?"

"We are from different lands, we speak different but same language and we came here for the same thing. I will not tell anyone of this conversation." Benny turned and walked away.

Ming Su was startled by the sound of footsteps in the grass behind her. She turned around to notice that it was Hai. Hai asked. "Are you okay Su?" Hai could see the pain in her face as the moon light reflected off Ming Su's tears. He stood in front of his little sister, bending down to pick her up. Ming Su wrapped her arms around Hai's neck and whimpered. "For some reason I feel like father is thinking about me right now. His heart is broken just like ours." Hai closed his eyes tightly to keep his tears from running down his cheek. In his mind he was sobbing for himself, Ming Su and for their father. "Everything is going to be okay Su, you will see father again. I promise. Hai stood, holding Ming Su as he felt her little body twitch. Hai glanced up at the heavens and sucked in a breath as he smiled. "Ming Su, Look! Ming Su sniffled and turned her head, looking up into the star lit sky. Hai asked. "Do you see it?"

"See what?" Ming Su asked. "Right there Su. The big bright star." Ming Su gasped with wide eyes. "That's the North Star?" Hai felt a little uncertain whether it was the North Star or not but under no circumstances was he going to put any doubt in his little sister's mind. He whispered. "See Ming Su. Mother is looking down on you right now, and see how the star twinkles? That is the twinkle in mothers' eye as she smiles back at how proud she is of you. Ming Su hugged her brother tightly. "I love you Hai." Hai pulled Ming Su tight against him and smiled.

9

Dawn was just beginning to break when Hai was loading Loco up with the mule cargo pack. Ming Su and Tommy were up, full of energy and ready to go.

The travel was slow and sometimes frustrating for Hai, who had to take his time with his long legs, high metabolism and perfect health. He knew that he would be much, much further along if he didn't have to walk at a slower pace and continuously stop for breaks to accommodate Hon and Tommy for a month as they grew closer to the State of Idaho. Gordy took to Tommy and Hon very well but Hai knew that Gordy would always remember his original master no matter how much the children loved him.

It was confusing to Hai as the environment continued to change from the Redwood Forest to timberland to high desert to timberland again. Keeping safety from elements was a continuous concern for the future of their journey. Horse and mule tracks, both shod and unshod, wagon wheels tracks running parallel along each other like train tracks leaving indentions in the ground from the weight of the cargo and many boot and shoe prints from human travelers on foot made following the trails easy, along with an occasional lost or discarded item such as a whiskey bottle, pot or pan, an article of clothing, prospector gear or even worse, human remains. It seemed to Hai that many prospectors and pioneers were more in love with discovering their fortune than the family that they once loved, cared for and cherished. To be incredibly inconsiderate and bold as to leave a once loved one's body dead, on the side of the trail without taking the time and burying it.

The sun crept in one morning without disturbing Hai as he slept. However the first to wake was Ming Su. She shook her brother quickly and called his name. "Hai, Hai wake up. Wake up Hai." He opened his eyes and saw his sister hovered over him. He whispers. "What is it Ming Su?" Her eyes were filled with tears, she pouts. "Tommy looks like he is almost dead."

"What? Tommy is almost dead?"

"No, he looks like he is almost dead. Come on." Hai quickly flipped the blanket off and sprung to his feet. He took a couple quick paces and jumped over Tommy before settling down on his knees. He looked at Tommy and said. "Oh no, Tommy is very sick... We better pack up Loco quickly and hope that we can find help soon." Ming Su fell to her knees, softly placing the side of her face against Tommy's chest as she wrapped her arms around him, she cried. "Tommy don't die, I love you so much." Tommy struggled to move his arm and placed his hand on Ming Su's head. She pushed herself up to look at her young friend in his half opened eyes. He forced a smile and lightly nodded. Ming Su whispered. "We're going to get you some help."

Hai was running frantic as he tried to pack all the gear and supplies on the mule pack that he already placed on Loco's back. He knelt down beside Tommy and Ming Su and stated. "Ming Su I need you to take Loco by the lead so I can carry Tommy." Ming Su looked at her brother with confusion and asked. "Why don't you put Tommy on Loco's back with the mule pack?"

"Because I think Tommy is too weak and he may fall off, I better carry him."

"Oh, okay, I'll take Loco's lead and follow you. Come on Gordy." After a few weeks of traveling, Gordy learned to understand Ming Su's commands even though her commands were spoken in Chinese. Gordy quickly ran to Ming Su and stayed by her side as she followed Hai with Loco's lead clinched in her little hand.

Hai was wearing down fast as he carried Tommy in his arms through the hot, dry sun. The 55 pound boy was not a lot, but 55 pounds being carried in ones arms could wear down any man after walking two or three miles over uneven terrain. Ming Su's extra responsibility took a toll on her as she tried to keep up with her brother while leading the stubborn mule. However, Gordy was not much of a problem at all. The old man seemed to have done a great job with training and discipline of the mutt while he walked the earth.

Hai suddenly stopped, lowered himself on one knee, placing Tommy in the tall green grass that stood about half way up Hai's calf. Ming Su caught up, let go of Loco's lead and knelt down beside her brother. Tommy fought to keep his eyes open as his face was pale white, clammy and his temperature felt higher than normal to Hai's touch.

The sibling's attention was taken off Tommy by the faint growl coming from Gordy. Ming Su snapped at him. "Quiet dumb dog." It wasn't a moment later when whinny from a horse caught their attention. Hai and Ming Su stood up quickly at the mere sight of more than ten men with long black braided hair, feathers in their hair and on their horses and animal skin covering their bodies with colorful bead work and paint on the horses about ten yards to their left.

Slowly a horse with a man and young woman riding it moved closer to the trio. The young woman climbed down from the large tan colored animal. Ming Su stared up in amazement at the quiet man who remained sitting on the horse way up in the sky while the young woman knelt down beside Tommy to examine his body. Hai stood back and watched the young woman, as he understood that she was trying to help him but Ming Su kept asking the young woman. "What are you doing to Tommy? What are you doing to Tommy?" The young woman looked up at the man on the enormous animal and said something to him in a language that Ming Su and Hai never heard before and did not understand. She motioned to Hai to kneel beside her. Quickly he heeded her invitation. The young woman pulled up Tommy's shirt, exposing his belly and a round red spot about the size of a large coin next to his naval and a swollen tick about the size of a pea. Hai's eyes opened wide before looking at Ming Su. He said to her. "It's a tick, he has tick fever."

"Is Tommy going to die?" Ming Su asked with worry in her voice. Hai slowly shook his head and replied. "I don't know." The man on the horse said something in what sounded like English but Hai and Ming Su still couldn't understand. But to their surprise Tommy whispered soft and slow. "They want us to go with them, they will make me better." Hai seemed a little hesitant at first then looked at the man on the horse and nodded with a questionable smile.

The man on the horse turned his head and shouted to the others behind him. Another man on a horse rode up alongside of him and hopped down onto the grass. He picked up Tommy and handed him to the first man on a horse. The horses turned around and headed away. The young woman motioned for Ming Su and Hai to follow her as she followed the others who were all on horses.

Hai took Loco by the lead before following the young woman with Ming Su and Gordy following close behind. It wasn't too long before Hai began to notice the young native woman leading their way. Ming Su looked up at her brother and noticed a look on his face that was very unfamiliar but was also soft and tender. She slapped her brother on the hip to get his attention. His face dropped when he noticed the make believe love sick look on her face as she kissed the air then pointed to the young native beauty. She began to giggle when Hai picked up pace, leaving her behind. They seemed to follow for a couple of miles until they entered a meadow surrounded by pine trees. Many teepees of thin logs and animal hide provided shelter to the many people who looked very strange to Ming Su. A large fire produced heat and light when darkness would be upon them. Many women of different ages sat around the big fire pit. Some were preparing food for the villagers to consume at a later time of the day, others grinding flour for bread from corn and grain. Children ran around and played in the meadow grass to keep them busy as their parents worked through their daily tasks. The elder woman of the village kept busy with preparing buck skin for clothing, Young warriors stood wading in the river as an elder instructed them on how to spear fish for a meal. The mountains not too far off in a distance were tall and beautiful with snow covering the caps. The birds of prey flew high and soared proud as they kept a sharp eye out for their next meal. Squirrels chirped and flicked their tails to warn others of their kind that danger may be among them. Dragon flies chased each other from reed to reed, perhaps trying to mate with one another or just a simple game of playing chase.

With Ming Su being lost in amazement of what she was witnessing a clan of young native children ran up upon her, startling Ming Su and Hai. Recognizing the frightened look on his sister's face he said to her with a big smile. "No worries Ming Su, they are friendly and want to greet you as their friend."

"Hai took noticed as an elder woman took Tommy from the warrior's arms and carried him into a teepee. Slowly he began to walk toward the teepee with concern for his young friend. An old Chinese woman dressed in buckskin approached Hai holding her hand up as a gesture to stop, and then she said. "The boy is very sick, tick fever. These people are your friends and they will make the young boy better. You and the other boy should come with me to my enclosure. Ming Su's face instantly looked angry as she began to snarl. "I am not a boy." But the look on Hai's face made her remember that she was Hon and not Ming Su. Hai winked at his sister and tugged on Loco's lead as they followed the old Chinese woman. The woman turned to Hai and stated with a smile. "You can call me Lost Doe, My given name is Milin. These people found me about three years ago after I was left for dead by the American men on a rampage through the forest to find the gold that drive most men to insanity. My husband and children are gone someplace in the mountains, perhaps dead or even slaves to the white man." She looked down at the ground and stated. "I don't think that I will ever see them again." Hai stepped forward and wrapped his arms around the old woman to show comfort from one of her own kind. Ming Su not knowing what was going on but understood her brother's gesture to the grieving woman wrapped her arms around her waist and looked up at her as Ming Su's hat fell to the ground. The woman looked down at the child with tear filled eyes and suddenly yanked her head back as her eyes opened wide. She whispered. "He is not a boy, he is a girl."

Ming Su smiled back at the woman as Hai put his finger to his lips. "There is a long journey still ahead of us and people must think they she is a boy for her own safety." Quickly she said. "Come with me." The siblings followed Lost Doe into her teepee. She directed them to sit on the ground. Lost Doe gathered bowls of pottery filled with fresh water and retrieved jerky from a pouch and handed it to her new friends before sitting down alongside of them. She said to Hai and Ming Su. "These people are good Indians. They will not harm you. They would die to protect you. But other people such as the American men and the even the Chinese men will take the young child and do horrible things to her out here in the wilderness. This place has no mercy and does not care about your life or mine. When you travel, be careful and cautious. I am your friend, Theses people here are your friends but no one else is. Trust me. Now come, I shall bring you to the chief. He may provide safety as you travel." The siblings quickly got up and followed Lost Doe out of the teepee and across the meadow. Lost Doe instructed Hai and Ming Su to stay by the fire as she went and spoke to the chief.

Ming Su said to Hai. "For all we know Long Doe is working with the bad men. We need to be cautious of her too for now. I don't want to be taken." Hai replied. "You are safe, Su." As he slowly panned around at all the strange people but his curiosity suddenly stopped when his eyes focused on a familiar native beauty. She noticed his stare and smiled at him, encouraging him to approach her. But to both of their surprise the warrior from the horse stepped in front of Hai and stared him down quickly. Lost Doe ran up to Hai and took him by the arm. She stated to the love stricken young man. "She is not our kind of people; she is not your kind of people. That man is her father Smoke Owl, and these people are very protective of their children, especially Smoke Owl and his daughter Flying Star." Hai threw his hands up and dropped them as the native beauty frowned causing her father to smile. Hai smiled back but his joy was quickly robbed from him when Smoke Owl's smile turned to a deadly stare.

Ming Su could see that her brother was annoyed with Smoke Owl. Hai sat on a short length of log with his back towards the fire, his head pointed to the ground as he kicked the heel of his boot into the dirt. Periodically he lifted his head enough to look under the brim of his hat at Flying Star. His elbows resting on his knees while pressing the fingertips of both hands against each other. Flying Star wasn't hiding her attraction to the Chinese immigrant. She kept smiling at him as she continued with her chores. Hai would smile back but tried to act inconspicuous when he noticed Smoke Owl glancing back at him. Ming Su laughed at the game that they all seemed to be playing as she found comfort on a length of log. Hai looked at his sister and grouched. "What is so funny?" He got up and stormed away in embarrassment. Instantly the smile disappeared from Ming Su's face as she cried out. "Hai, where are you going? Don't leave me here by myself Hai. Please come back." Nevertheless Hai kept walking away. However Ming Su's cries were heard not only by Hai who chose to ignore them but by Flying Star. Flying Star gave her father an unsettling look before setting down her basket and racing after Hai. Smoke Owl jumped to his feet and hollered something in his native language that Ming Su didn't understand but also fell on deaf ears of his daughter.

Lost Doe returned at that moment and walked over to Smoke Owl, encouraging Ming Su to rise from the comfort of the log and stand beside Smoke Owl. She looked up at him and smiled. "Smoke Owl." Lost Doe translated. "My brother Hai is not a dangerous boy, he is my protector. He understands how you feel towards the safety of your daughter because that is how he feels towards the safety of me. He will not harm Flying Star. He thinks that she is very pretty and likes her like you must like her mother." Smoke Owl set a light palm on Ming Su's head while barely expressing a smile. Suddenly Ming Su giggled as Smoke Owl stood up straight, puffing out his bare muscular chest as his expression turned bold. She quickly turned her head to take notice of what caught Smoke Owl's eye. Hai and Flying Star were walking side by side but Hai quickly stepped away from Flying Star to freely allow her to return to her father.

Flying Star stood before Smoke Owl. "Father I apologize for disobeying your commands but I am no longer a child. I am at the age mother was when she married you. I have that tickle in my stomach and the tightness in my chest when I look at Hai." She stepped back as her eyes slowly lowered to the ground while awaiting her father's response.

Smoke Owl held out his hand. "Come walk with me." Flying Star set her little hand into her father's hand that was at least twice the size and turned to walk away with him. "My daughter, you have been left as my only child. My concern is great for you. Try to understand that our people are not like most, we are not savages. We have great honor, great pride and our blood travels back for many, many generations of American Indian and no other civilization or culture. Our lineage must not go beyond the blood of our tribal families. But I do not want to restrict you from what you are feeling in your heart." He shook his head and let out a long deep sigh through his nose. "I must take some time and speak to Lost Doe, please send her to me." Flying star stepped away mumbling to herself. "Lost Doe, what does this have to do with Lost Doe?"

Moments later Lost Doe stood before the enormous warrior. "I am at the split in the road here Lost Doe, I also have too much work to get done so I cannot take the time to try to understand what attracts my daughter to that scrawny Chinese Boy. I have more muscles in my forearm than he has in his whole chest. I would like you to mediate between the two so there is no question of what is being spoken between the two. Ping Pi, Ping Su, oh Ming Su can go along with you. Perhaps walk down to the big bend in the river and back."

"I understand Smoke Owl."

"And bring that smelly mutt with you too."

Smoke Owl was one of very little emotion, not even his own daughter Flying Star could determine what he was thinking after watching how his daughter and an immigrant from China were interacting. The nearly six and a half foot tall warrior was very intimidating to the barely 5' 9" tall, 150 pound Chinese teenager. There was no doubt in Smoke Owl's mind that Flying Star had begun developing adolescent feelings for Hai so quickly but he also knew that romance between the two was much forbidden within the culture of the South-Western, Idaho tribe. He had no idea what he was going to do. To force them apart may encourage her to leave forever, but to allow a Chinese immigrant into the tribe could cause discrimination towards his daughter throughout the village.

Lost Doe led the way as the young couple walked along the trail barely speaking to one another, probably because of the language barrier. It was much of a surprise to find Ming Su following a few paces behind, giggling periodically at the two just ahead of her trying to break through the their communicative differences. Hai began to speak to Flying Star but quickly halted once he noticed the look on her face, realizing that he was speaking in a language that she didn't understand. Ming Su began to laugh at her brother when he patted himself on the chest with both hands like a gorilla and continued to say. "Hai, Hai, my name is Hai".

Ming Su got a real good laugh when Hai patted himself on the top of his head like a monkey and said. "Hai, Hai." She could tell that Hai was anxious to communicate with the native beauty and by the expression on Flying Stars face. Hai seemed to be only succeeding in looking like a fool. Ming Su decided perhaps that she should try to communicate with Flying Star.

Quickly Ming Su hustled to the lost couple. Taking Hai's hand with one of hers, then Flying Star's with the other to join them together. The expression on Hai's face presented accomplishment, success or perhaps even fulfillment.

However Flying Star presented a different expression of invasion or trespassing. Hai felt the physical tension in his arm as Flying Star began to loosen her grip in an attempt to let go, His smile quickly escaping his face. Ming Su quickly stepped in front of Flying Star, placed her hand over her heart and patted. Flying Star understood the gesture to be innocent and without threat. She smiled as she grasped Hai's hand into hers.

10

A few days had passed and there didn't seem to be anything separating the young couple and their sidekick, Ming Su. Smoke Owl decided that a fishing trip to the lake may be in order. He informed Lost Doe of his decision.

Traveling at a walking trot, Smoke Owl led three more horses. The first horse carrying Lost Doe and Ming Su. The second horse carrying Flying Star and on the third and taking up the rear was Hai. Lost Doe tagged along to translate between Smoke Owl, Flying Star and the Chinese siblings. With secret orders from Smoke Owl, to keep an eye on Flying Star and Hai when his back was turned. However she did seem to have very little interest in blowing the whistle on the young love birds.

To Ming Su, traveling on the horses felt like hours and many miles, but realistically the well-traveled path to the lake was less than a mile through the enormous pines. The tall green grass surrounded the lake that reflected the blue sky and clouds above.

As the party was dismounting the horses Smoke Owl pointed out an American Bald Eagle feasting on a salmon or trout about a hundred feet from them. However the bird of prey was startled by Smoke Owl approaching the water and took to flight. To Ming Su's surprise as the eagle took refuge in the sky a brown wing feather spun to the ground. Unknowing what the American Bald Eagle feather meant to the American Indians, Ming Su chased the feather down.

Smoke Owl stood stout as he held the feather high above his head as she spoke in his native language. The feather was then handed to

Flying Star. She cut a strip of buck skin from her clothing to use to tie the eagle feather onto Ming Su's hat band.

The sun wasted no time climbing to its highest point of the day attracting many different animals to the big body of water to drink. Black Bears, Deer, Elk, Coyote and Mountain Lions were some of the species that paid no mind to the humans while looking to hydrate themselves in the cool mountain water.

Smoke Owl announced to Lost Doe and Flying Star. "Time for a fishing lesson, I must show Chinese boy the proper way to catch fish." However with Ming Su and Hai over hearing something that sounded interesting from Smoke Owl they turned to Lost Doe. She explained that Smoke Owl was going to teach Hai how to fish. A confident look overcame Hai's face. He retrieved the fishing spool from his sack that he carried. He looked around in the grass for a grasshopper. On that particular hot day he found a good size one to tie the line around the body of the bug close to the steel hook. The bug would not be enough weight but Hai wanted the live bug to float and kick its legs, so he looked for a small long skinny pebble. After placing it a few inches from the bug he tied it loosely.

Hai unraveled a bunch of line and put his foot on the spool while holding the slack with his left hand before he threw the bug and pebble with her right hand into the lake. The bug and pebble flew many, many feet before landing in the water. As usual the pebble fell from the lose knot leaving the kicking grasshopper to fight for its life as it tried to keep from drowning. Hai looked at Smoke Owl and smiled as he got a hit. To everyone's surprise a large rainbow trout breached from the surface of the water as it swallowed the grasshopper and the hook. Hai grabbed the spool off the ground quickly and walked toward the water as he wrapped the line around it while backing up to pull the fish onto the grass. Smoke Owl couldn't believe that he had just been out fished by that boney Chinese boy. The trout was about two feet long and would no doubt ably make a great meal.

Hai did not seem to be very impressed by the way Smoke Owl paddled out into a canoe and used a type of spear to try and impale a fish as it swam close to the surface. Even to a well trained and experienced native warrior, Smoke Owl missed many more fish than he actually caught.

The sun was very hot. Stomachs were rumbling and the idea of smoked trout on the open fire sounded good. Smoke Owl help Lost Doe onto her horse, Hai helped Ming Su up on Lost Doe's horse right behind her. It was like an unsaid competition to get to Flying Star to help her up on her horse but Hai bounced back off of Smoke Owl's chest, giving him the room to help his daughter up. Hai and Smoke Owl stared off for a moment before breaking into laughter. Smoke Owl charged Hai, bending down and scooping Hai up on his shoulder before spinning him around a few times and setting him on his horse.

Smoke Owl once again led the way while babbling on about his grandfather when it came time to learn to fish. Ming Su could barely understand anything so she depended on Lost Doe for interpretation. Flying Star and Hai rode side by side saying few words due to the language barrier. Out of nowhere a mountain lion appeared at the top of a rock formation hovering over Hai riding next to Flying Star. The horses became frantic and almost unmanageable to handle. Hai However was able to maneuver his horse putting himself in between Flying Star and the cougar. With a loud growl the big cat let it be known that it was threatened by the unwelcomed trespassers. There was barely any time for Smoke Owl to react with his Hickory bow and arrows. He struggled to regain control of his stallion and was deprived a clear shot before the mountain lion leaped from the top of the rock formation. Flying Star screamed as Ming Su and Lost Doe could only watch helplessly. The mountain lion's feet hit the ground. Smoke Owl aimed the best he could and released an arrow, piercing the heart of the savage beast. However, not before it had already done its damage.

Ming Su laid a wake most of the night with ember coals of the fire casting the only light to the darkness. Tears covered her face as she sniffled. Lost Doe didn't know what to do or even what to say. She just slept close to the child to comfort her and to make her feel safe from any and all dangers. Hard for Ming Su to feel safe at all, considering how quick and easy the mountain lion took the last of her family away from her. She also knew that even though the mountain lion was no longer a threat, there were other threats awaiting her. Ming Su suddenly rolled over, facing the older woman, causing Lost Doe to open her eyes. Ming Su looked into the old Chinese woman's eyes that held an ember highlight and whispered. "I have to go to Bannock Village." Lost Doe shook her head and replied. "There is no one to travel with you now, it is too dangerous. A mountain lion or bear would be sure to get you."

"I have nobody now, I don't care. I came to America with my brother Hai to find gold and reunite with our father. I cannot travel with Tommy without my brother. So Tommy must stay here. My brother showed me how to hunt and how to fish. I will take the mule, Loco with all our supplied, my brother's rifle and his knife and I will make it to Bannock Village and with any luck I will find my father and we will find gold together. And somehow, I just don't know how but I will have to tell him that his only son is now dead. I hate America and now I cannot even go home" Lost Doe sat up and looked down at the child lying on the deer hide. Shaking her head she said. "I understand how you feel to be left alone and have nobody, but it's foolish for you to go on alone. It is too dangerous child. If men found you they would hurt you and even do much worse than you could even imagine. You must stay here with me." Ming Su got very agitated. "I didn't come to America to live with you, Lost Doe and Smoke Owl. I came with my brother Hai to find gold and our father." She sprung to her feet, bent down and hugged the old woman and said. "I will go now. Please take care of Tommy and let him know that I love him very much. He is the little brother that I always wanted." Then she walked toward the exit of the teepee. Suddenly she stopped and whispered. "I need you to promise me that when Tommy is a little older that Smoke Owl will show him how to use his father's pocket knife that he keeps in his pocket." The old woman nodded her head as a tear ran down her cheek as she said. "Ming Su, you are leaving the one boy that you just said was the little brother that you always wanted. I am sure that you are the big sister that he always wanted too." Ming Su lunged forward and threw her arms around Lost Doe. "I'm sorry." She said before letting go and running off.

The central fire remained burning as the village slept. The fire pit spread about eight feet in diameter surrounded by logs for sitting.

Ming Su struggled to get the mule pack on Loco's back but the pack was too heavy and Loco was too tall. She fell to the ground in defeat and began to sob. Suddenly she was startled by a hand on her shoulder. She looked up to see that it was Lost Doe. Lost Doe whispered. "Here, I will help you with the pack, sadly I cannot stop you from going, so I will help you as much as I can, just bring your dog, he will warn you of danger and protect you with his own life so you can travel safe." She whispered back. "Gordy is Tommy's dog, he will want to know where he is when he gets better."

"I will tell Tommy that you took Gordy for protection, he will understand," Ming Su let out a light sigh and said. "Okay."

The woman struggled to pick up the pack and get it onto the back of the mule. Ming Su picked up her brothers rifle and slung it over her shoulder. Lost Doe smiled but was also concerned that the butt of the rifle was merely an inch from the ground. She removed the rifle from Ming Su's shoulder and adjusted the strap to make it tighter and shorter before handing it back to the young traveler. Ming Su unfastened her belt and slipped Hai's knife on to it before refastening it. She looked up at Lost Doe with a sincere expression, wrapped her arms around the old woman and said "Goodbye." She whispered "Gordy, come on." She patted her leg before unfastening Loco's lead from the log post and began leading the mule out of the village in the direction of the glow on the other side of the mountains. Lost Doe stood in tears as she watched Ming Su, Loco and Gordy disappear into the darkness.

Smoke Owl's eyes opened quick and wide as he was a woken by an unfamiliar sound of a mule's bray and a dog's bark off in the distance. He looked at his daughter lying close to him as she slept in peace. Smoke Owl once again heard the mule and dog further in a distance.

Ming Su walked toward the glow that continued to get brighter and brighter as the night turned to day. She pushed on with her stomach rumbling and aching for what seemed like days but without darkness or night. As her legs were about to give in and the rest of her body was about to collapse from exhaustion and dehydration. She came upon a brook not more than two yards across as the sky was beginning to turn gray just before night. She retrieved a metal cup from the mule pack and sat down on a boulder by the brook. Loco and Gordy enjoyed the cool mountain water alongside their master. Suddenly an aroma filled the air. Ming Su pointed her face to the first stars outs as she tried to figure out the direction the bread and broiled beef was coming from. Then she remembered a trick that her father had showed her in China. She picked up some dry pine needles and rolled them in her tiny hands and watched which direction the light breeze carried them. Then she knew that she needed to search in the direction the wind was coming from. She didn't want to make any sound so she tied Loco to a small dead pine tree and demanded Gordy to stay. Being careful of where she stepped and her footing she slowly walked toward the wind. Her journey was short as she quickly came to a clearing with two covered wagons and what looked to be American families. Slowly she made her way to the side of one of the wagons with the other wagon on the other side. Between the wagons a large campfire burned pine as fuel. Ming Su hid behind the rear wheels, under one of the wagons. There she watched a big beef roast on a rotisserie and fresh bread cooling in a heavy but shallow pot. In front of the wagon she noticed a man brushing a horse in the firelight, three young Chinese girls about Ming Su's age or a little older sitting on a blanket looking up in the night sky, pointing out stars and one woman feeding the fire with fresh pine. Ming Su wondered why three Chinese girls were traveling with an American man and woman as she watched the woman. Meanwhile the aroma of the broiling beef was driving her taste buds crazy. Periodically she would look at the man brushing the horse and the Chinese girls on the blanket counting stars. Before she knew it the woman walked away to converse with the man brushing the horse. Ming Su made her move. She pulled Hai's knife from its sheath and crawled around the wagon wheel on her hands and knees before taking the sharp blade and cut a hefty slice off the roast. Not having any other utensils she used the blade of the knife like a spatula and tore a chunk of bread before disappearing in the darkness.

A few minutes went by before the woman noticed a chunk of bread was missing. She stormed over to the Three Chinese girls and began to scold and question them where the bread was but they couldn't understand her to give her a logical explanation. She slapped each one of them on the top of the head then stormed over to the man brushing the horse but his answer seemed to lead her nowhere as well. Agitated she began to pan around at the ground in search for fresh foot prints.

Ming Su felt pretty proud of herself giggling as she walked quickly back to the brook where she left Loco and Gordy. Switching the hot beef from one hand to the other and back as it heated her little hands. Gordy began to growl as he heard Ming Su rushing toward him until he heard her voice. "Shut up Gordy, you dumb dog."

She set the bread and beef down in a small pot that was hanging from the mule pack on Loco's back. Then removed a blanket from the pack and set it down on the ground. Gordy continued to whine at the scent of the beef that he wanted to fill the emptiness in his stomach with. Ming Su kept whispering. "Shut up Gordy." But he didn't stop until his new master sat down on the bed roll with the beef and sliced a piece off to feed to him.

The sky was completely black when Ming Su realized how tired she was and called Gordy to roll up alongside her. With them both having full bellies of beef and bread, they faded off to sleep under the dark clouds that chased away the stars.

Ming Su's sleep seemed to be uninterrupted until drops of rain began to splatter on her face in the early dawn. She struggled to get up and roll up her bedroll. After placing it on Loco's back she grabbed his lead and began to hustle toward the two covered wagons but to her disappointment the wagons were already gone. Gordy ran around the abandoned campsite with his nose to the ground, sniffing anything that would cause any interest as the rain began to fall at a steady pace.

Out of nowhere. A hand from behind grabbed Ming Su by the shoulder. Startled she turned around to see the tall American man who was brushing the horse glaring down on her. He snarled. "I had a good feeling that the little thief would return for more. And I was right." He grabbed Ming Su by the opening of his coat and swatted her across the face, causing her hat to fall to the ground. The man's eyes opened wide as he noticed. "You're not a boy, you are a little Chinese girl." He chuckled. You just added to my payday. Ming Su yelled out. "I'm boy, my name Hon, I'm boy." The man quickly lost his patience and shouted through the falling rain. "We'll get to the bottom of this right now." He began to pull Ming Su's coat off and then her shirt. Ming Su screamed with everything that she had. Gordy ran up from the side and locked jaws on to the man's pant leg. The man tried kicking his leg but had very little luck as Gordy pulled him to the ground, giving his master a chance to run away. The man retrieved his revolver from his holster and fired a shot at Gordy, with a yelp, Gordy took off into the rain. The man got to his feet and spotted a faint image of the girl running away. He began quickly after her but was stopped in his tracks by an arrow piercing his chest and heart. Smoke Owl quickly set another arrow as he heard a woman scream and the sound of gun fire. Smoke Owl was struck in the shoulder, spinning him completely around to take dead aim at his assailant. He released the arrow catching the woman in the chest.

Ming Su saw that Smoke Owl came to her aid. She ran up to him and threw her arms around him. After a moment she stepped back and looked up at the tall warrior holding his left hand over a bloody wound on the front of his shoulder. She asked him as the rain had almost come to a halt. "What are you doing here?" He looked to his right and about ten yards away stood his daughter, and Lost Doe. She ran to Lost Doe, looking up at her, she asked. "You told him?" Lost Doe shook her head as Smoke Owl stepped up and said. "I already knew." She looked at Smoke Owl with confusion and asked. "You speak my language." He smiled as Lost Doe replied. "Yes, I have been teaching him and his daughter." At that time Gordy came limping up to her, she knelt down and quickly looked him over. Gordy yelped in pain from Ming Su's hand brushing on his hip. She looked at the palm of her hand to discover blood mixed with rain. "Oh no." She cried as she hugged the mutt. "You've been shot." as she whimpered. Quickly she sprung to her feet shouting. "The other girls, there are three more other Chinese girls, they are in danger.

Lost Doe shook her head and stated. "It's okay child, they are safe, they will come back with us and eventually be with their family again soon." Ming Su looked at Smoke Owl, Flying Star and Lost Doe with concern. Then Flying Star knelt down and looked Ming Su in the eyes and said. "Trust us, they are fine. Right now we need to tend to your dog, so you must come with us, you will be safe. Ming Su stepped back shaking her head with disappointment or even fear in her eyes. She grouched. "I cannot. I must go to Bannock Village." Smoke Owl stepped forward and put out his hand for Ming Su to take but she refused. "I have to go to Bannock Village, my father is there." She cried. Smoke Owl looked at Flying Star. She returned a smile and said. She needs her father as I do you. Her brother is dead and we are all she has until she can reunite with her own father." Smoke Owl anxiously growled, then let out a sigh through his nose. "Okay, we will go back to our village first but the dog will be no good for traveling. I will do what I can to get you safely on your way by sending two young braves to help you get to your father." Ming Su smiled and asked. "Do you promise?" Smoke Owl turned and walked away. Leaving Ming Su in confusion. Flying Star smiled at Ming Su and said. He will keep his word. It is his honor to do so but I thought that your father abandoned you and Hai."

"He did, but I have no family left so I must find him."

"I understand but we must catch up to my father and Lost Doe now." The two girls hustled to catch up.

Ming Su was amazed at how fast that they returned to the village until she noticed the trail that she took was on the other side of the village and must have been a trail that circled around. Flying Star escorted Ming Su into Lost Doe's shelter and the three sat on an elk skin.

Flying Star began to speak. "Ming Su, the forest is a very bad place. All it took was one bite from a little bug to make your young friend sick."

"His name is Tommy." Ming Su stated with an attitude. "I am not trying to upset you Ming Su. I am your friend. "

"You are not my friend... My brother is dead because he was protecting you from that stupid cat. I have nobody now." Flying Star could feel Ming Su's grief. Lost doe felt the tension and she step in. "Ming Su, you can't blame Flying Star for Hai's death. It was not her that controlled the wild cat's way of thinking. The mountain lion acted on its own instinct. We know that Hai was your brother and that you loved him very much but the grief of his death is not solely yours. It is ours too. In some shape or form, we all have grief and a certain regret for his death. Take a moment and think about Smoke Owl."

"What about Smoke Owl?"

"Have you not come to the conclusion that Hai's death is weighing very heavy on him?"

"No! Why would I?" Lost Doe lifted her pottered jug and took a drink of water from it. "Ming Su, Take a look at Smoke Owl's stature. To look at him, we all know that he is a big strong warrior with much responsibility, one day he will be chief. There are rules of this tribe that has been kept and obeyed for generations. You know that he could see in his daughter's eyes the love that she wanted to have for Hai but deep in her heart she also knew the rules and traditions forbidding her from having any romantic relationship with an outsider, especially a boy that had traveled from another land. Smoke Owl is like any other father; he wants his daughter to be happy. Smoke Owl didn't have complete authority over changing the rules and regulations but to make his daughter happy and in hence make Hai happy as well, he was going to present the situation and the circumstances to the council but now he feels like that he made a grave mistake. He lifted his hand and allowed

Flying Star and Hai to spend time together as courtship but he quickly learned that breaking the rules or traditions led only to Hai's death instead of happiness for his daughter. Smoke Owl is crying out in pain within his heart for the mistake that he made."

"What mistake did Smoke Owl make?"

He escorted all of you down to the river. If he would have obeyed the rules and tradition then Hai would not have met his demise by the attack of the mountain lion." Flying Star looked down at a caterpillar inching along the floor. "I was wrong to show interest in Hai, I knew that it was wrong but..." Ming Su rose to her feet, wrapped her arms around Flying Star. "It is nobody's fault, except the mountain lion."

A few moments of silence passed before Lost Doe whispered. "Child you must be careful, you will be all by yourself. Tommy is too weak to travel and now Gordy is wounded and will not be able to accompany you to protect you." Ming Su stood straight up like a soldier at attention. "Hai taught me to be brave, to be strong and to be smart. I would like to leave tomorrow morning. I shall spend today with Tommy and Gordy and say goodbye to Hai." She turned and looked at Lost Doe. "Will you help me to go through all the gear that is packed on Loco so that I only travel with what I need?" Lost Doe nodded while staring at the ground.

Ming Su stood at the end of a pile of rocks with her head hung low. She sobbed as she looked around at many other piles of rocks where she knew the ancestors and families of Flying Star and Smoke Owl rested. She ran her right sleeve over her right eye and repeated with the left sleeve over the left eye. "I am sorry Hai. I am sorry that I teased you about Flying Star, I am sorry that I put the extra burden on you with Tommy coming with us, I am sorry that my legs are so short to be able to keep up with you. I will find our gold and I promise to live a good life within your honor, my children will know how brave and smart their Uncle Hai was. If I have my own son then I will name him after you. Please watch over me from the stars my big brother, help keep me aware of danger that may be hiding around the corner. I will always love you Hai. Goodbye." She was surprised to see Flying Star standing in the grass with a frown on her face. "He would have made you a good husband." Flying Star shook her head. "No! He could have never been my husband, not because of rules or tradition, but because if he wasn't lying in the grave before you then he would be protecting you on your travels to Bannock Village and I would not go with him. This is my home and once you leave tomorrow I will always wonder if you completed your journey. Forgive me for presenting a misunderstanding within Hai's heart and mind."

"I promise you Flying Star, I will be back one day to see you." They embraced. Ming Su asked. "Where is your mother, do you have any brothers or sisters?" Flying star took Ming Su by the hand and led her to another grave. "This is my mother, and here beside her is my younger sister, Rain Frog."

"What happened?" Flying Star walked over and sat at the base of a pine tree in the grass facing her mother's grave. She closed her eyes and took the passing wind into her lungs. "I was eight years old. My sister was almost seven months. It was the white man. Father was a young father himself, obviously not as wise as the chief or the elders. I remember that it was very cold that time of year but the snow hadn't fallen yet. One of the other young warriors came running into the village with word that there was a caravan of white man wagons with horses and supplies on their way to Boise but they were trading along the way. Father had a skull and pelt from a Grizzly Bear that he had killed when he was in the North Country. He traded with the white man for a hunting knife and some blankets. He knew that he was not getting the best part of the trade but keeping his family warm was a priority to him. He had no idea though that the blankets were carrying a disease that we later learned was Smallpox. For some reason father and I were not affected but mother and Rain Frog were. Mother and Rain Frog broke out into a rash all over their bodies that turned into blisters. Rain Frog would cry, cry, and cry but wouldn't eat or drink. She died first. Some of the other villagers came down with the same rash and blisters. They would all vomit. Their bodies got very hot and sweaty. Nobody had any idea where the sickness was coming from but father knew that the only contact that anyone had outside the village were the blankets. Right away he gathered them up and threw them in the fire but not before mother and three other villagers had died. For weeks nobody would get close to father and me. The following Spring we discover by other people like us throughout the mountains had died of the same disease the same way. That is why father is so protective of me. He will not forgive himself if something happened to me too.

11

The sky was still dark when Ming Su's sleep was interrupted by a heavy tap on her shoulder. She was instantly startled when she awoke to a large male silhouette but was relieved when she realized that it was Smoke Owl. "It's time to go." Ming Su gasped. "You are going to take me to Bannock Village?"

"Bannock Village about a five or six days walk. Two of my warriors will travel two moons with you, when you wake we will be gone."

"You are going to leave me in the middle of nowhere?"

"No! Wagon road is easy to follow, but is dangerous for a young girl. You must dress as boy again to fool the bad men. The young boy will stay here and be looked after by Lost Doe, The wounded dog is not good for big travel, he too shall stay here until fully healed and strong again."

"Gordy is Tommy's dog, He should stay with Tommy anyways."

"You must travel light and be prepared to run at any time, you must leave the mule here. There is a papoose outside with clothing, jerky, water and other supplies." Ming Su gasped in surprise. "My dress, what about my dress?" Smoke Owl smiled. "Yes, it is in the bottom of the papoose. Keep Hai's knife on your belt like you have. Fill your water every chance that you have."

"Father, father, please." Cried out Flying Star. "Ming Su is a smart girl, she has been taught well by her brother as I have been taught well by my father. I am confident that she will keep herself safe. So please, Beavertail and Firebug are waiting outside. Smoke Owl grunted before exiting the teepee. "Ming Su asked. "Firebug?" Flying Star chuckled. "Yes, Firebug likes to play with fire.

Ming Su stepped over to Lost Doe and wrapped her arms around the elder Chinese woman. "Please take care of Tommy and Gordy." Tommy remained lying on the elk skin petting Gordy. His heart broke as he watched Ming Su wave to him and Gordy before exiting the teepee. Lost doe placed her hand on the side of Tommy's shoulder. "She will be fine, you will see her again, I promise. Tommy wept. However, outside the teepee Smoke Owl picked Ming Su's papoose up off the ground and placed it over Ming Su's shoulders. The great warrior took a knee, looked Ming Su in the eyes. Ming Su was surprised to watch Smoke Owl's face transform from a serious Indian warrior to a soft loving father as a big smile developed on his face. Ming Su threw her arms around the stout man and embraced him for a moment before turning and removing her new knife that Cheng had given her in San Francisco and handing it to Smoke Owl. Smoke owl knelt and kissed Ming Su on the cheek. Ming Su stepped over to Flying Star and said. "I will see you again someday."

Moments later Smoke Owl picked Ming Su up and placed her on a horse. He told her that all she had to do is hold on that Beavertail had hold of the horses lead. Smoke Owl and Flying Star stood and watched Ming Su. The three horses and their riders disappear into the darkness.

12

After two days of traveling with Beavertail and Firebug, Ming Su woke the next morning to find herself alone in a field of knee high grass. That was when she realized that she was all alone. She lied on her bed roll listening to the morning bird singing their songs as they greeted a new day. The sky was blue with random white billowy clouds making their way across the sky from West to East when she heard horses snorting. She kept low, looking through the tall grass to watch a wagon drawn by horses make its way by on the wagon road.

She soon found herself following some American travelers at a distance. She figured that they were potential prospectors on their way to Bannock but she was a little unsure if her guess was accurate. The day was long and tiring, trying to keep up with the wagon but far enough back to not be seen by the travelers. As dusk fell upon them, Ming Su decided that it would be a good time to take a nap; she understood that the American travelers would have to attend to their chores around the makeshift camp on the edge of the river.

Later when she woke, she could smell the stew in the air. Ming Su slowly and quietly snuck over to the metal pot and removed its lid as it simmered over the open fire, hanging from a steel tripod. She thought. "Dog vomit but I am hungry." The aroma of the stew filled her nose but soaked her mouth. She took the wooden spoon that one of the braves carved from a piece of cedar from her back pocket and helped herself to the fine stew. She continuously looked around to evade from getting caught. Suddenly out of the corner of her eye she noticed a metal drink cup sitting on a small wood crate. She hustled over to get it. Looking into it, she couldn't help but notice the smell and sight of black coffee. Quickly she dumped it out and ran back over to the stew pot. Taking the cup by the handle and scooping some stew into it before placing the heavy lid back on the black pot and running back to the woods. She sat behind some bushes that still left her a good view of the camp, not to mention the stew pot. In no time her belly was full but now she was thirsty. She watched and listened as two men and a woman along with a young girl completed their chores and finally gathered around the fire to eat what stew was left. When the woman removed the lid she began to cuss the younger man. But he had no idea what he was being cussed at for. Ming Su felt bad for the man for taking the blame for what she did as she sat behind the bushes with wide eyes hoping that he wouldn't get into too much trouble. The man tried to convince the woman that it was not his doing. But she did not want to listen until she went to fetch her cup of black coffee but was frantic to discover that it was missing. She began to look around on the ground and was finally satisfied when she came across a small boot print that was not from her or anyone else in her party. She walked over to the older man and whispered in his ear. A moment later he got up and un-holstered his revolver. He looked around on the ground for other boot prints and quickly came across a set walking towards the woods where Ming Su was hiding. Overcome with fear Ming Su began to run deeper into the darkening woods. The man could hear the sound of something or someone running through the brush but could not see from where he stood at the edge of the forest. After a couple frustrating moment and a grunting sound of dissatisfaction. The man holstered his weapon and headed back toward the fire to eat his meal. He looked at the woman who was apparent to be his wife and told her. "It was more than likely a youngster looking to get something to eat." The woman snarled. "Well it looks like they did." She sat down alongside her husband to consume her dinner. When their daughter finished her dinner she retrieved a violin from the back of the wagon and began to play.

Ming Su was all bundled up in her bed roll when she heard a familiar sound. She sat up and listened. A smile grew on her face as she listened to the peaceful easy melody travel through the forest. There was no doubt in her mind that it was the same type of musical instrument that she enjoyed dancing to in San Francisco But it was more soothing and relaxing as the night drew later and later, chasing away all her worries as she faded off to sleep.

It was chilly and fog had settled over the river when Ming Su woke the next morning. The sun climbing higher into the sky was proving quickly to make it a very hot day. She took her last gulp of river water from the stolen metal cup from the night before and made her way to her feet unfastening her belt and pulling it back two loops to allow her to slide the belt through the handle of the cup before refastening her belt before kneeling to gather up her bed roll and tied a rope around it to be placed back in her papoose. She then headed back toward the river. Her legs ached as she began walking along the river's edge with the sun to her right.

After walking for a while Ming Su's belly was beginning to rumble from hunger and from thirst. She heard a big splash in the calm part of the river then spotted another fish jumping for bugs. An idea crossed her mind. She retrieved the fishing spool from her sack that her brother once carried. Remembering a trick that Hai had showed her. She looked around in the grass for a grasshopper. With luck on her side she found a good size one. She tied the line around the body of the bug close to the steel hook. She knew that the bug would not be enough weight but wanted the live bug to float so she found a small long skinny pebble. After placing it a couple inches from the bug she loosely tied it. She unraveled a bunch of line and put her foot on the spool. While holding the slack with her left hand she threw the bug and pebble with her right hand and all her might. The bug and pebble flew many yards before landing it the water. As she hoped the pebble fell from the loose knot leaving the kicking grasshopper to fight for its life as it tried to keep from drowning. Ming Su squatted down and before she knew it she had a hit. A large rainbow colored fish jumped from the water as it swallowed the grasshopper and unsuspectedly the hook as well. She picked up the spool and quickly walked toward the water wrapping the line around it backed up to pull the fish closer to land. She wrapped the remaining line quickly as she walked forward and backed up again until the fish was on dry ground. She couldn't believe her eyes. The trout was half the length of her. Realizing that she couldn't eat it all by herself, and didn't want to kill it but she was still hungry. Ming Su thought about throwing it back in and trying to catch a smaller fish but wasn't sure if another fish would bite. Sitting on the ground she watched the massive fish flop around thinking that it could feed about six people then she got an idea as she noticed a familiar covered wagon coming toward her. Standing up she picked the heavy fish up then walked toward the wagon. The younger man that got cussed out the night before approached her on a horse as the wagon slowly made its way up the path. Ming Su looked up at the man on the horse with a smile as she squinted from the bright sunlight. The man climbed down off the brown mare and squatted down in front of Ming Su. But feeling scared all of a sudden Ming Su stepped back. She could hardly make out his English when he said. "It's okay. I won't hurt you." About that time the wagon came to a stop and the woman climbed down. She smiled as she approached Ming Su. The man stood up and backed away. Ming Su gestured as she held the fish in her arms to offer it to the woman. The woman took the fish from the young Chinese girl then stepped back. Suddenly her face dropped as she let out a sigh when she spotted the metal cup on Ming Su's hip. Closing her eyes she shook her head then backed away before heading back to the wagon. Ming Su unfastened her belt and removed the cup. The young man put his hand out and shook his head and said. "No! You can keep it." Then he climbed back up on his horse. The woman came around from the back of the wagon with a little sack and handed it to Ming Su. She said. "Bread" as she held her hand to her lips. Ming Su smiled and took the sack. Her face lit up when she saw many little biscuits. She bowed to the woman in thanks and then backed away.

Ming Su watched the rider on the horse and the wagon as they passed. Then she caught another grasshopper and tied the line around it. Tying on another pebble then throwing it in the water near a tree branch but the pebble didn't fall away. Instantly the grasshopper sank but before Ming Su could pull the line back in, it got tight. She pulled on the line and wrapped it around the spool. To her surprise it was not a rainbow trout like she thought it would be but a smaller fish with a real big mouth. She removed the hook with ease and put the spool back in the sack. She removed a single piece of cloth from her papoose that she would use to bathe, and removing the biscuits from the little sack she wrapped all but one of them in the cloth before placing them in her papoose. Ming Su ate the biscuit that she left out, leaving her mouth even more dry. But luckily she still had the metal cup.

Finally she used Hai's knife to clean the fish with the big mouth then placed the rest in the small sack, head first as so the fins would not catch the cloth, before she walked over to the river and place it in the water for a moment as she filled the metal cup with cold mountain water and took a drink. She carried the little wet sack in one hand as she carried her papoose of belongings over her shoulders. With some food and refreshment in her stomach she headed on.

The sun was losing its heat and its height in the sky as Ming Su came across a small rock formation where a campfire was. She figured that it would be a good place to camp for the night and enjoy her fish. After sitting her stuff on the ground she went to gather some wood for the fire. To her surprise as she was picking up a stick, she noticed a thorn bush with black berries on it. The berries looked big and juicy but Ming Su was not sure if they were edible or even if they tasted good. She picked a little one off the bush and placed it into her mouth. Her face lit up with a smile after tasting the sweet but sour tickle on her tongue. Quickly she began picking the biggest ones from the bush and placing them in the metal cup, filling it fast.

Ming Su placed the wood alongside the fire pit and placed a bunch of dry grass in the pit. After taking the matches from the papoose, she lit one and got the fire going. As the fire burned the grass and wood, turning it to ember coals she finished preparing the fish by attaching it to a stick to use as a type of long skewer. She remained kneeling as she slowly turned the stick to get the fish cooked all the way through and all over.

The little cloth sack was dry by the time that the fish was finished cooking. She spread the sack out and used it as a plate to place her meal on, which consisted of fresh Bass, a biscuit and a handful of black berries. She hustled to fill her metal cup with fresh cold water then returned to finally enjoy her meal.

It was almost dark when she spread out her bed roll and used her sack as a pillow. With a fully satisfied stomach and a cool breeze, she was feeling pretty good lying next to the ember coals while staring up at the bluish black sky filled with the little white dot of stars, thinking about her brother Hai as she drifted off to sleep.

… "Ming Su, Ming Su, I got it. I figure out how we can get the money to go to America to find father." Ming Su looked up at her brother with her big brown eyes. "We don't have anything to sell. Father sold everything and took the money." With great excitement Hai explained. "No, No, listen to me Su. Tigers are worth a lot of money right now. Nobody has been hunting them like father said. I know how we can do it." Ming Su shook her head. "For some reason I don't like this idea already."

Ming Su woke by the sound of a horse snorting. Her half opened eyes were met with a hand covering her mouth. A man in the darkness rolled her over and tied her hands as she screamed then he placed a cloth in her mouth and tied another around her head to stop the screaming. The man took the other end of the rope that bound her hands and tied it off to the saddle on the horse. He climbed up in the saddle and signaled the horse to move forward keeping it at a slow but steady pace that was still too fast for Ming Su's short legs, forcing her to run at a slow pace. Breathing from her nose was difficult as she ran causing her to lose her breath and fall to the ground. The man dragged her for a few yards then stopped. He climbed down out of the saddle as another man on foot rushed up to him. He looked down at Ming Su and noticed the cloth around her head and turned her over. He growled at the other man. "We don't want boys, just girls."

"Do boys squat when they relieve themselves? I saw her yesterday." He got a closer look at Ming Su's face and replied. "Dang, she is a girl." He removed the cloth and gag before tapping her on the face to wake up. Ming Su opened her mouth to scream but the man yelled. "No!" Startling Ming Su and encouraging her to keep quiet. The other man untied the other end of the rope from the saddle and tossed it to the man with Ming Su. He began walking slow as Ming Su was forced to walk with him. The walk seemed long to the young Chinese girl, but was actually less than a half mile. They ended up at a camp. Ming Su was forced to sit down against a small tree and was tied with the rope to the tree.

She sat awake for what seemed like hours, watching the two men and listening to their meaningless conversation as they passed a bottle of whiskey back and forth. She knew that the men were not going to hurt her but was afraid that they were going to try and sell her. Nonetheless she was confident that it was just a matter of time until they both fell to sleep.

Ming Su waited patiently until the first man fell to sleep and not too long after the second man did as well. There was no doubt that she needed to escape and worked up a plan. But she needed to get one boot off first and then possible the other. She pushed on the heel of the sole on one foot with her other boot. After struggling and intense pain to her leg from it feeling like she was going to pull it out of its socket she managed to get a boot off even though the rope was tied around them. There was then enough slack to maneuver her legs out from the binds of the rope which allowed her to move both her legs and strategically work her right boot to her bound hands in front of her belly. Once she managed to get the boot knife out of its case she quickly cut the rope and found freedom. She wasted little time putting her boots back on. But she needed to get free and not be tracked and hunted by the men when they woke and noticed that she was gone. So she ran over to the wagon and cut the two horses free with her knife but pulled the reins through the metal ring and guided them along with the other two horses out of the camp, far and away from the men.

Ming Su felt that she traveled quite a distance once the sun began to rise. She came across a big wall or a building with no roof. There were many men all dressed the same in blue uniforms. Some were loading wagons, others were unloading a different wagon. As Ming Su got closer she caught the eye of an older man dressed as the others. He had white hair and a thick white mustache. The man approached Ming Su with a smile. But Ming Su felt uncomfortable and could not trust the man too get too close. The man could tell that the little girl was afraid so he began to speak to her. "Hello little lady. I am Colonel Brigham. I am friendly and I am not going to hurt you. This place is Fort Boise and all these men are soldiers." Ming Su didn't understand too much of what the man was saying. She reached her hand out with the reins in her grasp and said. "Bannock Village."

"Bannock, Bannock." He thought. "Oh! You mean Bannock City. It is a long way to go for a girl that is all by herself. Ming Su looked to the man like she didn't understand him but was able to state in English. "Father there."

"Hmmm, Oh I see, your father is there. But you know that it is very dangerous for you to be traveling alone. There are a lot of child abductors." Ming Su nodded her head with her eyes wide open in complete understanding. "Horses belong to child abductors, the bad men. They tried taking me. I must get to Bannock Village now." The man hollered to a soldier. "Dempsey, take the reins to all four of the horses and put them in the stable."

"Yes Sir." The man replied as he took the reins. "Whoa, whoa soldier." cried out the Colonel. "Fetch me that new Chinese interpreter, ah ah, Z,Z,Zh."

"Zhang Sir, his name is Zhang. Right away Colonel."

"Send him to my quarters."

"Yes Sir Colonel Brigham."

Colonel Brigham reached out to take Ming Su's hand, he wasn't too surprised when she pulled away and stepped back. Quickly he put his hands up and waved. "I'm sorry. I am not going to hurt you. Are you hungry? Do you want to eat?" He put his hand to his mouth." Ming

Su got the idea and showed gratitude with a smile and followed the Colonel.

Ming Su's feet were dangling from the chair that she was sitting in at the table in the colonel's quarters munching on an apple in one hand and grasping another apple in her other. She stated. "Bannock Village, father in Bannock Village, must go." At that moment Zhang walked in. "Did you ask for me sir?"

"Yes Zhang. I need you to get information from the girl here. I want to know why she is traveling alone, but she has an Indian papoose that she was carrying on her back and why is she going to Bannock City."

Zhang asked Ming Su the questions in Chinese. Ming Su responded. "My name is Ming Su. My brother Hai and me left China many weeks ago to find our father in Bannock Village, but Hai was killed by big mountain cat. Indian people helped me get to here. But bad men tried taking me two times because I am girl so I dress as boy to look like boy. Will you help me get to Bannock Village?" Zhang interpreted Ming Su's information to Colonel Brigham. Brigham thought for a couple minutes while looking at the map of Idaho. "Okay, let her know that we will bring her down town to catch a stagecoach to Bannock City, Explain to her that it is about a nine hour ride on the stagecoach but she will be safe. I wouldn't expect the driver to charge anything for her passage but if he does I will cover it. Those four horses are now the property of the United States Government. You and I will ride to the stable down town at dawn to see her on her way. Have the cook prepare a couple sandwiches for the girl, fill her canteen with water. I also want a hearty supper brought in here to her. She will be eating in my quarters tonight. And one more thing, I want two trusted guards at the door tonight as she sleeps protecting her, I don't trust half of the deadbeats in this battalion and I think considering the circumstances that I find it imperative that she is well protected from everyone. In fact I will sleep in the great room tonight."

"Yes Sir, Colonel Brigham." I'm on it."

13

It was late in the day; chill began to fill the air when the stagecoach arrived in Bannock City. With many weeks of travel with travelers who spoke English Ming Su understood enough English to be confused when the driver shouted. "Bannock City." Ming Su looked up at the driver and asked. "Bannock Village?" The driver Looked around with an ignorant expression. Shrugged his shoulders and smiled as he responded with an unsure tone. "Yeah I suppose." Ming Su smiled and gave the friendly driver a quick hug before climbing down from the stage. She stood amazed as she watched as a finely dressed American woman and a finely dressed American boy step from the doorway of the stagecoach. The woman had a long Green dress on with a big hat that had flowers attached to it. Her mannerism represented money. Perhaps she was family to a lucky minor who had struck gold and felt that she needed to act the part as many people would when they forgot their days when they had nothing, not even a sliver of bread to fill the gap in their growling stomachs. Her apparent son was about Ming Su's age, Ming Su's heart throbbed as she smile at the young man dressed in dark gray trousers, with a matching coat, a black tie over a white button down shirt, topped with a light gray big brimmed hat. They may have noticed Ming Su but didn't acknowledge her. She wasn't as clean as them, she wasn't as rich as them and in their mind she could not have possibly struggled through the hardships and turmoil as they did. A Chinese child did not deserve their attention for even a second. Ming Su watched as a middle aged Chinese man removed the fancy and expensive luggage from the roof of the stagecoach and hand it down to another before carrying it away, leading the mother and the young man into the hotel. She walked to the back of the stagecoach and stepped out of the way.

Suddenly Ming Su was startled at the snap of leather and the team of six horses being signaled to mush on. She quickly stepped back to watch the stagecoach pull away and disappear into the cool dust. She picked up the papoose, put her arms through the shoulder straps and began walking. People from different races and cultures watched her head down the main street. The architect was completely different from what she remembered in China, it was plain and simple, signs of American and Chinese lettering painted on them. The people were dressed different and the Chinese were not so proud as they were when they were in their own homeland. Prostitutes of Chinese and American women made vile comments at the apparent young boy. However Ming Su felt a sense of satisfaction every time that she was recognized as a boy.

The sun was beginning to sneak down behind the mountains to hide, leaving the Bannock City to become darker by the minute and colder by the second. Ming Su had no idea where she was going to spend the night. Main Street was full of people but there was no one who knew Ming Su, not to mention anyone who knew who Hon was, which made her feel all alone and very afraid. Cautiously she made her way down Main Street continuously turning around to watch her back and become familiar with her new surroundings but was instantly startled when she turned back around and bounced off a woman's long dress. She fell back onto the ground and stared up at a young Chinese woman. Ming Su's eyes opened wide as she recognized the face looking back at her to be her mother. She squeezed her eyes tightly closed and reopened them to be left in disappointment, realizing that her mother was not standing before her but was still deceased. A soft voice from the Chinese woman standing above her said. "I am sorry little boy." She held out both her hands. "Let me help you up." Once Ming Su made it to her feet the woman gasped and whispered. "You are not a boy at all, but a precious young girl." The woman took Ming Su by the hand and said. You should not be out here all alone. Where is your family?" Ming Su shook her head with a frown. The woman said. "Come with me child. You will be safe, many bad men here that will hurt you or even worse." Ming Su hustled with the woman down a walkway between a restaurant and a blacksmith's shop to a door leading into a single room behind the restaurant. The room was dark even though a single wax candle burnt in the corner as it sat on the end table alongside of the bed. Clothes hung on ropes that were strung between the walls in different directions and different heights. The woman asked Ming Su. "Are you hungry?" Ming Su nodded her head as she stared at the woman.

A moment later the woman placed a bowl of stew in front of Ming Su as she climbed up on a chair at the table. Ming Su thought to herself. "Does every Chinese-American make dog vomit to eat?" But she was too hungry and knew that she couldn't be ungrateful so she watched the woman with every bite she took off the metal spoon then she smiled and stated. "I am Ming Su from China. My brother usually calls me Su and I like it." The woman sat down across the table from the lost little lady and stated. "Hi Ming Su, I am Lanying. Can I call you Su?" Ming Su smiled and nodded. Lanying didn't know what so say to get a conversation started between the two. She reached under a cloth that was sitting over a plate and removed a cookie from it, then placed it in front of Ming Su. Looking around she said. This is where I live. I came here with my husband last year but I haven't seen him in many months. I had to beg for a job here at the restaurant so I had a place to live. I keep the floor swept, wash the dishes, help cut up the vegetables for stew and sides and wash the linens that are used for napkins, table cloths and cleaning rags. They give me a little money at the end of the month that helps me to pay for things that I need. I don't expect to ever go home so I will make America my home and maybe one day my husband will return with a big sack of gold or I will find my own gold." Ming Su may have been young but she could tell that Lanying was lonely and needed a friend. She finished her stew and picked up the cookie. Her smile grew from the sweet taste of the pastry. Lanying said. "I get to eat all the extra food that is made at the restaurant. I don't have to worry about going hungry like many of the prospecting families here."

"You are very lucky Ming Su replied. Lanying stared at the young girl for a moment as she ate her cookie and then asked her. "Where is your family Ming Su, I mean Su?" Ming Su sat silent as her eyes filled with tears. "Oh I see, you don't have any family do you? What about your brother who calls you Su?" Ming Su shook her head. Lanying let out a sigh and asked Ming Su. "Would you like to live here with me? You will have to earn your keep and help out but I will keep you safe." Ming Su sat in silence as she stared in the sincere eyes of the woman and then softly nodded. Lanying said. "For now you need to get some sleep. We start early but we end early too. Tomorrow is Sunday and I will show you around town and help you become familiar with the town. But don't trust anyone except me and Mr. Kolinski, the owner of the restaurant."

Ming Su sniffled and wiped her eyes. "How do I know that I can trust you or Mr. Ko- Ko-Kowacky?"

"You mean Mr. Kolinski, but good question. Why don't you get some rest for now. First thing tomorrow after work you are getting a bath."

"I have been traveling for a long time. I would like to bathe right away if I may and would it be too late to get me some fresh clothes?"

"You are amazing young child. A young lady who knows what she wants. Would you like attire for a boy that you disguise yourself to be or would you like an attire for a young lady that you are?"

"I have gone weeks dressed as a boy, I would like to be a girl again. I have some money, not a lot but maybe enough for a dress. I do have a pretty dress with me but it needs to be cleaned."

"A girl you shall be then. But listen to me closely. There are many, many bad men here in Bannock City who would be looking to abduct you. It is hard to tell who is who. Some are American men and others are Chinese men too. So you must be very careful."

Ming Su lifted her shirt and retrieved Hai's knife that was in its sheath from her belt and held it out for the woman to see. "Just the same Ming Su, it may be in your best interest to refer to me as your Aunt Lanying. I don't have too much of a name or respect from the people here but they do know who I am and know that I work at the restaurant. Mr. Kolinski is the owner of the Restaurant and I will let him know that my niece has come to America to live with me. He will make sure that you stay safe with me."

"Must we not tell the truth?"

"It is for your protection."

"You don't want to be my mother?"

"The people here know that I do not have a daughter or a child for that matter. Aunt Lanying will have to do my child." Ming Su nodded her head and smiled to be courteous to the woman.

Even though the darkness had fill the sky, the night was still young and the mercantile was still open for business. Lanying and Ming Su headed out to the street to make their way to the mercantile. Ming Su stayed close to her older counterpart but still felt comfort knowing that her brother's knife was still tucked inside her belt. She continued to scope around at all the people, horses and wagons that covered the dusty dirt street. The noise was more than one could imagine as she almost had to yell for Lanying to hear her when she asked. "How many people live here?"

"The last that I heard it was about seven thousand; people come and go every day. There are people murdered almost every day, rape on adult woman and young ladies like you are quite common too. Many travelers lose their belongings to burglary and theft. This is the last place that you want to be all alone. You are so fortunate to have made it all the way here from San Francisco, not to mention China. Danger surrounded you but somehow you made it here."

"I didn't travel alone. My older brother Hai traveled with me and we had some help from a man we knew in San Francisco."

"What encouraged you to come to Bannock City?" Ming Su looked at the ground and shook her head. "Where is your brother now?" Ming Su shook her head again. "Don't worry child. You take all the time that you need to share with me. I am patient and I know that you have been through a lot just getting here." They walked without speaking for a couple moments until Ming Su asked. "How much farther?"

"It is right up the street" Lanying stated as she pointed. "We are going to the Chinese mercantile. The American people can be very mean after dark and a lot of bad things can happen. It is better that we stay with our own this evening and not make trouble or let trouble make its way to us. Besides the owner Longwei has taken a special interest in me."

"What do you mean, a special interest?"

"He thinks that I am pretty and likes me in a very special way."

"You mean that he wants to be your husband and you to be his wife?"

"Something like that."

As anticipated by Lanying. Longwei's face lit up when she walked into the mercantile. "Lanying, cold night tonight. You need good handsome husband to keep you warm at night." Lanying released a fake cough and looked down at Ming Su with a smile. "Longwei, I would like to introduce you to my niece Ming Su. She just arrived here from China this evening."

"Oh a niece. I didn't know that you had a niece. She is pretty, she looks like you too. She must be your sister's daughter." Lanying and Ming Su looked at each other chuckling. "Yes, she is my sister's daughter."

"Yep, this is my Aunt Lanying."

"Well, what can I do for you tonight Lanying and Ming Su?" Ming Su pointed to a dress on the wall. It was light blue, with white trim. However Lanying said. "I don't think that dress is a good idea right now. That is more for special occasions, how about the long brown dress with the long sleeves and the white buttons. It will keep your legs and arms warm since winter is close. In the spring we can get you some pretty dresses that are short for the warm weather. Ming Su walked over to the dress hanging on the wall. "You want me to wear this? She asked with concern. "It will make me look like and American traveler."

"You are now American Su. Besides you are not going to want to get such a pretty dress dirty from feeding the pigs, cows and chickens. You will have chores like I said Su." Ming Su dropped her head with a long sigh. "Okay Aunt Lanying. We will get that brown dress. I suppose that I have to wear ugly boots on my feet too." Lanying and Longwei looked at each other exchanging smiles. Lanying bent down to whisper to the little girl. "Su, we don't want to draw too much attention to you as a girl."

"I know, the bad men will notice me a lot easier if I stood out more, but I still don't like it." Longwei snapped at Lanying. "Are you out of your mind to allow your niece to come to America? The men do not bring their families unless they plan on staying in America. Wives and children are sold to slavery and sex trades. Not just America but Bannock too. Hundreds or thousands of people come and go every day to and from Bannock. Whatever you do, do not turn your back on her because come the next day she may be miles from here on her way to a mining camp to be ravaged over and over by the American scum. And don't misunderstand me Lanying. Many Chinese men and women are involved in abducting the children and getting them sold as slaves of all sorts. Because when it comes to making easy money, people become more evil."

"Longwei, I didn't know that she was coming. My sister had passed away, she had no place to go so she made her way here from China. I will do my best to protect her but we both know that there is nobody here that can protect her. When the Marshall comes around, he couldn't care any less. But I am stuck. I have to do my best to be her family. If she got abducted then she would bring a good price and I know that. So please do not lecture me. If you want to be helpful then help me protect her."

"Okay Lanying. I will let people know that your niece is here in Bannock City but to be honest Lanying. I don't see her evading abduction for more than a month or two, so I wouldn't get too attached."

"Just get me the dress Longwei. I must get her home to take a bath and get to bed. Ming Su will start working by my side at the restaurant tomorrow. Mr. Kolinski will look out for her too."

It wasn't a common practice but Lanying was short on time and still needed to wash Ming Su's clothing, therefore once Ming Su finished her bath, Lanying used the soiled hot water for cleaning the laundry. A rope strung from one wall to the parallel wall acted as a clothesline to hang the clothes to dry. Even Ming Su's dress from Cheng's Mercantile in San Francisco

Ming Su lied under the covers on her back in Lanying bed holding her wooden horse in her grip as she pretended to make it trot over the wrinkles or folds on the heavy blanket, listening to Lanying sing a Chinese song in her native tongue while she finished her unexpected added chores.

Lanying left the single candle burning in the metal can to illuminate enough light to see within the walls of the room as she climbed into bed alongside Ming Su. She whispered to the young girl. "I am very concerned for your safety and welfare Ming Su. I am sorry that I cannot be your mother but I will do my best to honor her." Ming Su reached inside the neck of her nightgown and pulled out the pendent attached to the chain around her neck. She held it up for Lanying to see and said. "This is the North Star, the only star that never moves. That is where my mother is, she lives among the stars. A sickness took her from father, Hai and me in late winter. Father soon abandoned Hai and me. He came to America without us. Hai used me as bait to lure the tiger to his trap so he could kill it for its meat, fur and bones so we would have the money to journey across the big ocean to San Francisco I don't know if my father is here in Bannock City but it is where he was going. A Chinese man in San Francisco said that father is travel with crazy American men who kill all animals for fun, drink a lot of stinky water from the tall glass bottles. I would like to try and find my father here. Do you know who Fong Wei is?"

"I am sorry but I don't."

"You and him are all I have except for Tommy and Gordy."

"Tommy and Gordy? Who are they?"

"Tommy is a young American boy who was traveling with us that got tick fever and may have died at the Indian village about a seven days walk from here. Gordy is his dog that should be with him. The bad men tried taking me two times while I journeyed but I got away. The first time, the bad man shot Gordy with his gun so that is why Gordy didn't come with me."

"Ming Su I wish that I had the right words to comfort you but I am sorry that I do not. I do understand your feelings. I miss my husband who brought me to America for a better life. For all I know he is dead but I try to believe that he will come back for me someday soon. So for now I do what I can to survive... Enough for now. Let's try to get some sleep. Tomorrow we start early. American breakfast is very busy at the restaurant and in between breakfast and lunch we must tend to the animals and feed them." Ming Su rolled towards Lanying and kissed her on the cheek before rolling away to fall to sleep.

14

Ming Su adapted to life in America's Bannock City, Idaho pretty well. The word got around quick within Kolinski's Restaurant that Ming Su is under Lanying's supervision and his protection. Ming Su quickly became a familiar friendly face to the regulars and the residence that dined at Kolinski's but also to the local criminal element.

"Wild turkey was plentiful in the mountains around Bannock City so with President Abraham Lincoln's proclamation to make the last Thursday of November to be celebrated as the national day of Thanksgiving. It was less than a week away. Most Americans had little to no idea what Thanksgiving was all about except that turkey was usually the main dish. And a feast always attracted a large crowd. Hundreds of hard core mountain men would come from the depths of the forest to gather for this great feast. Many vegetables such as potatoes, carrots and green beans were stored away for the 3rd annual celebration, whereas other side dishes would have to be brought in from far away like the cranberry and pine apple. For desserts were cherries, apples, pumpkin, squash and the ever tasty sugar. Needless to say the rotting or bad vegetables and fruits needed to be disposed of, which made good food for the livestock.

Ming Su noticed the first snow falling from the sky as she tossed apples, potatoes and carrots to the pigs and the chickens behind Kolinski's. Her attention was drawn to Main Street by the sound of a dog's bark. She stood waiting in anticipation for the dog to come into view. The barking got closer and louder, encouraging her to walk towards the street. Lanying yelled to her. "Ming Su don't wonder off. The crowd is too plentiful." But Lanying discovered that her words did not travel far enough for Ming Su's ears. Suddenly out of the corner of Ming Su's eye she caught a quick glimpse of a familiar dog. She yelled. "Gordy, over here, come on Gordy." But like Lanying, Ming Su's words didn't travel enough to be heard by the dog. She dropped the wooden bucket of overaged vegetables and ran once again with all her might and speed. She could see that Gordy was following some men on horseback traveling at a galloping pace. Many thoughts ran through Ming Su's mind as she ran after Gordy, ducking around horses, wagon and people that were in her way. Lanying ran out to the street to see but Ming Su was already too far away.

The next thing that Ming Su knew, she was being tied up in the back of a covered wagon. She thought. "How careless could I be?" As little as she was, she knew what was happening when it didn't take much for a stranger to grab her off the street. Covering her mouth to prevent her from screaming and eventually gag her. However, she did manage to bite the stranger's finger and let out a scream that was on deaf ears considering that the crowd of people, livestock and machinery were much louder. Without warning her eyes were covered by a dark hood after a strip of cloth was tied around her head to prevent her from screaming anymore, lastly she felt her arms and legs being tied tighter. She was weightless as her body was picked up and transferred to another wagon to be placed inside what seemed like a wooden box. Once the lid was close, everything went darker than night. Even though she could see through a little hole in the hood, day light seeping through the cracks between the weather beaten wood slats. Her panic and the lack of fresh air in the wooden box robbed her of all her energy, forcing her to quickly pass out.

Ming Su had a woken while the wagon was still in motion Unknowing how long she had been sleeping. Nonetheless she could hear men talking and laughing, she figured that it was probably the driver and one or two passengers. Their conversation was muffled and overpowered by the rattling and creaking of the wood wagon and pounding of the horses hooves against the dry ground. Travel of the wagon seemed to last and last before coming to a halt. Conversation between the men became clearer but she still didn't understand all their English language. However, she was more than certain that she was in serious trouble. Being locked in the box was just as terrifying in the dark as it was claustrophobic with very little room to move. She could only lay there and listen to the horses weening as well as dogs barking. Howling echoed throughout the forest making it evident that she was no longer in Bannock City being well aware that she had been abducted by the bad men. She was also aware that their plans were more than likely to sell her to make a lot of money. There was no doubt in her mind that she had to escape at the first chance that she had. For all she knew the buyer could have been waiting for her to arrive and standing right by the wagon. Waiting to find out just became more and more frightening for her. She thought in her mind that she needed to come up with a plan. First thing first though. She had to get out of the wooden box. She began to kick her feet to make a ruckus in hopes that the bad men would let her out and remove her restraints. When the lid of the wooden box was opened, she let out a sigh of relief. She was confident that her plan began to work. It would be the ignorance of her abductors for under estimating her. Although she acted as it was when she was picked up by what appeared to be a big man. He removed her dark hood and the cloth covering her mouth. Drama was her next step. Instantly Ming Su began to scream as loud as she could as her echoes screamed back at her from the forest. The man stood taller than any man that she had even seen. He wore a worn out prospectors hat, had green teeth of built up crud as his breath smelled of whiskey. A red shirt covered with overalls and a long gray coat kept him warm. He mocked Ming Su by screaming back in her face before he chuckled. "Nobody is going to hear you way out here in the woods. We are over seven miles from town. So any ideas that you have about getting away from us and walking back to town, you can just forget it. You will for sure be killed by a wolf, bear or mountain lion if the snow and the cold don't kill you first." Ming Su resolved to crying. Only to be mocked again by the man rubbing his eyes and acting as if he was crying in an attempt to torment her. He slapped Ming Su across the face and told her to shut up. Ming Su's attention was drawn to an old but mean looking woman walking towards her with a metal cup. Her dirty gray hair was short like a man. She wore a shirt and trousers that were too big for her frame but still looked like a man. The scariest thing about the old woman was her eyes that sat way into her skull. She tilted the metal cup to Ming Su's lips and told her to drink. Ming Su took a sip of the cold water and asked for more. The woman quickly obliged her. The abductors really did underestimate their prisoner as they never realized that Ming Su was scoping her surrounding by moving her eyes while she sipped from the metal cup. There was a building to her left that looked as if it could be a mercantile or a trading post in a large clearing. Like most buildings in the Bannock City area it was constructed of pine boards but without paint of any color. However, no other structures or buildings were noticed except an outhouse about twenty adult paces from the mercantile. It looked much older than the mercantile by a few years. Perhaps it was built by used materials. It was hard to tell with it all weather beaten with no paint.

The sound of a big dog barking caught her attention. She notice that there were six of them that looked like they could be wolves tied together and a little mysterious looking wagon with no wheels but wooden tracks on the bottom. When she finished her refreshment, Ming Su looked at the ground but slowly looked around to try and notice other things that may be of some kind of help for her to plan an escape. The scent of stew blew by her. She mumbled to herself. "Smells like that dog vomit, I hope that they don't expect me to eat that." She sat with her feet tied together dangling from the wooden tailgate of the wagon while using a wood crate labeled. "Whiskey" as a back rest. Although the thought of the stew turned her stomach she was hoping that her abductors would offer her some but to her disappointment and relief they didn't.

For what seemed like an hour her stomach growled and ached for some fulfillment that never came. The late November air was starting to cool down quickly as the sun disappeared behind the great pines and mountains. The big man stood within a couple feet of the Chinese captive, possibly to intimidate her and discourage her from trying to escape.

Ming Su was eventually set on an elk skin by the campfire to use as a place to rest. Her hands and feet still tied together, she had no choice but to lay on her side with her feet towards the campfire. She laid and watched the four men and the old woman walk around, occasionally engaging in conversation, grouching at one another, laughing and carrying on as they passed around a couple bottles of whiskey. The more that they drank the whiskey the more drunk they all became and the more everything seemed meaningless to Ming Su, and made little to no sense to her. She thought to herself that the five abductors would sleep half the day away tomorrow and be suffering from hangovers while she sat there and froze on the cold ground?

Ming Su waited hours for the sky to turn black. There were no stars and no moon to give any light to the darkness at all. Just a breeze that seemed to be picking up throughout the forest and the howling echoing through the mighty pines. Ming Su understood the language barrier between her and her abductors. However she knew how to say, "Outhouse." In English. She said to the man sitting on a log next by the fire and whispered. "Outhouse!" He snarled back at her. "Do you got to go?" She nodded her head. The scruffy and smelly man hollered to the old woman, instructing her to bring the girl to the outhouse. The old woman looked at Ming Su and began laughing hysterically. "What would happen if I didn't bring her to the outhouse?" The four men began laughing. One said. "You'll be cleaning the mess." The woman growled as she made her way to her feet. She untied Ming Su's feet then helped her to stand up. Shocking her abductors Ming Su collapsed from the weakness in her sleeping and cramped up legs. The old woman kicked her on the thigh and demanded Ming Su to get up. Ming Su struggled to her feet. Once standing, the woman tightly held on to Ming Su's arm to prevent her from trying to run off. When they got to the outhouse the woman untied Ming Su's hands and told her. "Hurry up, don't try anything stupid, I'll be right here waiting for you."

Ming Su almost gagged as she opened the dried out wooden door. The stench or human waste was almost unbearable. However, it had no effect on the old woman who hung a lantern from a hook hanging from the ceiling before Ming Su entered. Ming Su looked around for any potential ways to escape. She looked down in the hole leading into the pit and immediately decided that she was not going to climb in to hide. But after further investigation noticed a slat that was lose at the top and pulling away from the structures back wall. Making unnecessary noise was completely out of the question. It would probably only lead to Ming Su getting caught trying to escape. She climbed up on the seat and peaked out the crescent moon cutout in the door, listening hard as she tried to hear the men talking outside but the wind blowing the tree tops together resulted in the branches crackling against one another, muting out their conversation, encouraging her to realize that the men probably couldn't hear her either. She pushed on the slat as close to the top as she could, forcing the nails to slip out of their worn out holes in the frame. She was startled and gasped when she heard the old woman banging on the door and shouting. "Hurry up in there, you deviant slant eyed brat." Ming Su shouted back, "Minute," before turning the lantern down then pushing on the slat once again. She became excited when the nails lost their grip allowing the slat to slowly fall. Quickly she reached out through the opening to catch the board before it fell to the ground. The woman knocked on the door again. Ming Su shouted. "Belly hurt, minute." the woman shouted back. "For crying out loud, will you just hurry up? I don't have all night." Ming Su removed the elk from covering herself and tossed it out through the opening as she chuckled with confidence and squeezed out onto the ground. Listening and trying to keep an eye out for the old woman she leaned the slat against the opening and before grabbing the elk skin and fleeing into the forest.

Faster and faster she ran through the dark woods in the supposed direction that the wagon traveled from. While thinking to herself. "That was the easy part. Now how do I get back to town?" She knew that she hadn't eaten a bite all day and the water that she drank would only last a while to quench her thirst. None the less, sticking around would only make her future worse than she could ever imagine. Knowing that she was little and could hide easily behind a tree, brush, log or a boulder, it still didn't hide the fact that she was tired and hungry. Her weak and hungry state made her not very fast compared to a full grown man on her heels. She stopped to rest once she was out of breath and felt safe. Her little hands were quickly absorbing the cold. She was relieved to find that she did not lose her mittens that were in her coat pockets. She also thought about abandoning the elk skin that Lost Doe slipped over her head but she figured if it kept the Indian people warm in the cold weather it should do the same for her.

Looking behind her she noticed through the trees a lantern that was probably being carried my one of the men on horseback. Looking around she gasped at the sight of another lantern that was still a distant away but just the same, closing in on her. Being lost in the middle of nowhere she knew that it would be easy and even more dangerous to get disoriented if she tried to make her way back through the forest of the pitch darkness of the night. She decided to lie down at the base of a fallen pine and covered herself with bushes, leaves and anything else that would make her not look like a little girl silhouetting in the darkness. Time dragged on as she laid still in anticipation and fear, hoping that the lantern lights would pass her by and eventually fade away.

She woke the next morning as the sky was brightening to the new day. The clouds were dark, the air was cold as the wind continued to blow harder and harder. However, not more than twenty yards away the big man with green teeth was passed out against the base of an enormous Ponderosa Pine with an empty whiskey bottle clenched in his worn out leather glove. Ming Su felt confident that it was safe. She slowly sat up while looking around frantically hoping that other than her sleeping guest that she was alone.

Snowflakes began to fall one by one. Fear struck her hard once she realized that she would leave tracks once the snow started to accumulate but took advantage of the dry ground while she could and began running towards the wagon road. Once she stepped on the road, she looked both ways. Somewhat fresh wagon tracks were evident along with horse tracks from two horses. She was sure that it was the wagon road that she traveled in on and headed in the opposite direction of the trading post. After walking for a while, she noticed two horses with riders in the distance coming towards her. She panicked because she didn't want to get caught again. The only alternative was to duck back into the woods and hide behind a pine tree with hopes that she was not spotted by the two men. Being as quiet as possible she was quite strategic as she made her way around the pine slowly as the two men on horses passed by. The riders seemed silent from the distance giving Ming Su confidence that she evaded them too. She snuck back onto the road. However, as soon as she began walking the weening of a horse in the near distance caught her attention. She ducked back into the woods to hide once again. She listened carefully and could also hear a second horse and the rattle of a wagon traveling at a trot. She took refuge behind another big pine as the wagon passed. Her suspicions were evident when she spotted one of the men from the trading post and the old woman sitting beside him. Her heart jumped up into her throat as she began to cry in fear for her young life but the wagon passed on by as she once again worked her way around the back side of a big pine tree, hiding from the view of the bad man and woman.

Ming Su's stomach ached as she pushed on through the high wind and low mountain temperature. She began to grow weaker to the point of almost giving up after the snow began to fall harder and faster. The thoughts of never seeing Lanying again troubled her mind, creating her to panic. Her doubts of her father laying eyes on his beautiful daughter had practically disappeared. It was only the memory of her brother Hai that gave her the strength to keep moving. Other thoughts crossed her mind such as making a camp fire but that thought was a moot point considering that the smoke would send off a scent and would visibly be seen from anyone passing by. The last thing that she wanted to do was give her whereabouts away, especially to the bad men. She began to wonder about how many hours she had been walking through the lonely forest but so much had seemed to happen that she really had no idea. That she was cold and it was just going to get colder if she didn't make it back to town before night fall.

For some reason it didn't really seem to occur to her that she was leaving tracks as the snow got deeper and deeper, covering her soles, then her toes and as time passed, her ankles as well. She stopped and turned around. It was discouraging to see her tracks so plain in the ankle deep snow behind her. Anger struck her hearts. She screamed. "How could I be so stupid?" Realizing that she screamed out loud she looked around her in hopes that she was not heard. Slowly she began to walk. She chuckled uncontrollably. "I have to be the only crazy, absent minded person to be traveling through this stupid blizzard." Nonetheless, she pushed on.

The cool breeze transformed into a brutal wind causing the falling snow to seem more like trillions of little white flies frantically flying around as the mighty pines swayed high into the white void, causing their branches colliding with one another, crackling and screeching. The sound was so loud and frightening that it seemed like the sky above was about to collide with the earth. Eventually to be proven once the smaller and weaker branches fell to the ground coming to abrupt stops with a loud thud and an explosion of fresh snow. She cringed and ducked in hopes to not be a target for the falling limbs.

In the not too far off distance howls echoed through the blank white. Fear struck Ming Su with a vengeance as her mind tried to determine what the howling sound would be and how far off it really was in a forest considering that echoes traveled for miles. There was no doubt in her mind that she would make a tasty little petite treat for a pack of wolves or even coyotes. Her visibility was reduced down to just a couple yards as she struggled to see the once laid out trail covered with the same white that was all around her. It was like being trapped inside a white billowy cloud. Making it almost impossible to keep her eyes opened from the frozen little flakes that continuously swarmed around her face. The knitted scarf that covered her nose and mouth developed a skin of ice from her breath that got thicker in the below freezing temperature. Her elk hide poncho only did so much to keep

Ming Su warm from the elements as her muscles ached, causing her to shiver. Suddenly the echoing howls seemed even closer. Frightening her enough to spin around and around in fear as her young heart raced as fast as it did the day before she left China. Once she stopped spinning, panic set in. "Where are my foot prints?" she asked herself. Suddenly the wind stopped momentarily for her to get a quick glimpse of the foot prints that she was leaving in her wake. She let out a sigh and turned around with comfort in her heart, knowing that she was not leading herself back into the lions' den.

Ming Su's exhausted body was weakening by the minute. She lifted her legs high to take what should have been simple steps. Her knees just wouldn't bend that far in the deep snow. She thought. "If I fall, I would be hidden by the snow and my body may not be discovered until Spring." She shook her head and fell to her knees in exhaustion. Deep inside her heart and mind she could hear her brother Hai. "Get up Su, get up." She began to hallucinate, seeing the bad men surrounding her and coming in from every direction. Tears instantly filled her eyes as she cried out. "Nooooo!" But she was quickly startled when out of nowhere a brown rabbit lunged out in front of her from behind a large boulder sitting on the side of the wagon road. Instantly Ming Su lost her balance and fell forward in the snow. A moment passed as she lied their laughing at the little cuddly fur ball. She rolled around in the snow trying to see which direction the rabbit had run to. She knew that there would be no way that the bad men would be out in the blizzard looking for her. So catching the rabbit would make it a great opportunity to have a tasty meal. Unaware of where the rabbit took refuge to, Ming Su scuffled to her feet to try and see its tracks though the quick falling snow. Moments passed before a streak of gray rushed passed her feet and up alongside the boulder. She laughed deviantly as she rushed after it. Grabbing hold of the side of the boulder and saplings sticking up from the snow to help give her balance and speed as she followed the frightened animal up alongside the boulder and then behind it. A large hole caught her attention. It was obvious to her that the rabbit used the hole as a home. The hole was rather big in diameter as Ming Su studied it. She thought to herself. "I can get in there." She wasted no time dropping to her knees and fighting through the snow to make her way into the hole.

There was plenty of room in the hole. Ming Su could almost sit up. She removed her right mitten and reached into her coat pocket to retrieve a small tin containing wooden matches with the white tips. She lit one on a rock to give her a little bit more light as she wiggled her body deeper into the hole. Pushing with her feet and pulling with her elbows, further and further into the hillside. As expected the match burned out about the time that she lied on her side and rested her head on a tree root. Once again she retrieved a match and struck it against another rock before rolling onto her back. Her attention was drawn to the little sparkles in the soil but she paid little mind considering that she was still on the hunt for the rabbit. She just had no idea where the rabbit could have gone off too. However, realizing that she was safe from the snow, it didn't seem all too cold since the wind wasn't blowing in the hole. She said. "This is actually very comfortable. I will rest here for now." Even though her stomach was aching from hunger pains she closed her eyes and faded off to sleep.

Ming Su was awoken by a tickle on her nose. She was startled but didn't panic, what little light that was coming in from outside she could tell that she had a visitor or was the rabbit welcoming her as a visitor? She looked around and noticed another rabbit, then another and before she knew it she come to realize that there were many rabbits living together in the hole. Slowly she reached out and petted the rabbit on its back. It seemed very skittish but also seemed to enjoy the feel of its fur being stroked. Ming Su smiled and giggled until the rabbit sprinted towards the exit. One by one the other rabbits headed toward the exit as well.

It took Ming Su a couple moments to realize that the rabbit hole was pretty bright and that the storm must have passed and the night had turned into a new bright day. She turned around and crawled her way back through the hole to discover a sunny morning. Taking a deep breath of fresh mountain air into her little lungs while leaning with her back against the boulder she found the strength despite her hunger pains to move on.

Moments later as she made her way down from behind the boulder and stood on the wagon road she came to discover that there were at least three sets of wagon wheels and many sets of horse and dog tracks that was when she come to realize that the wagon with wooden tracks was probably drawn by the team of dogs that looked live wolves but with her stomach aching she followed the tracks towards town. Walking in the wake of the dogs and horses, the snow on the wagon trail was still hard on her petite and short legs through the deep snow. Her hearts remained tight in her chest by unknowing how far ahead of her the bad men were. Either way she was sure that the tracks would lead her to food and to shelter in Bannock City and not a settlement or another town.

Walking in the wake of the wagons and dog sled was still very challenging considering the uneven terrain beneath the snow, hidden rocks, tree limbs, clumps of dead grass and holes. The sun had crept across the sky but Ming Su still found herself lost in the middle of nowhere. As the minutes passed her steps became shorter and fewer. She was weak, tired, starving and dehydrated. She began to worry as the sun was quickly falling and the cold was moving in even faster.

Three days of traveling with no food or water except melted snow for an unknown amount of miles had taken its toll on the young Chinese orphan. Daylight once again disappeared as a black sky opened up to its speckles of glowing stars. The moon looked like a slice of apple giving a little bit of light on the dark wagon trail as it reflected off the snow from the night before. Falling branches from the trees echoed throughout the forest striking fear into Ming Su's heart and mind.

Ming Su came across a small boulder that she decided to sit on and take a break. She allowed her heartrate and breathing to slow enough to allow her to hear people talking and laughing, music playing and animals crying out their individual calls. A slight breeze carried the scent of American food cooked on an open fire. Pork, vegetables, warm bread, cinnamon cake or perhaps apple pie from this seasons apples. Ming Su's lungs expanded as she stood to her feet, suddenly a burst of adrenaline overtook her body and she began to run towards civilization. Losing traction with every few steps didn't discourage her at all, she was on a mission and it was not too far off. The chatter and laughter got louder and louder, the smell of the food was all around her. The animals speaking in their language was so loud and monotonously overwhelming. Then came the stench of the people who hadn't bathed in weeks or even months. There was no doubt in her mind that she was in the town that she recently called home once the animal waste on the main roads filled her sinuses. She gagged and choked a couple times as she tried to slow down her breathing while running but found that it was not very effective. Stopping at an all American restaurant, she quickly opened the door and entered before closing the door behind her. Leaning back against the wall she closed her eyes and took a deep breath of the delicious foods filling the air. A man suddenly placed his hand on her shoulder. "Come on with me, I will buy you dinner." Ming Su's eyes opened wide in as she panicked. She slapped the man's hand away, opened the door and ran off into the street but she quickly recognized the buildings and knew where she was, the only problem was that she still had about half of a mile to go and the last thing that she wanted or needed was to be spotted by any bad man that would take her far away. She knew that she didn't have the strength to fight back nonetheless, escape again. Suddenly she spotted one of Longwei's employees. She ran up to him and made her presence known. The Chinese man's eyes opened wide as he gasped. "Su, where have you been, Lanying is worried out of her mind about you. Come on, let me get you home." Ming Su grabbed tightly on to the Chinese man's hand, showing no attempt to let go. But to her surprise she noticed that they were walking straight towards one of the bad men who had taken her three days earlier. She snapped her hand from the Chinese man's grip and took off running towards Kolinski's Restaurant. The Chinese man cried out. Ming Su, Ming Su where are you going?" Ming Su kept running, catching the attention of the bad man. When the bad man focused on the child running away he realized who it was and yelled. "I can't believe it, there she is." But with the crowd of people in his way, he didn't have any chance of pursuing Ming Su.

The wooden door opened quickly, catching Lanying by surprise. Ming Su wasted no time slamming the door behind her considering how scared out of her wits she was. Lanying rushed to her and fell to her knees embracing the missing youth. Ming Su cried and trembled as her fear escaped her heart and invaded her body. Lanying asked. "Su where have you been all this time? Do you know how dangerous it is here? There are bad men who would swoop you up like a bird of prey and take you away forever." Ming Su was not ready to stop crying. She just kept nodding her head very fast. A moment passed before she calmed down enough to look at Lanying and confess. "The bad men took me when I ran after Gordy the other day. They took me way out into the forest. I escaped and came back." Lanying held Ming Su tight and felt her frozen to the bone. "I want you to get out of those clothes and sit by the fire." Ming Su cried out. I can't my body aches too much, help me. Please help me Lanying." Lanying helped Ming Su strip down to nothing at all and wrapped her in a warm blanket. Lanying stated. "Just sit by the fire. I will get you some chicken soup from the kitchen. Just stay warm, you are safe now." Lanying covered Ming Su with a second blanket before she left out the door.

Ming Su was slowly sipping on the chicken broth from a mug when she began to explain in detail of her three day ordeal. With no food or water, the continuous snow fall and the cold, as well as how she feared that she would never see Lanying or Mr. Kolinski again. Lanying closed her eyes and whispered. "You are so brave child. How could such a young girl suffer so much loss in her life at such a young age and triumph over such an ordeal with strength and determination to make it back here to her home?" Ming Su didn't say a word as she found comfort in Lanying's arms. They sat embraced together until the fire was starving for another log. Lanying stuffed two smaller logs into the coals before she fetched Ming Su a fresh set of clean warm clothes. Ming Su declined on taking a bath due to being even colder. She stood in front of the fire getting dressed as Lanying picked up her cold, damp clothes from the floor. She shook the elk hide, filling her eyes with surprise. Little specks of gold dust sparkled by the light of the fire as they fell to the floor. She turned to Ming Su with concern. "Ming Su this is odd, where have you been to get gold dust on your clothes?" Ming Su gasped. "The wooden box in the back of the wagon that the bad men put me in." But Ming Su really knew better as she recalled the little sparkles in the rabbit hole reflecting off the lit matches. Lanying's excitement quickly turned to disappointment. She tossed the elk skin in the corner of the room. Lanying said. "I just want you to forget about all of what had happened. We need to get some rest tonight. The day after tomorrow is a big American celebration called Thanksgiving, it has something to do with some foreigners giving thanks to the Indians for saving their lives or something of that sort. The restaurant will be very busy all day long; we must work hard and work fast. So let's get some sleep. We will be starting early tomorrow and the next day. Tomorrow will be for making pies, cutting up vegetables and potatoes and baking lots of bread rolls."

15

A worn out wooden tomato crate made a fine step for Ming Su that put her at the right height to scrub the Thanksgiving dishes. The loop around her neck was tied in a knot to shorten the apron that was almost as long as she. The sides were wrapped around her sides and looked like a dress with the strings wrapped around her hips two times and tied in the front. A sliver of cloth wrapped around her head and tied off, holding her hair out of her face and off her shoulders, protecting it from the dirty dishes water and soap.

Even though her sleeves were rolled up to her biceps, they were still soaked from dunking the dishes into the water. To her left the dishes kept piling up faster than she could wash them. The plates, the bowls, the coffee mugs and of course the metal eating utensils. A metal bucket was used to scrape the uneaten food into, only to be recycled by feeding the unconsumed food to the chickens and pigs.

Lanying had just finished scraping the cut vegetables from the cutting board into the big Calderon along with about 20 pounds of beef chunks, herbs, spices and other flavorings for lunch and dinner the next day. But when she noticed the dishes piling up alongside her counterpart she rubbed the back of Ming Su's shoulder. She stated. "Let me do this Ming Su, you take a break. I know there is a lot to wash but you will get used to it in time. Go get a cookie and rest a few minutes."

Lanying pushed the tomato crate out of the way with her foot the moment Ming Su stepped down. She watched her grab an oatmeal cookie from the ceramic jar and head towards the dining room to rest at a table with four chairs strictly reserved for the staff. Ming Su sat watching a young American woman talk to Mr. Kolinski. She couldn't make out what either of the two were saying as she just munched on her cookie and stared. Suddenly the woman opened up a wooden case that was lying on the table and removed a wooden instrument of some sort with a lot of strings. It reminded her of a Erhu, a Chinese stringed instrument used to make music. But she didn't pick it up to play it in the usual way; she tucked the base under her chin and ran a stick over the strings. To her amazement it was the same type of sound that she recognized in San Francisco that she was dancing to and the sound that she heard on the trail as she fell to sleep that one night. She closed her eyes and began moving her head from side to side as the chatting and laughing minimized in the restaurant. A moment passed before she jumped out of her chair to run back into the kitchen to get Lanying's attention. "Come on, I want to show you something." Lanying followed Ming Su. That is the music that I like. Lanying smiled and began to take it in as she swayed to the soft melody. Mr. Kolinski took notice and smile at the American woman while nodding. The woman began to walk around the tables playing her instrument for the customer's enjoyment. A young American boy followed her around with a little metal bucket, watching the restaurant customers toss coins into it. Lanying turned and walked back into the kitchen leaving Ming Su to enjoy the music. But Ming Su's joy was quickly robbed from her when a familiar loud, annoying laugh was heard from merely yards away. She looked around through the crowd like a cat looking through the grass for a rodent. Ming Su gasped with wide eyes. It was two of the bad men and the woman who had abducted her Sunday morning. She slowly slipped down off the dining chair and ducked down as she made her way into the kitchen. Hustling to Lanying's side, she looked up at her with fear in her eyes. "They found me." Lanying looked at the child with confusion then realized what she meant. She asked. "Are they out there?" Ming Su nodded her head. "Yes, two men and an ugly older woman at the table with the knife mark." A few weeks prior Ming Su and Lanying were witnesses to two men that had gotten into an argument and one slammed the tip of his knife blade into the top of the table, leaving a deep mark. "Lanying asked. "Do you think that they saw you?" Ming Su quickly shook her head. "Okay then good, let's sneak you out the back door and into our room." The duo moved quickly. Once inside their room Lanying instructed Ming Su. "Under no circumstances do you unlock that door and open it for anybody but me. Do you understand?" Ming Su's eyes were wide as she nodded and replied. "Yes!"

Lanying walked around the front of the restaurant to enter. Right away she scanned around for Mr. Kolinski before rushing to him. She explained to him the situation and where the unpleasant customers were sitting. He said to Lanying. "Yeah, they have been in here many times before." He turned and rushed away. After looking around at the different people he grabbed a young American boy by the arm and seemed to give him instructions.

Minutes later the American boy returned with Sheriff Williams and his deputy. Kolinski filled them in on the matter. Sheriff Williams stated. "Oh yes, Mrs. Murphy and her two sons Jacob and Oliver. I have never known a more criminally consumed family as them. I'll take care of this, come on deputy." Kolinski and Lanying stepped back to their restaurant duties for the Thanksgiving feast. Fortunately another one of the kitchen staff kept up with the dishes. Lanying turned and exited the kitchen, sitting at the table where Ming Su sat earlier. She overheard the sheriff as he approached the table where the Murphy family claimed control. "Jacob and Oliver Murphy, I see you brought your mother in for some Thanksgiving turkey and other sides. What else brings you losers into town? It wouldn't be a young Chinese girl would it? The big loud one took his hat off and placed it on his knee. Took a couple more chews of his turkey and stated. "Sheriff, what my brother Oliver and I do is none of your business but if you want to, we will be more than happy to make it your business."

"You know Jacob, if I didn't know better, I would take that as a poor attempt to threaten me."

"Oh, no, no sheriff, not at all. The business that we have here today is that we just brought momma for Thanksgiving dinner at this fine restaurant. We don't want any trouble sheriff but I am concerned about your accu, accu, accumilation about something with a Chinese girl. Are you accusing me of something Sheriff?"

"No! I just know of this little Chinese girl that was abducted last Sunday."

"Oh Sheriff that is horrible."

"Yeah, I say that I would have to agree, not to worry though, she is safe with her family now, after she out smarted an ugly old woman and escaped from an outhouse that had a slat that was not properly secured. And the funny thing is, her little fingers are pointing in the direction of you three. What do you all say to that accusation?"

"Oh yeah, accusation, that is what I meant to say, that's the right word. But we don't know what you or some Chinese girl is talking about sheriff. Perhaps you would want to fetch her and bring her to stand before us, just to make sure that she really is pointing her fingers at the right people."

"I know all about you three. You think that you are untouchable because you're some distant cousins to George Grimes and his buddy, whatever his name is that was suspected to have killed him but blamed it on the native Indians. Either way you are too lazy or too stupid to find your own gold so you kidnap young Chinese girls or purchase them from their parent with the promise of giving them a better life but in turn you sell them to the highest bidder to be sold as sex slave and eventually prostitutes. So don't try to pull the wool over my eyes you pile of cow manure. If I had my way, you would all three be hanging from some tree right now. I think that they are done with their Thanksgiving dinner deputy. Make sure that they pay for their meal and get rid of them. I don't want to see you three in my town again." The sheriff stepped back and watched the Murphy brothers and their mother get up before they were escorted out of the restaurant.

Christmas and the New Year had passed with a new name for Bannock City. In December of that year, 1863 by the order of the New Idaho Territorial Legislature, Bannock City, Also known as West Bannock was given the name Idaho City to avoid confusion with Bannock, Montana, a little over 300 miles away.

Ming Su seen many people come and go from Idaho City and experienced more snow fall that winter than she could ever imagine. She kept her hair at shoulder length throughout her first winter in the American North-West. Some of the regulars at Kolinski's Restaurant knew Ming Su as a sweet young Chinese girl that would help out at the restaurant on occasion. Very few would question why a boy her height and weight answered to Hon. That disguise would prove to be a good choice considering that the Murphy's had no intension on obeying the sheriff's demands. They knew that Ming Su lived in Idaho City and they were looking for retribution. There was no doubt that Ming Su would bring a good stack of money if to be sold to the skin trade.

Ming Su's birthday was celebrated in the American way on March 22nd. There was a private party for her at Kolinski's Restaurant in the back room. Very few people were invited, present were Mr. Kolinski, Lanying, Lonqwei, and Susan, the woman with the violin. It was the first time that Susan had played solely for Ming Su. Ming Su danced around to the music. She giggled as she noticed Longwei and Lanying dancing hand and hand. Taking it upon herself Ming Su grabbed Susan's sons hand to dance with him. He was a little reluctant at first until Susan quickly whisper at her son. "Joseph!" And he began to dance with Ming Su.

A woman from the kitchen staff brought in a beautifully made chocolate cake and set it on the table alongside a stack of little plates and forks. Eleven candles were burning causing Ming Su's face to light up. Lanying told her to make a wish and blow out all the candles. Everyone smiled as all eleven flames bent away from her and disappeared. Mr. Kolinski placed a long item with a cloth covering it on the table, stepped back and bowed the best way that he knew to be tradition for Ming Su to understand it as a gift. She removed the cloth to be left in aww. Lanying gasped as the sight of the brand new violin. Mr. Kolinski could barely balance himself as Ming Su threw her arms around the middle aged American man and hugged him tight. Kolinski didn't know how to react considering that he had never been married or had any children. He bent over and kissed Ming Su on the top of her head. "Happy Birthday little lady." Ming Su wasn't concerned about the cake at that particular moment. She wanted to make beautiful music like Susan. Susan once again opened her violin case and removed the violin from it. She positioned the violin on her shoulder and instructed Ming Su to do the same with hers. Her student quickly understood how to hold the bow properly before pulling it across the strings and watching Susan's violin put out a beautiful note. However, when Ming Su pulled the bow across the strings, her violin let out a loud eerie sound. The crowd got a quick laugh at the expression on Ming Su's face. The teacher instructed Ming Su to stand on the chair. Susan set her violin and bow down on the table and stood behind Ming Su. She showed Ming Su where to hold the neck to give room for her to place her hand. With her right hand she placed it on top of Ming Su's right hand and began moving Ming Su's hand that was holding the bow. Ming Su was amazed that she was making such beautiful music with a few flaws as Susan guided her hand with the bow. After a couple moments Susan let go of Ming Su's right hand and let her move the bow in the same sequence as Susan was showing her. The music wasn't as clean and crisp as it was when Susan was helping but Ming Su got the idea and seemed to feel confident that practicing will prevail in the end. She dedicated herself to about a half hour every evening with the determination to play beautiful music like Susan. To Lanying the tune was embedded in her brain to where she hummed the melody day after day at work.

16

Three weeks later, to the day Ming Su decided that she would head out on her two day journey to find the boulder where she spent the night with a family of rabbits. She had no idea what she was going to tell Lanying when she returned, she just knew that Lanying would worry all night because it was not the right time to tell her where she went and why. Ming Su dressed up as if she was Hon, her long ebony hair had to be hid under her hat. For safety she slipped her belt through the loop of Hai's leather knife sheath before she headed out. There wasn't a single doubt in her mind that she wouldn't recognize the boulder. What she wasn't sure of was, were there any forks in the road that she would come upon that she don't remember. The last thing that she wanted was to wander onto the wrong wagon road and end up traveling in the wrong direction. Realizing that it took most of the day to get back to Idaho City from the boulder because she was cold and weak, her biggest challenge was actually the snow and the continuous loss of traction as she walked. So in her mind she had no idea how far that she needed to walk back into the forest until she ended up at the boulder. Finally she stopped and grouched at herself. "Ming Su, stop it. Stop thinking about it," as she headed into the restaurant to grab some oatmeal cookies, four bread rolls, a cinnamon roll and a couple slices of breakfast ham to stuff in her bed roll before she sat down to have pancakes and bacon for breakfast.

As soon as Ming Su took to the street her mind quickly dwelled on her very imperfect plan. She asked herself. "Is it really a good idea to go by myself, or even go at all? Would Lanying go with me even if she told her the truth right now?" She thought about recruiting Joseph but decided that it would not be a good idea if she got them both lost. She couldn't trust the sheriff, or his deputies, not to mention the staff at Kolinski's Restaurant. They were all adults, so they would more than likely want to control everything themselves of the whole expedition. She had every doubt in the world about going but she knew if she didn't then she would never know and she would fail to keep her word to her brother Hai. Needless to say. She headed on.

The wagon road was easy to find, she remembered it well when she exited the forest. Where the main street forked to the left. Standing in the middle of the wagon road she dreaded the thought of the long hike ahead of her. Being physically fit for long hikes like she was when she first came to Idaho City was not the issue, it was getting lost or abducted again that was attacking her heart. Fear or not, she knew that she had to go.

After walking for what seemed about a mile a tree formation all cluttered together became recognizable. Instantly being reminded that she was on the right road even though everything was no longer white but of all natural spring colors. The wagon road reminded her of the road that she and Hai traveled the morning that they left China. The dead tan grass was turning green. Trees were sprouting their little buds of leaves. Wildlife was all around but not attempt to be a nuisance as the rodents played and chased each other, the birds flew, testing out their Spring wings through the warm air. Mule deer followed close by in hopes that Ming Su would offer them something to eat as they showed no fear of a human presence.

About another mile in she began to think about the return trip. She said to herself. "Once I get there, I have to walk all the way back. Hai this better be worth it. Otherwise you can find your own gold." Many travelers passed. A few people on foot, some on horseback and a couple horse drawn wagons. However her head was always turned downward or away. To the other travelers she looked like a boy walking by himself with a bed roll tied with rope, slung over his shoulder and a water canteen slung over his other shoulder. She made it a habit to count the number of travelers that she passed and then turned around to recount them. She was always suspicious of someone recognizing her as a girl and trying to sneak up behind her. Most of the times she just thought that she was being paranoid but after being abducted three times already. She wasn't taking any chances of being vulnerable again.

The violin melodies that Susan had been teaching her played on in her mind and helped to keep her thoughts away from the long hike, the bad men and her belly rumbling. In reality the thought of how far she had been walking and how far she had left to go, completely escaped her mind until she spotted the boulder ahead of her about twenty yards. Her discomfort or even fear forced her to stop in her tracks as she stepped to the side to look all around her to memorize her immediate surroundings. Being clever and killing time as travelers approached from ahead, she knelt down to look as she was tying the laces on one of her boots while closely watching and listening for other people talking or horses snorting. Evidently leaving any foot prints or tracks in the mud by the boulder would be a giveaway to anyone who may notice. When both directions were clear she headed up the hill where she was adjusting her boot laces then worked her way through the weeds, brush and rocks to the top of the hill at the back of the boulder. It seemed reasonable to use an enormous pine tree as cover considering she had clear view of the road in either direction. When she felt the time was right by no other presence besides herself. She tossed her bed roll and her canteen toward the hole leading into the ground. After one last look in both directions and without hesitation she crawled down the hill, into the hole.

It took a few moments for Ming Su's eyes to adjust from the bright sunny day to the darkness of the hole stretching deep into the hill. Her heart began to pound erratically when she noticed little sparkles of sun light reflecting off the nuggets of gold. Thoughts of being rich entered her mind. She grabbed her bed roll and set it under her head as a pillow while she turned onto her back. However her excitement was not powerful enough to keep her from fading off into a deep sleep.

Memories of her family invaded her dreams. It felt so real to Ming Su as her mother, father and her brother Hai were living well with money and gold spread all over the furniture and rugs. Fong Yeo standing tall with a Chinese business suit on, a long pipe wedged in between his lips as he slipped a custom gold band with a large diamond onto his wife's finger. Hai standing just as stout as his father, stroking his hand along the orange and black fur of his domesticated tiger and Ming Su sitting side saddle on a white stallion, in her beautiful lavender dress while spinning the umbrella resting on her shoulder.

Her nap was quickly disturbed by a horse snorting just merely feet away on the other side of the boulder. She looked around as if she was trying to recognize where she was, doing her best not to make any sound. The pounding of the horses walking drew further and further away, encouraging Ming Su to let out a deep breath before realizing that she was actually alone and not with her family. Provoking her to break down into tears as her heart ached.

Ming Su stared at a large sparkle of gold as she rubbed her mother's North Star in between her thumb and fingers for a few moments before forcing herself to get up. She pulled Hai's knife from its sheath and began to chip at the hard soil and rock. She chipped and dug with her fingers on the bottom, then on the left side before the right side and even on the top. It was intriguing to her at the amount of gold nuggets of various sizes from the diameter of a pea to the size of a musket round that she accumulated in such a very short time. It was easier than she thought it would be to fill a cloth sack up about the size of an adult's hand. However, having the filled sack of gold in her possession could easily prove to be dangerous if the bad men or anyone else were to become suspicious of her before she reached home. She grabbed her canteen, popped the cap and took a long drink of the cold well water. Suddenly she realized. "If I head back now it will still be light when I get there, Lanying won't worry or ask questions." Heading back immediately became the plan but first she had to pour most of the water out onto the ground and then dump the little sack of gold nuggets into the canteen. She didn't know much about weight but she knew that gold was pretty heavy and that her canteen could not feel heavier than a full canteen of water and to her it felt just right.

At that point the sun was beyond the mid-day hover so Ming Su decided that she better get going. As she stood up she quickly ducked back down, hoping that the two men walking towards the boulder did not see her. She waited and waited as she listened to the conversation between the two about bear hunting got louder then faded away.

She worked her way back through the weeds, brush and rocks to the location where she headed up the hill and headed back down onto the wagon road. She looked behind her, there was nobody, she looked ahead but the two men had already turned around the bend.

Her excitement and probably even her adrenaline kept her walking at a fast pace but she felt that she should not walk faster than the men ahead of her so she kept a steady distance. Her journey back wasn't very different then her journey out. She passed many men walking towards her, others on horseback and an occasional horse drawn wagon. Lucky for her, nobody recognized her as Ming Su but as a boy traveling alone.

Lanying was not home when Ming Su walked through the door. Ming Su assumed that she must be visiting Longwei as usual at that time in the afternoon. However, it was perfect for Ming Su. She was anxious about finding a safe hiding place for her gold. A sudden thought crossed her mind. "Do I call it my gold or the gold or do I call it our gold. I guess nobody else was with me and I found the gold, which would make it my gold. Yeah! So my gold it is."

She stood in the middle of the room, slowly spinning around in hopes that a hiding place would come to mind then she remembered a loose two inch diameter knot in the pine slat behind a painting that Lanying hung to hide the unsightly knot in the wall. She removed the painting from the protruding nail to allow her to pry the knot out with Hai's knife. She hustled to get a spool of sewing thread from the drawer and cut off a length. One end she tied off to the protruding nail before she poured the nuggets and water into the little cloth sack. She did however keep out four of the bigger nuggets before tying the sack closed with the other end of the thread and feeding the sack into the hole on the wall. After replacing the knot she rehung the painting and stepped back to make sure that it was straight. She chuckled with pride at her great achievements while she picked up a cloth to sponge the water up off the floor.

Less than a moment passed before Lanying pushed the door open and entered from outside. Ming Su looked up at her and said. "I spilt the water from my canteen. But I have something that I want to show you."

"What is it? Are you okay?"

"Yes, I am wonderful." Ming Su stood up and held her hand out containing the four nuggets of gold. Lanying questioned. "Ming Su, where did you get that, you didn't steal it did you?" Ming Su wanted to be honest with the woman who gave her so much love and caring but she wanted to protect the rabbit hole from everyone, even her best friend. She felt that she had no choice for now but to lie. On the outside she was excited but on the inside she felt ashamed when she explained to Lanying. "I was walking in the woods and spotted these four gold nuggets lying on top of the mud. There were a lot of boot prints so I think somebody lost them or dropped them by mistake. I really don't know who they belong to."

"It looks to me that they belong to you now Ming Su." Ming Su thought with a smile. "Yeah! My gold."

"But Ming Su, I think that we should bring it to the gold exchange, or we will have Longwei do it for you." Ming Su agreed. They rushed out the door with Lanying closing it behind them.

The gold exchange was next door to Longwei's Chinese Mercantile and Supplies. Longwei agreed to act as if the gold was his, perhaps from a prospector who purchased some supplies but paid with the gold nuggets.

The clerk at the gold exchanged weighed the four nuggets of gold and determined that the weight totaled out at sixteen grams or just less than half a Troy ounce, selling for $10.34. Ming Su could hardly contain herself, considering that Lanying makes $5.26 per week but also got free housing and Ming Su was earning about $1.96 per week as a part time wage.

The trio went back over to Longwei's and settled in the back office. Longwei handed Ming Su $10 and explained to her that he usually keeps 10% but since it was her first transaction he would only charge her .34 cents instead of $1.03. Ming Su didn't seem too excited about giving up the .34 cents or $1.03 but Lanying explained to her. "Nothing is for free Ming Su, not even ones services. Longwei is a business man and his time is valuable, so you have to pay him for his time. Do you understand?" Ming Su sighed. "Yes, but it still doesn't make it right." Ming Su reached under her coat and pulled out Hai's knife. Lanying's eyes opened wide. She asked. "Ming Su what are you doing?" Ming Su set the knife down on Longwei's desk and asked. "Will you please have this sharpened for me? It has gotten dull over time. I believe that my father was the last person to sharpen it. He gave it to my brother Hai before he left for America so it means a great deal to me and I don't want it to be dull. You never know when you need a sharp knife." Lanying and Longwei chuckled. Longwei nodded and replied. "I will have it ready for you later today but it will cost you 5 cents." Ming Su growled under her breath and stated. "Okay, but it better be sharp."

Ming Su was so proud when she and Lanying stepped outside. However, it did weigh heavy on her heart to give her guardian half of the cash but deep inside she knew that Lanying wouldn't accept it. Nevertheless Ming Su plotted another plan and purchased a nice dress for Lanying to accompany the man who had a special interest in her to dinner.

Even in the mid 1860's, $10 only goes so far. Ming Su decided that it was imperative that she returned to the rabbit hole on a regular basis. It was hard for her and her young mind to comprehend that many Chinese immigrants and American prospectors search year after year to find their fortune in gold that never comes to light and by the evil of the Murphy's family; she stumbled upon what she referred to as her family's fortune in gold. At the time the rabbit hole was so important to her because she thought that she was honoring her father and brother

Hai but as time went on it turned more into an obsession to become the richest Chinese immigrant in Idaho City, Idaho. The problem that bothered her most was how the Americans treated the Chinese. They were discriminated against, shunned and targeted for violent attacks. The woman and children, mostly the females were considered expendable and worthless with the exception of serving the American man and the skin trade such as prostitution and rape.

Ming Su made it a bi-weekly commitment to return to the rabbit hole, but never carried more back than what she could fool people with by carrying about a pound of gold in her canteen. In fact a pound of gold pretty much filled her canteen but she needed to leave room for water just in case she needed a drink or she was searched. Fortunately for her, no one ever stopped and searched her.

Ming Su's hard work paid off quickly after she purchased a small pick ax, small shovel and a spoon. She thought about just taking a spoon from Kolinski's but she knew stealing was wrong. In two months she had a little over $1100 in gold stashed away in many different hiding places. June through August turned out to be the hottest summer that Ming Su ever experienced at that point in her life. Nonetheless she did become very creative with the place that she stashed her gold. Watching the carpenters build houses and other buildings, she developed an idea. By use of a hammer she was able to pull the one of the slat with the knot from the wall where her and Lanying lived. To her surprise the studs were six inches deep and two inches wide and twelve inches on center with a ten inch space between them. It was perfect for hiding her gold.

Ming Su contracted one of the carpenters to make a wooden box. It was made from one inch thick pine, two feet tall, nine inches wide, a thickness of five and a half inches with one end capped off. She placed the wooden box with the opening at the top into the space between the two studs and secured the top with two nails. The slat with the knot was re-nailed to its original position.

On Ming Su's spare time she would gather up the gold from her various hiding places. Some gold was in little sacks, some in children's socks, others tied up in old linen dining napkins. One by one she would feed the bagged gold into the knot hole and let it drop into the wooden box before replacing the knot and the painting. She did have a problem however. There was a lot of soil in the rabbit hole that contained gold dust and tiny specks of gold because all she was taking were the pea size pieces and bigger. On occasion she would see the men down at the river panning for gold. Some would be panning through the soil from the river bed and the shoreline while others carried large sacks of soil, sometimes by horses or mules to dump into their pans to swirl around, leaving the heavy gold behind at the bottom of the pans. With that in mind she knew that it was not anything that she was really interested in doing but she also knew that there was a lot of gold hidden in the soil. She decided that she would come up with a plan over the winter to mine the gold from the soil. Because before she knew it, the hot summer cooled down to a mild fall and then a cold winter once again. But on her last trip to the rabbit hole that year she decided to by-pass the boulder and follow the wagon road deeper into the forest. She needed to know exactly where the trading post was and how far that she walked to get back to town.

It seemed like that the distance between the rabbit hole and the trading post was about the same distance that she would walk to the rabbit hole from town. She was surprised to see that there were three wagons in front of the trading post and four small canvas tents pitched off to the side. Perhaps they were gold prospectors or hunters, but the thought that frightened Ming Su the most was. "Could the other people be there to purchase Chinese girls or even sell them to the Murphy's for a less price so the Murphy's could make a great profit?" Either way she felt that there was no reason to tell Sheriff Pinkham when she got back to town. Sheriff Williams wasn't able to do anything before and she felt without any evidence of other abducted children being held captive that Pinkham couldn't do anything now. However she realize that even if there were any children being held captive that the chances of them being gone by the time she got back to town, convinced the sheriff and then returned would be great. Feeling frustrated she began wondering why she even wasted a day for nothing.

Ming Su decided to hide behind a big pine and watch the travelers come and go on foot, on horseback and by wagons heading to and from another town called Placerville according to a hand painted sign in the shape of an arrow. She understood why the wagon road always had people coming and going on it as she went to the rabbit hole and back. The trading post was potentially a place to stop and get supplies and something to eat. But it puzzled her why the Murphy's were not so worried about her being out in the open all tied up. Once that thought set in. Ming Su came to realize that maybe she will inform Sheriff Pinkham of her discovery just the same.

Some of the travelers brought merchandise or supplies into the trading post while others carried merchandise and supplies out. Some sat around the big fire pit and consumed whiskey from the clear glass bottles while others just drank coffee or tea. On occasion, what smelt like beef steaks would be placed on the grill over the open fire to cook and Mrs. Murphy would continuously return to the fire pit to flip the steaks and sometimes remove one or two, placing them on a metal plate. A steel tripod held a big pot of some kind of stew that Ming Su figured was probably the vile smelling and tasting dog vomit. It was no surprise to Ming Su when Oliver Murphy came out of the trading post and advised one of the travelers that were spooning mouthfuls of dog vomit into his mouth that he should be getting going soon if they wanted to make it to Idaho City before dark. The traveler licked the spoon before he dumped the rest of his stew into the fire and handed Oliver the empty bowl and spoon as they stood and carried on a conversation. It was obvious that Ming Su too had lost track of time and didn't want to be traveling after dark. Nonetheless, she didn't want to leave without seeing the inside of the trading post either. After thinking for a moment she kicked up some fresh dirt with the heel of her boot to rub ground in filth over her hands and face before following Oliver and the traveler into the trading post. Being disguised as a Chinese boy Ming Su felt more than confident that she would not be recognized but kept her hat tightly on her head and her face pointed to the floor to hide her eyes. Slowly making her way around the inside of the trading post she noticed pelts from elk, deer, rabbit, coyote and wolves along with mining supplies, hunting rifles, knives and camping gear. Her recon was not completed when without warning the loud annoying voice that she knew to be Jacob Murphy yelled out. "What do you want kid? This is no place for slant eyed pain in the neck." Ming Su stepped up to the counter focusing on a glass jar of jerky strips. She disguised her voice the best that she could despite the fact that she was standing in the lion's den. "Two jerkies." Jacob snarled back as he popped the metal lid off the glass jar. "One penny, then be on your way." Ming Su set a copper coin on the counter before grabbing two strips of jerky and heading out the door. She could barely breath as she ran to find refuge behind the big tree once again. Jacob and the traveler came out the door not long after. They exchanged a few words before Jacob slapped his hand on the back of the travelers coat and returned into the trading post. The traveler walked over to a covered wagon and set a package on the driver seat before hustling to the outhouse. Mind Su ran to the covered wagon and climbed into the back for a free ride home.

17

Ming Su was becoming a little concerned about how the front of her shirts had begun to prove evident that she was a girl and not a boy. She felt that privacy was beginning to be an issue as well, even towards Lanying. She decided that she would let Lanying in on her little secret.

One evening while Lanying was resting her feet by the fire Ming Su removed the painting from the wall. Lanying asked. "Why are you taking that painting off the wall?" Ming Su picked up the hammer and pulled the nails out until they were released from the studs. Lanying watched in concern but didn't say a word. To Lanying, having Ming Su around was never boring and always an adventure. There was no doubt that the girl was up to something.

Ming Su removed the slat from the wall to reveal the wooden box which caught Lanying's attention. She slowly rose to her feet as pain rushed through them and she hobbled over to Ming Su. Ming Su reached into the wooden box and pulled out a little cloth sack. She smiled at Lanying and instructed her to hold out her hands. Ming Su poured the bag of little gold nuggets into her guardian's hands. Lanying's eyes opened wide as her chin dropped then she took a deep breath. "Su, where did this come from?" Ming Su wrapped her little hands around Lanying's bicep and guided her to the chair to sit. Lanying listened closely as Ming Su confessed her little lie and explained to her why she felt that she needed to keep it a secret and then what encouraged her to bring it all to light now. However, Ming Su neglected to inform Lanying where exactly the rabbit hole was. All she mentioned was behind a boulder about three miles into the forest. Lanying explained to Ming Su. "You obviously have a lot of gold, I don't want any of it, it is your fortune that you sought out. But we must keep your gold a secret. I will purchase a scale from the American Mercantile to weigh out the gold for you. The price of gold has not changed. It is still $20.67 per Troy ounce, I know this from Longwei. We cannot have anybody trying to take advantage of you and conning you out of your money. As we rest in bed tonight I will figure out the best thing to do." Ming Su nodded her head quickly a few time and stated. "Lanying, you have been like a mother to me and you gave me a good safe place to live with good people around us. I think it is time that I pay you back with this gold."

"Su what are you talking about? It's been a pleasure, you don't owe me anything."

"The truth is that I need my own room, you need your own room. I am a growing girl and I need privacy as you do too. I would like to buy us a house but I am not even twelve years old and that still isn't old enough. Will you take some of the gold and buy us a house?" Lanying smiled staring at the floor before looking up at the mature young girl. "Yes, I will speak to Longwei tonight and have him find us a house." Ming Su perked up with a sincere smile and tone. "If not, we will have one built." The duo began to laugh with joy.

That night Lanying could hear Ming Su's long continuous breaths as she slept. Many thoughts went through her head concerning her young friend. She knew that the word of Ming Su's fortune would bring danger to her. Men are killed every day around Idaho City over their gold claims, stashes of gold and fortunes. She didn't like the idea of making regular gold exchanges for cash at the local gold exchange. There is too much gossip, too many con artists, and not enough security. She decided that the best bet was to have different men that she could trust to make predetermined exchanges on a rotating schedule so nobody would catch on and they would be paid 5%. She contemplated that 5% may not be enough but considering that each predetermined amount of gold may be about a pound or so. 5% would pay out at over

$15, not a bad payday for thirty minutes of work. Then she thought that it takes her three weeks to make that kind of money and decided that $5 per transaction would be more than enough.

The next morning she noticed Edmond in Kolinski's. An American man in his middle twenties from Utah with a wife and two children at home. He seemed to be an outstanding honest family man trying to get rich quick. Lanying approached him and asked to speak to him. Edmond accepted the invitation and sat at the table with Lanying. She said to him. "I have discovered a little gold of my own but being a well-known employee here at Kolinski's I am very cautious about going to the gold exchange to cash it in. I am willing to pay you $5 to secretly take exactly one pound of gold and collect the cash for me." He chuckled. "$5 is not a lot of money for exchanging a pound of gold for three hundred some odd dollars."

"No it's not, but it is a lot of money for less than thirty minutes of light work."

"What do I get for keeping my mouth shut?"

"I will fill it with a slice of cherry pie and you won't be able to say a word." The two shared a laugh. "Okay, I'll do it."

Every two or three days Lanying would approach another man that she knew to exchange more gold. However, she did make sure that the weight of the gold was never consistent and she always had a good idea of how much cash should be returned to her. It really did matter just in case one of the men decided to take some of the gold for himself. Lanying did trust the men but she also knew that one could be tempted when it comes to money.

By the time the winter had passed all of Ming Su's gold had been turned into cash. But now she was challenged with the task of hiding the cash. Some was hid in the

wall where she hid the gold. She had no reason to think that it wouldn't be safe, neither did Lanying until they came home one afternoon and found their dwelling ransacked. Fortunately the money was still hidden in the wall. However, it encouraged Ming Su and Lanying decided on a home. The recently built Audette home had just become vacant since William Audette had passed away and the rest of his family moved to Boise. It was a priority for Ming Su to find a hiding place for the cash. Almost right away she found the perfect place in the wall behind the dresser in her bedroom. Unfortunately, Lanying was becoming very concerned about Ming Su's childish decisions and demanded that they take a stagecoach ride to Boise. She felt that behind the dresser was more than an obvious place if the house was to be ransacked like their room was. She made immediate travel plans for her and Ming Su.

Ming Su and Lanying were returning from Boise on the stagecoach. Many horses and wagons were rushing from the direction of Idaho City as the stagecoach got closer and smoke begin to fog the air. The driver stopped the coach and hopped down to have a word with Lanying and Ming Su. "I feel that I should let you know but I think that there may be a fire somewhere ahead, possibly even Idaho City." Lanying replied. "Yes, we can see and smell the smoke, leaving us quite concerned. I suppose that would be the reason for everyone passing us on the road."

"I believe so Lanying. Hang tight and I will get you home." Ming Su whispered. "That's if home is still there."

With the buildings and houses constructed of mostly wood from pine trees that were logged and processed from the surrounding area, the town of Idaho City suffered the first of four devastating fires in May of 1865. Lanying and Ming Su were in complete despair when they returned to discover that over 80% of the town burned to the ground, The sheriff's station was gone, the jail was gone as well as Kolinski's, Longwei's and the Audette home.

Lanying and Ming Su stood in front of the stone foundation where their house once stood covered with black coals. They stared at the ground in disbelief. Mr. Kolinski approached them with tears in his eyes, he dropped to his knees. "It's gone, it's all gone, my restaurant has been burned to a crisp. I have no choice but to retire, sell the land for what I can get for it and go back to Southern Nevada." Lanying asked. "What happened?"

"The last that I heard the fire was set by an arsonist at Cody's Saloon on Montgomery Street. It burned everything on that street and then come back down the other side and spread so fast from the wood buildings being so dry and the wind blowing. Idaho City never had a chance." Ming Su stepped over to Kolinski and put her arms around him. She cried out. "It will be okay Mr. Kolinski. Please don't cry." He patted Ming Su on the back of the hand and replied. "You have such a good heart Su. I don't know what I am going to do though. I have to go home broke." Ming Su looked at Lanying and they began to smile. Kolinski felt a little insulted for their inconsiderate gesture, jumping to his feet he snarled. "What could possibly be so funny at this place and time?" Ming Su responded. "It is not going to be your problem Mr. Kolinski."

"What are you talking about Su? It is my problem. I have nothing left."

"Mr. Kolinski, just last week you were talking about selling the restaurant and retiring. It is a nine hour ride to Boise on the stagecoach and a ten hour ride back."

"I know that, but what point are you making?" Ming Su looked at Lanying then back at Kolinski. "Lanying and I talked about many things. We would like to buy your restaurant so you can retire."

"Su, you are both crazy. I appreciate the offer but there is nothing there." Lanying stepped in. "Yes there is."

"What?"

"Prime real estate property. We decided on buying the restaurant before the fire, so we will work together to rebuild the restaurant. With all the work that had to be done here in Idaho City there will be many, many hungry mouths to feed. So this time next year we will have it appraised and we will negotiate an amount for the land and the restaurant as well as everything in it."

"Why would you two do such a crazy thing, I thought I taught you better than that Lanying." Ming Su threw her arms around Kolinski's waist and looked up at him and smiled. "Because we love you Mr. Kolinski, you have done so much for us."

"Perhaps but you don't owe me anything." Ming Su sarcastically responded. "Perhaps, but there are over two hundred businesses in this town but we don't want to buy a saloon, or a store or even a bakery. We don't even want to buy another restaurant. We want to buy Kolinski's." The six foot, two inch tall, 240 pound man with thin hair on top of his head broke down in tears as Ming Su hugged his waist. He mumbled. "It's a deal ladies, it's a deal… Where do you expect to get the money though?"

"We will tell you but it is imperative that you keep it between us because we actually need your help too."

"Absolutely, what is it?"

"Well, I would say to lets go talk in the house but it too is gone. But believe it or not Mr. Kolinski. Su is probably one of the riches people in this town. We just got back from Boise from making a cash deposit of a very large sum to the First National Bank of Idaho."

"How is it that I am finding out about this now and where did she get all the money?" Ming Su chuckled. "I came here to find gold and that is exactly what I did."

"I am not sure that I am understanding. You work for me." Ming Su laughed. "Mr. Kolinski, it is a cover. I don't want anyone else to know that I have the money that I do but people would wonder how I would be able to purchase a lot of the things that I have if I didn't work."

"But you are only thirteen years old. They would expect you to get money from Lanying."

"Perhaps, but anyway, I have several 5 pound sacks of soil from where I get my gold. They have been there all winter and are hidden under the leaves and brush in an old stone foundation of a burned down cabin out in the woods. The first one was too heavy for me to carry comfortably for over three miles. One day I followed what I thought may have been a deer run but turned out to be a grown over wagon road that ended at the burned down cabin."

"So what is it that you need from me?"

"I need somebody who looks like a prospector, with a pack mule to accompany me there and carry out the sacks of soil. And I need a very, very, I mean very honest person to pan through each sack of soil down at the river for the gold trapped in the soil for a handsome compensation." Kolinski sighed. "Have you met Jim Pfeiffer?"

"No, I haven't had the pleasure to. Who is he?"

"Jim Pfeiffer is a retired Pastor from Sacramento who travels now that his wife had passed away a couple years ago. I can vouch for this man. I never met a more honest person and his luck at discovering gold has not been very good despite his praying. So let me talk to him. I also assume that there will be more sacks of soil from your undisclosed location?"

"You assume right Mr. Kolinski."

The town got back on its feet pretty quick. Buildings were going up all over the place, caravans of wagons carrying supplies and equipment were coming in from Boise and other towns around the area every day. The lumber mills around the region could not turn out lumber fast enough for the number of swinging hammers and cutting saws. However, many businesses and houses were rebuilt using brick. Prospectors who were not prospering very well took on jobs as lumber jacks, mill workers, brick layers and laborers as others help rebuild the town too.

The reconstruction and other restaurant affairs were left up to Kolinski while Ming Su and Lanying traveled to Boise for a month's stay while their house was being rebuilt and Jim Pfeiffer panned through twenty seven 5 pound sacks of soil.

Ming Su and Lanying returned in the beginning of July. They went back to their duties at the newly rebuilt restaurant. There was a lot of question around town on who paid to have the Audette house rebuilt to begin with. People felt that a Chinese woman and a child could not possibly make enough money working as help at a restaurant. Nonetheless the most common conclusion was that Kolinski lent Lanying the money.

18

Ming Su became a little grief stricken at the word that on July 23, 1865 Ex- Sheriff Sumner Pinkham had been shot and killed by a professional gambler named Ferdinand Patterson while waiting for the carriage to bring the Ex-sheriff back to town at the pool fed by the warm springs, two miles west of Idaho City. Pinkham took a special interest in protecting Ming Su. He had heard about the Murphy's abducting her and frequented Kolinski's Restaurant. To Ming Su he was more than just an average customer.

To the clerk at Lonqwei's Chinese Mercantile, Bojing had his own suspicions about Ming Su and how much she was spending money at the Chinese Mercantile on a restaurants' helper's part time wage. Not to mention other places around town. Things were just not adding up.

Bojing encouraged his daughter Nuying to befriend Ming Su to find out where she was getting all her money to buy the best clothes and the best house hold goods.

As friendly as Nuying was she found it to be an almost impossible task. She tried befriending Ming Su but Ming Su could not trust the overzealous daughter of the mercantile clerk. She kept up with her position spying on Ming Su and many times on Lanying while reporting back to her father. Ming Su was becoming very suspicious of Nuying since Nuying kept bringing by traditional Chinese food to their house and running into her and Lanying on the streets all the time. Ming Su was very reluctant about returning to the rabbit hole because she had a feeling that she would be followed by Nuying. Nonetheless she also knew that there were not too many more weeks left before the first snow fall.

The days were getting shorter. The leaves on the trees were starting to turn colors. Ming Su decided that she evaded Nuying enough and had to get more gold. She dressed up as Hon once again and headed out on her journey to the rabbit hole. But as she suspected, her disguise was not fooling Nuying. Her father had informed her that Ming Su sometimes dresses as a boy so men would not take a second look at her. However, Nuying could not figure out why Ming Su would be dressed as a boy today unless she was up to something. The question was. What? She gave plenty of space between herself and Ming Su. Nuying thought that she was being clever hiding behind trees and ducking behind bushes. Nonetheless, Ming Su still knew she was being pursued by the mercantile clerk's daughter. Ming Su acted as a boy when she passed others on the street and the wagon road. On a clear day Ming Su could make the three mile hike to the rabbit hole in about an hour or so. She also had her doubts that Nuying could keep up.

Periodically Ming Su would turn around quick to notice Nuying quite a distance behind her. The deviant side of Ming Su was fighting to express itself. She didn't stop at the boulder that hid the rabbit hole, she continued on by it and once she turned the bend she ran up the hill quickly and hid behind another boulder to keep watch. She was willing to let Nuying continue walking deeper and deeper into the forest on the wagon road to teach her a lesson. Suddenly Ming Su became frightened not only for Nuying but from the memories of her own experiences. In a not too far off distance into the forest she could hear horses and a wagon rattling as it traveled down the road towards her and eventually Nuying. She got a good look at the driver and realized that it was Jacob Murphy, her former abductor. She was overcome with fear once again but not for herself, but for Nuying. Ming Su was instantly struck with a horrible dilemma. She felt the urge to yell to Nuying to warn her but she would be jeopardizing her own safety. She watched as Nuying walked around the bend and waved at the oncoming wagon. Ming Su said to herself. "Stupid Nuying, stupid, stupid, stupid." The wagon came to a stop. Jacob Murphy acted very friendly and polite as he hopped down from the wagon and without hesitation swiped up his next payday. Ming Su knew that she had to do something but had no idea what. She watched Jacob put Nuying in the wooden box and closed the lid as he did to her. All Ming Su could visualize was Nuying in pain that was being inflicted on her as her father cried from the disappearance of his daughter. She knew that she couldn't bear the guilt if she didn't try to do something to save the nosey daughter of the mercantile clerk. She had a good idea that Jacob would have to turn the wagon around in the clearing down the wagon road to bring the prize back to the trading post so she devised a plan.

Ming Su stood behind a large pine tree when she heard the wagon and horses returning. She said to herself. "I was right." She prepared herself as she stood just a couple feet from the wagon road but higher than the driver. With a stone firmly in her right hand and another grasped in her left. She wanted to give Jacob what he deserved, mainly to kill him or leave him for dead but she didn't want his death on her conscience any more than she wanted Nuying's disappearance on her conscience.

She watched the horses pass by as she tightened the muscles in her right arm and with all her adrenaline rushing through her body. She threw the stone, striking Jacob on the side of the head. Jacob fell from the driver's seat resulting to him falling to the ground and rolling down the hill. She risked her life to climb up on the moving wagon so she could pull back the reins to stop the horses. She cried out. "Nuying, it's me Ming Su." She jumped into the bed to unlatch the locking mechanism on the wooden box and pulled the lid open. Ming Su yelled. "I am going to untie you but you have to stop moving around and you have to run with me as fast as you can back to town." It seemed like all her fingers were thumbs as she struggled to untie Nuying before grabbing her by the hand to help get her up. "Come on Nuying, we got to run." She looked down at Jacob lying at the bottom of the hill. "He is still knocked out." Ming Su and Nuying jumped down off the wagon. Ming Su instructed Nuying to help unhook the horses and spooked them to run off. The brake on the wagon was not engaged, leaving it to roll back off the road and down the hill. The girls watched it as it flipped and flipped before it slammed to a stop against a mighty pine tree.

The girls ran as fast as they could past the boulder and the rabbit hole as they headed back to civilization. Their speed and pace slowed as they got further from the scene of the incident. Ming Su was wise and she knew that a lot could happen before they got back to town. She stopped and looked behind them about a quarter of a mile to make sure that Jacob was not following. Ming Su slowly turned her head with her eyes still hidden behind the brim of the hat, looking at Nuying and shouting as she pushed her to the ground. "Stupid girl, stupid, stupid girl." before storming off. Nuying yelled to her. "Wait Ming Su, don't leave me, please." She struggled to her feet and ran after Ming Su. Ming Su continued to walk at a fast pace as she lectured Nuying. She held up three fingers. "Three times, do you know what three is? Three times the bad men tried to take me but I was lucky. You are too stupid to be so lucky. If I didn't know that you were following me then you would still be tied in that wooden box. You would have no supper tonight. That man and his brother and their friends would have done horrible things to you. Yep, that's right. There are more than just him, even his mother is a part of their schemes. They would have made sure that you would have never seen your mom or dad again. Why were you following me anyways?" Through Nuying's sobbing and tears she managed to reply. "I wanted to see where you walk to all the time." Ming Su stopped and turned to her. "Nowhere, I walk to nowhere. I just like to go for long walks but I have learned to be very careful. Do you think that I like wearing boy's clothes? No! But a Chinese girl cannot be out here in the forest all alone. A boy, they usually pass by. I walked all the way here from San Francisco and I have learned of the dangers that are lurking. And for now on my walks better be without you, because next time I just may look the other way."

"You wouldn't do that."

"Do you want to take that chance?" Ming Su turned and walked away leaving Nuying. Nuying yelled. "I just want to be your friend." Ming Su turned back around and charged towards Nuying, pointing her finger in Nuying's face. "I understand but I don't want anyone as my friend. My only friend is my Aunt Lanying, she is the only one that I can depend on and the only one that I can trust. So when we get back to town you go your way and I will go mine and just leave me alone for now on."

Ming Su didn't have any gold to show Lanying, all she had was a horrible story that she shared about a wasted day. Lanying asked the child. "Are you afraid of the forest at night when it is at its darkest?" Ming Su thought for a moment and replied. "No! Why should I be?" Suddenly her face lit up. "That gives me an idea Lanying. I can leave in the middle of the night when the full moon, half-moon and quarter moon is at its highest to give me just enough light to see the wagon road. I have been to the rabbit hole enough times to know how to not stray off course."

"That's right child. Travel without your lantern so nobody can see you coming or going. When you get there sleep until the sun comes up, gather your gold then make your way back here."

Two nights later, after the town had died down, Lanying dressed up as a man and accompanied Ming Su dressed as Hon to the end of town to see her on her way. However Ming Su was terrified of the forest at night when it is at its darkest. She walked slower and easier to be quiet as possible. For some reason she didn't understand why noise traveled louder and farther at night. After walking about a mile she could still hear the night life coming from town. The good thing was that the darkness made it much easier to see lanterns or torches coming from ahead or from behind, giving her plenty of time to duck behind a boulder or a tree.

After returning the next day Ming Su noticed a face from her past. She chuckled to herself. "No way, it can't be. It's impossible." He didn't look like a little boy anymore. He was taller and looked a lot stronger. She quickly approached him and looked up at him with a big smile and said. "The orphan from San Francisco." It took him a moment to realize. His eyes opened wide. "Ming Su? Or should I say Hon?"

"Thomas? Or should I say Tommy?"

"Other men call me Tom now." They threw their arms around each other and embraced. An American walking by backhanded Tom on the arm and snarled. "Men don't hug men in America." The lost friends stepped back and began to chuckle. Their language barrier had become less intense since Ming Su had been learning English ever since she arrived in America over two years prior.

Ming Su felt that she could trust Tom and invited him to her home. She asked him. "How did you get here?" Tom smiled and replied. "I am not an Indian, I wanted to find gold too since we left San Francisco. After I was not sick anymore I lived with Lost Doe, she was actually a great mother figure but I still wanted to prospect for gold and I remembered you always rambling on about Bannock Village."

"Ah! Bannock City, now it's Idaho City."

"Yeah I know, some of the people in Boise didn't know what I was talking about. And beside that I wanted to be with you. You are my family. I am sorry about Hai; He was like a big brother to me too."

"Yeah! I know, I miss him so much... Come on."

"Well anyways, Smoke Owl discovered an American family who got lost. He helped them get back onto the wagon road. Come to find out that they were going to Boise from California some place. Smoke Owl gave them some food and supplies in exchange to bring me to Boise with them. It wasn't a long journey, just a few days. The dad, Mr. McAllister met some prospectors who were on their way to Idaho City and they allowed me to ride in their wagon as long as I promised to help around the camp for the two nights and earn my way. So Here I am... But Ming Su, did you find your father?" Ming Su shook her head and stated. "Kind of." Tom looked at her with a confused look on his face and asked. "What does that mean?" Ming Su got frustrated. "Tommy, I really don't want to talk about it right now, come on, we are almost there."

Tommy snarled back. "You better respect me woman and call me Tom like I said."

"Okay Tom." Ming Su snapped back.

Tom was blown away as he stood in front of the house where Ming Su lived. It was white and it was enormous with many windows and black shutters "Is this where you live Ming Su?" He asked. She smiled and replied. "Yes, I live here with a matured Chinese woman name Lanying. She took me in and I call her Aunt Lanying. Tom's first words when he stepped into the house was. "Wow! It must have taken a lot of money to buy all this nice stuff. Where did your Aunt Lanying get all her money to have such a nice house and all this nice stuff? Did she discover her fortune in gold?" Ming Su had to think quick. "No, not really. I think her husband discovered his fortune in gold and then he left and I think he left her a bunch of gold." Ming Su hated the idea about lying at Lanying's expense but she was beginning to feel like Tom was asking too many questions concerning money and property. She was becoming very suspicious of Tom so she figured that she would inform Lanying of the situation and the tale that she shared with Tom to throw his potential thinking off course. Tom began walking around, running his hands over the carved wood on the furniture, adjusting paintings on the wall and looking very suspicious to the point where Ming Su felt uncomfortable for bringing him inside the house. Suddenly she suggested. "I am hungry, are you? Let's go get something to eat. I will buy. I get a weekly allowance and have some saved up."

"Allowance? What's allowance?"

"I get money from helping Aunt Lanying at the restaurant, she manages the Restaurant down the street and I help out a lot. In fact, she should be there now and I can introduce you."

"What kind of work do you do at the restaurant to get an allowance?" Ming Su shrugged her shoulders. "I wash dishes, clean tables after people are done so they are clean for the next customers, I feed the animals and take out the garbage."

"How much do you get for allowance every week?"

"I don't know. It doesn't really matter. You sure do ask a lot of questions though."

"Well I was thinking maybe she would give me something to do so I can earn an allowance until I find my gold." The two friends began walking down the busy street, Ming Su asked. "Are you going to be a gold prospector Tom?"

"Absolutely and I am going to be a boss too. While everyone is working their tails off for me, I will be counting my money."

"Tom, I don't understand. This doesn't seem like the Tommy that I knew."

"I'm not. I am older, wiser and determined to get rich and there is absolutely nothing that is going to stop me."

"Where did you learn this talk?"

"From the prospectors that I came in to town with or course. Mr. White really seemed to know what he was talking about at the campfire both nights after dinner. He told me not to take any horse manure from anybody and to take what I needed to get by until I made it big." Ming Su didn't seem to like or appreciate what she was hearing from her old friend that she considered a little brother. But to change the subject she asked. "Where is Gordy?" Tom shook his head. "I really don't know Ming Su. The second day after leaving Smoke Owl he got away from me and never caught up. Mr. McAllister wasn't going to take the time to go looking for him. I figure that maybe a cougar or a bear got him. I am sorry. Ming Su." Ming Su got angry. "You were supposed to take care of him. He was your dog but he was my dog too." Tom lashed back. "Don't be mad at me, you are the one who didn't take him with you." She snarled. "Because he had a bullet wound, he couldn't travel at the time."

Ming Su's excitement wasn't so much blooming when she introduced Tom to Lanying. In fact Lanying picked up on Ming Su's irregular attitude. She asked. "Ming Su, will you come with me for a moment?" Suddenly Tom yelled. "Come on woman I am hungry, are you running this place or not?" Lanying and Ming Su looked at each other with great concern.

"Lanying, it was a mistake to let him come with Hai and me from San Francisco. He is only ten years old and he is so disrespectful to me and now to you too. I don't know what to do. We cannot let him stay at the house with us. He saw everything in the living room and asked where you got your money. I had to be dishonest, I told him that your husband left and left you a bunch of gold."

"I agree with you Su. I just met him and I don't like or trust him. Let's let him fill his belly. Meanwhile I will go talk to Longwei. Maybe he can find Tommy or Tom, whatever his name is a tent to stay in with some type of chores to do so he can learn to earn his keep. But whatever you do, don't bring him back to our home." Ming Su shook her head, her eyes opened wide. "I won't, I promise."

Once Tom was filled up with house stew, chocolate cake and a slice of cherry pie Ming Su escorted him to the Chinese Mercantile to see Longwei. Tom asked. "What are we doing here?" Ming Su was hesitant to say but she knew that she had to. "Mr. Longwei will get you a cot in one of the tents so you have shelter, he will find chores for you to do too so you can earn your keep and some allowance." Tom's expression was nothing more than disappointed. "I thought that I was going to stay with you in the big house with all that nice stuff. We are supposed to be family. I am not staying on some dusty cot in some musty tent. I'm staying at your house with you and your aunt."

"I'm sorry Tom but you cannot. We haven't seen each other in over two years. I barely knew anything about you when you got tick fever. The way that you act now, I feel like I know nothing about you. Or even want anything to do with you."

"What is that supposed to mean?" Ming Su shook her head without losing eye contact with Tom. "I don't trust you anymore Tom and to be completely honest with you. I want you to leave me alone." Tommy snarled. "Fine, I'll find my gold without you. I don't need some stupid slant eyed immigrant in my life or in my country for that matter. Why don't you just do every American a favor and go back to China." Tom kicked the dirt with the heel of his boot before storming off. Ming Su watched in sadness as her traveling companion disappeared into the crowd. She whispered. "I never thought that I would ever regret convincing Hai to bring you with us." She turned around and headed back to the restaurant. As she stepped up onto the porch to enter the dining room she made eye contact with an elder Chinese man sitting on the thick planks with his back resting in the corner between the wood slatted wall and the railing. The man's clothes were old and grungy. He had not had a shave in months judging by his scruffy beard. He looked overly thin and undernourished. His head tilted to the side as he tried to make eye contact through his aging blurred eyes. Ming Su made no attempt to show her recognition of the man. However, her stare never changed as she opened the door and entered the restaurant.

Lanying could tell that Ming Su was grief stricken when she entered the kitchen. Lanying set her hand on Ming Su's shoulder and stated. "I am sorry about Tommy." Ming Su looked up at Lanying and shook her head. "It's not about Tommy or Tom."

"What is it about then child?"

"Will you make sure that the old Chinese man with the long beard on the patio gets something good and nourishing to eat at least twice a day or as long as he is around?"

"Oh my goodness child. Are you really grief stricken over a homeless man?"

"Lanying, I just feel for him. Perhaps it is that I discovered what he came to America for." She whispered. "Gold, and he probably lost his family and everything."

"You have no reason to feel responsible for him for any reason. You need to know who you are. You need to start thinking about you and your future. One day you will be old enough to take care of yourself and I will move on, probably marrying Longwei or something. But start thinking about you and your future a little more than spending money on other people to help them out, and help yourself out."

"He is a man like my father with old Chinese tradition. He just needs a little help."

"I don't understand your thinking Ming Su?"

"What do you think? He probably left his son and his daughter to die in some old one room shack. I know that I owe nothing to him. He does have to eat though. Goodness Lanying. More food is wasted than what twenty of that man could consume every day."

"Su, your safety is my concern. I have always protected you and I always will, even if it's your feelings. I shall have someone bring the old Chinese man a bowl of stew with a couple bread rolls and tea." Ming Su bowed her head and closed her eye before walking off.

The old man's face lit up when a Chinese member of the kitchen staff set a bowl of stew, two bread rolls and a mug of tea in front of him. "When you are finished just leave the dishes here. Come back right here tomorrow for lunch and for supper." The man looked at the young Chinese man with concern. The young Chinese man replied. "It is Lanying's request that you are given two meals a day. And for dinner a sweet dessert will accompany your dinner." The old man watched the young man walk away in disbelief that someone was actually being nice to him or at the very worse to his pride, feeling sorry for him. Ming Su watched from the window as the old man devoured his stew and bread roll in a matter of minutes before sipping his tea and setting the tea cup into the clay bowl on the patio beside him. She thought about what it was like when her mother was still alive and to be a part of a loving family who knew only poverty and was accepting of it for she felt rich with love from her mother, father and her brother Hai. She quickly wiped the tear from her cheek when she heard Lanying's voice behind her requesting her help.

19

Day after day Ming Su's heart ached to see how the man had to live. She knew that the old man must have spent every cent that he had to travel from China to Idaho City. She wondered if he met any friends along the way like she met Flying Star, Smoke Owl, Lost Doe and eventually Lanying. It was certain though that he no longer had anybody to share a cup of tea with, to sit around on a log and talk about life in general. As much as she wanted to make herself known to the old man she knew that she had to sacrifice to keep what was hers.

Meanwhile it took Tom a couple weeks to accept reality and overcome his anger and disappointment towards Ming Su. He understood that Ming Su was right and the way that he departed was not very appropriate especially to a girl who begged her brother to take him along with them on their journey to seek out gold. He seemed to feel like an apology was in order from him and approached the front door of the house and knocked on it in hopes that Ming Su would answer but only discovered that the door never opened. Tom had no idea what Ming Su's daily routine was or the schedule that Lanying worked at the restaurant so he decided to head to Kolinski's. As he was about to leave he heard a noise coming from inside the house, it seemed like a good idea to him to walk over to the window to see if he could see anything. His eyes opened wide as he was quickly taken by surprise to see Ming Su on the other side of the pane of glass, raising his hand to knock on the glass he witnessing Ming Su moving her bed, encouraging him to become curious and lowering his hand and to move aside to where he could barely peek through the window. Looking around on the interior walls he noticed paintings of the Chinese culture. A shelf on the wall with little Chinese statues and figures perhaps purchased from the Chinese Mercantile. He watched as Ming Su rolled up the corner of the rug and wrapped her fingers around a handle to pull a little hidden door up from the floor. His curiosity really overtook him as his eyes were glued to the secret compartment in the floor. Ming Su removed a small linen sack from the secret compartment. She reached her hand in to retrieve a stack of currency. Tom was left in disbelief; he ducked down to sit in the ground while leaning against the house. "That lying slant eye brat. I can't believe it, she has money." He whispered to himself. "I bet her father found his gold and he is back out prospecting. I can't believe she lied to me."

Tom sat and pondered on the situation and how he was going to confront Ming Su about her deception before he made his way to his feet. Quickly he snuck over, across the road. There he sat on a stack of burlap sacks containing grain. The ten year old boy was full of energy like any other, sitting still and waiting was harder for him then he could ever imagine, especially since his adrenaline was rushing through his veins with anticipation. Nonetheless he began to get bored and anxious very quickly as the sun traveled slowly across the blue sky. With a bird's eye view of the house, Tom paid extra attention to the dark red door that entered the house. Without warning the door finally opened. It was Ming Su stepping through to leave. Tom slid down off the stack of burlap sacks and hid behind them so not to be noticed by his Chinese friend. He decided to follow Ming Su for a couple moments and got lost in the passing crowd too before heading back to the house

Tom didn't want to take any chances by just barging through the front door so he took the time to knock on the door once again to make sure that nobody else was there and to not make anyone who was watching very suspicious. After waiting for about a minute he looked around before pushing down on the thumb lever with his hand to release the latch, allowing him to push the door open. The door swung inward towards the right with a subtle creak. He left the door open behind him as he made his way into the room where he watched

Ming Su earlier. The bed was easier to move than he thought it would be, the rug folded over itself with ease and the 12" x 12" door in the floor opened without any resistance. Tommy reached in to grab the linen sack before placing it on the floor to open it. A smile grew across his face as he pulled out a stack of $5 bills with $200 stamped on the band wrapped around the bills. He whispered. "I can buy a whole ranch with this."

The sound of the front door slamming shut caught the undivided attention of the little thief. He jumped to his feet and grabbed a porcelain figuring from off the shelf and threw it through the window. But before he had a chance to dive through the opening in the glass Lanying entered the room and fired a shot from the pistol in her hand into the pine wood floor next to him. She yelled. "Tom, I had my feeling about you but I had no idea that you would be as stupid as to come into mine and Ming Su's home and try and steal from us." Tom pulled his fathers' knife from his pocket and quickly opened it before darting toward the door. Lanying fired another shot into the floor ahead of him. "Don't you dare to try to move, I have no compassion about not taking your life right now." Tom tossed the knife towards Lanying's feet and sat down on the floor with his back against the wall. Lanying hollered. "Ming Su." Tom was shocked to see the one person that he had the nerve to call family enter the room. Ming Su slapped Tom across the face and asked. "Are you trying to steal from me? I knew not to trust you. I guess Mr. McAllister or Mr. White were not the best influences to you that you thought they were." Tom still had the bundle of bills in his grasp. He threw it at Ming Su. "This has nothing to do with Mr. McAllister or Mr. White."

"Then why did you try stealing from me? If you needed some money, you could have asked." Tom chuckled. "Yeah! How much would you have given me, a dollar, maybe two? That was $200. I was going to buy me a ranch."

"You were going to buy a ranch with stolen money? What would you have told your future wife, your children, your grandchildren, that you worked your hands to the bones like a real man? Or would you have been dishonest with them as you are now and cowardly lied to them too?"

"Tell me Ming Su. How did you get all this money, from your father? My father is dead, my mother is dead. I had nobody, not even the girl that was supposed to think of me as a brother."

"Tom you have no idea what you are talking about. You destroyed our relationship"

"I know enough, and you can think what you want. But either way you still lied to me."

"You stupid boy, you are so ignorant, you know nothing, because if you did then you would know that my father is the poorest man in this town. He doesn't even know that it is me who makes sure that he eats twice a day while he wastes his life away lost in his regrets and sorrows. I said that I would find my fortune in gold and I did. I said that I would find my father and I did, but that is none of your concern now."

"Then some of that money should be mine. We left San Francisco together to find gold together."

"I owe you nothing. I came to America to find my father and to find gold with my brother Hai. Hai is dead and I owe you nothing. And if I wanted to I could even blame you for Hai's death considering that it was because of you and your tick fever that the Indian people took us in to help you, not me or Hai, but to help you. To basically save your life and this is how you repay me and Smoke Owl, and Flying Star and not to mention Lost Doe who you said was a great mother figure? But don't worry I am way better than one who would point fingers."

"What?"

"You were the reason why we were with the Indians. You got tick fever. If you never got sick then we would have kept going and maybe Hai would still be alive right now." Lanying stepped over to Ming Su and put her arm around her as she whispered. "Okay, okay Ming Su. That is enough. I need you to fetch the sheriff and his deputy." Ming Su continued taking deep breaths before responding. "Yes ma-am... Shoot him if he tries to get up." She stared at Tom as she left the room.

Apparently the gun shots were heard outside in the street and immediately reported to the sheriff. The sheriff and his deputy were running up the walkway when Ming Su opened the door. She pointed to the broken window and said. "In the bedroom to the right."

Lanying explained to the sheriff and the deputy what had happened. The deputy wrapped rope around the youngster's wrists. The sheriff pointed at Tom. Tom could see the anger in the sheriff's face when he stated. "Kid, there is enough dishonesty in this town, murder, rape, theft, abduction, deceit and now a ten year old boy trying to become a fugitive of the law. I will not stand for it in my town." Tom couldn't hold back from crying as he was being lectured by the lawman. The sheriff ordered. "Get him out of here deputy." Lanying asked. "What will come of Tom?" The sheriff sighed. "Unfortunately Tom is way too young to be kept in jail for any lengthy amount of time. You say that he has no parents so we can't release him to them but he did break the window and will need to pay restitution. However he did not get away with any money. It's just a bunch of manure but he will more than likely be transported to Boise to an orphanage and hopefully adopted to a family to work the farm but I wouldn't doubt if he came back to seek retribution one day but for now all I can say is that I am sorry that this had to happen. Ming Su I hope that you have not been too frightened over all this."

"I will be fine sheriff. We will take care of the broken window because I never want to see or hear from Tom again." The sheriff nodded his head and said. "I will need you both come by the jailhouse as soon as possible to give a full statement." He turned and walked away.

Lanying entered Ming Su's room to find her sitting on her bed sobbing. She sat beside the child and took her into her arms. After a moment Ming Su pulled away. "He seemed like such a good boy when we left San Francisco."

"Ming Su, he was feral, he was a con artist. He fooled both you and Hai. He didn't have anybody, the local merchants gave him food to eat and looked after him to a point but he grew up quick with the way that he had to live. They were probably excited to see him leave San Francisco. You and Hai were just the suckers who took the bait."

"Money is such a devil. I hate how the world thrives for it, steals for it, and even kills for it. China was so poor and I thought that I would have a better life here but I was wrong, all because now I have more money than I can do with."

"You sound like having money is a bad thing."

"Lanying, for me it is. My father has absolutely nothing, my brother is dead and now my friend tried to rob me. I just don't know what to think anymore."

The next afternoon Lanying and Ming Su walked to the jailhouse to give the sheriff an official statement. When they finished Ming Su asked to speak to Tom as he awaited his transport to Boise.

Ming Su stood back about four feet from the one inch steel vertical bars. She stared at Tom shaking her head. "Tommy why?" She pouted. Tom replied. "It's Tom and you lied to me Ming Su." she was stunned. "When did I lie to you?"

"You told me that you get allowance."

"I do, I just never said how much." Tom forced his face up between two of the bars and snarled. "I will be back and when I do, your father won't be the poorest person in this town anymore."

"No! he won't, but you still will." Tom chuckled as he pulled away from the bars and moved to the back of the cell.

Ming Su stepped out into the chilly fall air. She looked up but all she could see was the brightness of the sun glowing white behind the gray blanket that hovered above. She ran on, leaving Lanying to walk by herself.

Lanying walked through the door moments after Ming Su. She sat in the wooden rocker across from Ming Su who was rocking forward and back on the sofa. Ming Su stared at the wood floor and whispered. "I will leave in the morning before dawn to go to the rabbit hole, and return tomorrow, late in the day." Lanying asked. "Tom had gotten you very upset, hasn't he? But Ming Su, you have so much money hidden in this house that you don't know what to do with it, not to mention what is at the bank in Boise. If Tom would have gotten away with that stack of money, you probably wouldn't have even noticed it." Ming Su snapped. "It is good thing that he didn't get away with it because he would keep coming back again and again and again and all we know he may have even killed the two of us. I can't believe how stupid Hai and I were. We thought because Tommy was such a young boy that he could be trusted but he was feral as you said and the people in San Francisco took the opportunity to get rid of him at our expense. He should have just died of the tick fever." Lanying snapped back. "Ming Su, mind yourself. He is still a human being. You and I don't want him here anymore or less than the American people want you and I here. But he still is a human being, just as we are." Ming Su let out a sigh through her nose and looked at Lanying. "Tomorrow will be my last journey to the rabbit hole. The cold is coming quick and snow will be here soon. I am so tired of the rabbit hole Lanying. It has made me greedy and selfish. I can never seem to get enough. Enough is never enough. Is it my pride? Is it the challenge and the risk every time that I go? Do I go to toy around with the Murphy's? You are right, I don't need the money but I don't want anyone else to have it either." Lanying shook her head. "Someday you have to let go Ming Su. Perhaps one day you do find your father. It really wouldn't be a bad thing if you lead him to the rabbit hole." Ming Su got frustrated as she quickly thought to herself. "I can't believe that this woman hasn't figured it out about my father yet." Then she stated. "No! He would not be as careful as I. He would make a mistake and before we knew it, everybody would be at the rabbit hole digging until there was nothing left. But I do need to start thinking of something that I could do for my father. I just don't know what yet."

"You are a smart young woman Ming Su. I know that you will figure out something for your father."

Hon left out the dark red door before the Eastern sky showed any evidence of day. The muddy streets were solid ice, making walking a little difficult stepping onto the wagon wheel tracks, horse and human boot print that had frozen over. The horse drinking troths developed a sheet of ice, preventing live stock from quenching their thirst. The elements didn't stop other prospectors and travelers from filling the early morning streets of Idaho City. Occasionally Hon would be shoved or bumped by the inconsiderate and impolite people. Mean words would be expressed. "Get out of the way kid. Go home to your momma." And other demeaning comments towards the out of place young boy who should still be in his warm bed.

By the time Hon reached the wagon road the Eastern sky was glowing. The black of the night was turning the pine trees to green and brown. Before long the squirrels and chipmunks were on their morning hunt for anything that they could scavenge and bring back to their homes.

Ming Su Shivered as her body tried to warm up while she pushed on through the Idaho mountains. The three and a half mile walked seemed to last much longer stepping out of the way of wagons traveling from both directions. As usual, she kept her head hidden under the brim of her hat to keep from being recognized as a girl. Traveling light was a priority for Ming Su. With the cold weather setting in she didn't have to depend on too much water to be carried to keep her hydrated. Two or three pieces of jerky wrapped in a linen cloth, tucked in the inside pocket of her coat. As always Hai's knife secured to her belt. People passing by on foot, horseback and wagons didn't seem to have any time to want to talk to a Chinese boy. Things may have been different if they knew that she was actually a girl.

The day was brightening up despite the cold all around her that was causing her breath to remain constant little white puffs of steam. Hon reached the boulder without a hitch and climbed the hill at the point where she usually does to not leave any foot prints. The surface of the boulder was colder than she ever knew it to be.

She crawled into the rabbit hole which was originally about two and a half feet wide and about twenty feet deep beneath the hill. Ming Su thought about all the trips that she made, using a shovel, little pick ax and a metal bucket. Leaving the rabbit hole about twice the width and another ten feet or so deeper. She kept and extra over coat in a burlap bag to change into leaving her traveling clothes without any soil, dirt or gold dust attached to her clothing that would most definitely raise suspicions and questions and ultimately attract danger to herself.

With Ming Su's long day at the rabbit hole she took chance and filled her tin canteen with gold nuggets as small as a mustard seed and as big as a pecan that she managed to pick up with her little fingers and filled another five pound sack with soil. As usual she dropped the sack of soil off at the stone foundation on the way home. When she got home she immediately went into the kitchen where Lanying was enjoying a slice of apple pie and Chinese tea at the table. Ming Su laid the heavy canteen onto the table. Lanying was surprised when she picked it up and jiggled it. "Wow Ming Su, feels like you got about three times as much this time."

"That is why it took so long and I got back so late."

"Ming Su, I don't like you going out there by yourself. I was worried about you again. I am not liking the worrying about you when you go to the rabbit hole. I really hope that one day the gold that you found and the money that you have will be enough."

"Maybe a couple times in the Spring and then that will be enough I think."

"I hope so child, I hope so."

20

To Ming Su this was the coldest winter in Idaho City, it was by no doubt the worse than she could ever imagine, she knew snow in China but nothing like the mountains of Idaho. Sometimes the snow would be so deep that it towered over the average American man. The population obviously dropped since mining for gold in the frozen mountain soil was pretty much impossible. Some prospectors moved on, some lived in their covered wagons and tents while others returned home or took refuge from the snow and cold elements in Boise. Nonetheless the prospectors who prospered well, built cabins and homes to prepare for the winters and eventually sold them once they moved on

The Spring of 1868 Ming Su developed little interest in returning to the rabbit hole. She felt that she was above wearing boy's clothes and wanted to be recognized as a proper Chinese young lady. Lanying hired a stagecoach to carry the two of them on another nine hour trip to deposit more money into the First National Bank of Idaho, and to go shopping for new attire to properly fit a young lady. Lanying also hired the protection of two gunmen by the recommendation of the sheriff to escort the stagecoach to the First National Bank of Idaho in Boise. Upon the arrival at the First National Bank of Idaho the armed escort went their own way to register Ming Su and Lanying into an upscale hotel while being replaced with two fresh gunmen. They too were tall, well dressed and carried pistols on their hips while one of them carried a rifle as well, to escort the two ladies around down town Boise while they took to shopping.

The shopping proved to be exhausting for the two women. The late April sun was hotter than normal for Lanying and Ming Su within the City of Trees. Their cotton dresses were soaked by their perspiration even though their large brim hats kept the hot sun from burning the light skin on their faces.

Ming Su and Lanying spent three nights in Boise as they enjoyed shopping, dining out and a play. The morning of their departure Ming Su and Lanying were approached by the stagecoach driver. He asked them. "Would you be willing to allow that young Chinese man to accompany you inside the stage for the ride back to Idaho City?" The ladies turned to look at the young Chinese man, Ming Su looked at Lanying with a big smile. Lanying closed her eyes and softy nodded while stating. "Yes, that will be fine." Lanying could see that Ming Su had an instant interest in the well-dressed young Chinese man and also knew that Ming Su was no longer a little girl. The young Chinese man presented himself in a proper manner as Choy Lin from Seattle. He had an American accent but was fluent in Chinese and in English. He explained that his father had discovered gold in Washington not long after he was born in 1852. A descendant of a Chinese immigrant born in America.

The young man sat across from Ming Su as the stagecoach made its ten hour uphill journey back to Idaho City, accompanied by the first two armed escorts.

Choy was seeking his fortune in gold since his father refused to spoil him beyond the age of sixteen. Choy had no choice but to travel with the money that his father gave him to seek out his own promising future. Although he did decide to follow in his father's footsteps as a gold prospector he felt that he needed to break free of the family name and reputation in Washington as well.

Lanying sat in silence as she listened to the two young adults carry on with each other. Ming Su explained to Choy that her family owned one of the restaurants and she worked there periodically. Not necessarily a lie since Lanying was referred to as Aunt Lanying and she was considered family.

Lanying explained to Choy that the high point of the Idaho gold rush was now behind them and a lot of gold had already been discovered and mined. Ming Su interjected. "But there is more than likely a lot more gold to be discovered." Lanying smiled and gave a quick nod.

The stagecoach pulled up to the hotel in Idaho City a little after 6pm. Choy's journey had finally come to an end. He stepped out from the stagecoach and looked around with a satisfying grin on his face. The driver handed down Choy's suitcase to him. Choy set it down on the ground and demonstrated the gentlemen that he was raised to be by opening the door and asked Lanying. "Would you be so kind and give me the name of the restaurant and point in which direction that I would find it? I would like to stop by and see your niece Ming Su." Lanying was humbly impressed at the young man's manners and surrendered the needed information to him. Ming Su stared at the young Chinese traveler with a love stricken grin.

The driver wanted to get the horses to the stable to eat and rest up before returning to Boise in the morning but first he had to navigate through about twenty minutes of busy city streets, disrespectful and inconsiderate residence, wagons and prospector's. Once they arrived the driver carried the ladies luggage and packages into the house as the armed guards stood watch. The driver explained to Lanying that he didn't want to drop them off first to keep the young Chinese man from knowing where they lived. Lanying replied. "You did well Robert and we appreciate your concern and you always." Robert smiled as he set the last package inside the dark red door. "It's always a pleasure Lanying and your safety is always my first priority." He tilted his hat and walked away.

Ming Su removed all the books from the bottom shelf of a bookcase built into the wall to allow her to remove the bottom shelf. She placed the remaining money that was not spent in Boise into the secret compartment under the bottom shelf then replaced the shelf and the books.

Being gone four days there was a lot to get caught up on at the restaurant as well as other things that needed to get done. Ming Su and Lanying were up before dawn to head to the restaurant. Ming Su stepped up on to the patio. She noticed her father sitting in the corner between the wall and the railing sleeping. Ming Su immediately instructed one of the cooks to prepare eggs, bacon, toast and a cup of tea. She sat at one of the outside tables looking at the man with the side of her head resting in the palm of her hand and her elbow sitting on the table as she waited for the plate to be brought out to her. Once it arrived with the cup of tea, she waited for the cook to walk away before getting up and carrying the plate and cup over to her father and set them down on the table closest to him. She smiled and softly tapped him on the shoulder while whispering." Mister, Mister, please wake up, I have some breakfast for you. He slowly began to move around and opened his eyes. Suddenly his eyes opened wide as he took a deep breath. "Sing? Is it really you?" Ming Su stepped back and looked down at the wood deck. "I am sorry but my name is not Sing. Come up here and sit at the table and eat your breakfast." Ming Su sat across from the man. "My friends sometimes call me Su. My Aunt Lanying manages and runs this restaurant." Ming Su quickly realized that her father's sight was not very good by the way he kept straining to focus on her. He picked up a wedge of toast and dunked it into his tea. "My name is Fong Yeo. I apologize for calling you Sing. She was my wife of thirty six years. We struggled to have children at a young age but were not fortunate until I was almost 40 years old. She gave me a wonderful son and then six years later a beautiful daughter. Sing passed on a couple years back. I left her grave and our children in China to come to America to become a failure. I will never see either one of them again." He began to sob. Ming Su struggled to act proper and not let him see the tears in her eyes as she fought her emotions.

Ming Su returned to the kitchen after a bit with the plate in one hand and the cup in the other. Lanying stated. I don't understand why you keep feeding that man. He is just a man from china who has had the worse luck that anyone ever could. You don't know him. What is it guilt, because of Tommy or even Hai? He is just an added expense that we really don't need and now he is like a stray animal that will not go away. I think that we need to stop feeding him and have the sheriff run the old man off." Ming Su shook her head as she stared at a fork lying on the wood floor and began to sob. Lanying stepped to Ming Su and wrapped her arms around her. "I didn't mean to hurt your feelings child, I am so sorry. You have been so sensitive lately." Ming Su stepped back and looked at Lanying with an unrecognizable look on her face. "You really hadn't heard a word that I said to Tommy did you? The old man's name is Fong Yeo." Lanying's face went blank. "You mean your father Fong Yeo? Yes I did hear you, but for some reason it didn't make sense to me at the time. I just didn't put it together. I am sorry Su." Ming Su just stared at the woman. "We cannot tell him who I am, nobody can know."

"But he is your father."

"He is the foolish man who abandoned his children. He has no idea who I am. The thought of his daughter, Ming Su being here in Idaho City, Idaho, America probably never crossed his mind. It may seem to you that I am torturing him but I am actually nurturing him. Hai is dead because he left us, his suffering is all his own."

"Ming Su I never knew you to be so cold and without compassion, especially towards your own father... Do you think that you will ever tell him the truth?"

"Truth?... Believe me, all I feel is guilt when I don't think that I should. There was no truth when he believed in what he thought was waiting here in America for him. I think that it would only destroy him again if he knew who I was and that I am living his dream."

"I have an idea Su. I will speak to Longwei and see if he can set up a cot in a tent for Fong Yeo to sleep on and perhaps Longwei can find him some kind of work to make a little money." Ming Su chuckled. "That will make me feel a little less guilty."

The morning crowd began to grow as it usually did around 7 am and among them was Choy. It took less than a moment for choy and Ming Su's eyes to collide. Lanying took notice and chuckled. "Go ahead child, just be safe."

Ming Su spent the morning showing Choy around Idaho City. However her father weighed heavy on her mind. They walked by the horse stable to see the different colors of the horses. Ming Su asked Choy. "Do you know the difference between a paint horse and a Pinto?"

"I have no idea?"

"They are both characterized by their white spots but a Paint Horse is a breed and the Pinto is any breed of horse with spots." Choy chuckled. "Where did you learn that?"

"I overheard two men talking about horses one day and for some reason I always remembered that. Which it does remind me of some old friends that I need to go visit soon."

"Old friends?"

"Native Indian friends. Flying Star, Lost Doe and Smoke Owl."

"Smoke Owl. That is a weird name."

"Yeah, but he is an amazing Indian Warrior."

Ming Su brought Choy by to meet the sheriff and explained the situation with Tommy from San Francisco to the day he came down with tick fever and the day that he tried to rob her and Lanying. She also felt that it was appropriate to inform him of the romance between Flying Star and Hai and the wonderful brother that Hai was.

That evening Ming Su sat at the dining table across from Lanying, a thought crossed her mind. "Lanying I was thinking. I was wondering if there was a way that Fong Yeo could stumble across some gold. Wouldn't that make everything better for him? He finally finds his fortune in gold, it makes him feel like a man again by accomplishing such a great thing."

"What exactly are you saying Ming Su?"

"I am just thinking about what I could do for him. I mean, I have enough money that I could buy Idaho City if I wanted to, but I have no desire to which I think is a good thing too. But if father discovered some gold then just maybe he can become the father that I knew in China."

"I'm sorry Ming Su but I am thinking it now too. One of his children has died. There is nothing that would make him that same father again, especially knowing that his son died on a quest looking for him." Ming Su sighed and stated in a low calm voice. "Lanying, I am just so tired of living lies. My father should be in my life. I love him, I miss him and I am afraid that I am going to lose him again... I also keep dreaming about Choy and perhaps he and I will marry someday but I am terrified to tell him about my personal fortune. I know it's deceptive but can I really tell him about the rabbit hole or just keep leading him to believe that my fortunes comes from the restaurant? And then I would have to lie about how I got the restaurant. Another lie and another lie. I don't want to lie anymore Lanying. I lied so much just dressing as Hon. I know it was for my own good and protection but I have had enough with being dishonest. I want to be a well-respected woman like you."

"Child please don't put me on a pedestal. You know that I have dealt with a lot too with my husband abandoning me. I am ashamed to say that I sold myself twice to smelly inconsiderate American men to have money to eat until Mr. Kolinski took me in."

"I had no idea Lanying and am sorry, but you are still a great mother to me. I look up to you very much. But understand that I hate seeing my father living the way he does while his daughter lives in a nice house." Lanying shook her head. "Ming Su I am sure that I understand." Suddenly Ming Su got excited. "How about we set up a situation where my father, Fong Yeo discovers or finds a hefty sack of gold that somebody else apparently lost?"

"Yeah but we have to be very clever about it. I mean we cannot have somebody drop a sack of gold in front of him, Fong Yeo may just pick it up and give it back to the person. He needs to actually find it sitting somewhere that he wouldn't have any idea where it came from and he is forced to keep it but also someplace where nobody else will see it being dropped."

"Does anything come to mind?"

"Actually, yes! Ming Su. Longwei told me that he would have Fong Yeo work in the stables shoveling up the horse manure. We will have to spy on Fong Yeo and learn his schedule and routine."

"Then what?"

"Just trust me child, but we are going to need as much gold as you want to give him."

"Okay, I will go to the rabbit hole one more time for my father's sake. Whatever gold that I get will be his. But after that I don't want to go back. I want to be a woman. I think about marriage and having children of my own and teaching my daughter how to play the violin like Susan taught me, pass Hai's knife on to my son then watch the years roll by as I become a grandma. Oh the stories I am sure that I will be able to tell." Lanying chuckled. "You have so many already child. I am impressed by you every day but don't rush marriage. I know that you have a special interest in Choy but give it the time that it needs. If he wants you and loves you then he will wait. And since we are talking about it I should share something with you." Ming Su looked concerned. "What is it?"

"About a year ago Longwei asked me for my hand in marriage." Ming Su showed excitement. "Oh really? What did you say?" Lanying chuckled. "I said yes! Of course. But I also told him that it must wait until you are eighteen."

"But why? At sixteen I can get married."

"Ming Su the house is yours, as well as the restaurants but they cannot be rightfully put in your name until you are eighteen. Besides Longwei loves me, I am only twenty nine. there is plenty of time for me to please my husband after we are married and for me to have children too. Longwei is willing to wait until you are eighteen, and not a day less."

"Okay Lanying. When I am eighteen then you and I will both marry."

The next morning dawn had come and gone by the time Ming Su came in view of the boulder. She began to wonder if it was the same boulder or if by chance she strayed off course and was looking at a similar one. She turned to her left and climbed up on the hill but quickly concluded that the rabbit hole was no longer there. She thought if it could have been discovered by somebody else. As she stepped up to the rabbit hole she noticed that the pine tree had uprooted and fell on top of the rabbit hole, collapsing it. At that point she determined that it would be her very last time that she journeyed there.

Lanying was standing outside the Chinese Mercantile conversing with Longwei when Ming Su approached in a frantic state. Lanying's first thought was. Did the Murphy's or other bad men try abducting Ming Su again, but Ming Su cried. "It's gone, it's all gone." Lanying gave Longwei a certain look that signaled him to leave the two women alone to discuss their business. "Lanying the gold is all gone."

"What do you mean gone? I do not understand what you mean. What happened?"

"All I can assume is that all these trips and digging in the rabbit hole made the top and the sides very weak and the heavy snow put extra weight on the big pine tree and it up-rooted before falling on top of the rabbit hole and collapsing it. The top part of the tree must have broken on the boulder and rolled down the hill on the other side of the wagon road. I dug up about three or four pounds of gold but it was tough with all the roots and tree branches of the pine tree."

"Three or four pounds of gold should be plenty for Fong Yeo."

"Yes I know. I just never want to go back there again"

"It could be dug back up couldn't it Su?"

"I am just not interested anymore Lanying. I could have been in the hole when the tree fell."

About a week or so passed by. At about dawn was when Lanying took a sack of almost four pounds of gold and got it all muddy before planting it next to a small pile of horse manure. Lanying and Ming Su kept watch from behind a half wall. Fong Yeo stood over it, looking down at it as to try and figure out what it was before he bent down and picked the muddy white sack up off the ground. He held it high as he looked at it spin around and twist, hanging in his grasp, he shook it a couple times encouraging a smile on his face. After leaning his shovel against the wood post he then opened the sack. Instantly his eyes lit up. He took a step back and looked all around him to make sure that he was alone then began to laugh while reaching for the leather pouch that he kept hanging under his left shoulder and stuffed the sack of gold into it. Ming Su followed her father around while Lanying went to work at the restaurant. Approximately midmorning Fong Yeo made his way to the gold exchange. Ming Su hid outside to follow where he went next. To her surprise it was to Kolinski's Restaurant. Ming Su had to hustle around the back so she could be seen by Fong Yeo coming from the back as if she was working. Ming Su greeted Fong Yeo. Fong Yeo handed his estranged daughter two one dollar bills. Ming Su shook her head. "No! I do not want your money. It was a pleasure providing you with meals." The excitement scattered from Fong Yeo's face as he stepped back and looked around as if he was embarrassed. He noticed a table with a Chinese family who were drinking tea and eating dry toast and smiled as he handed the money to Ming Su and stated. "I will pay for their meal, give them a good breakfast and some dry goods to take with them and I would be very grateful." Ming Su smiled as she fought to hold back her tears of joy as she watched him exit the front door. She followed Fong Yeo once again but her joy quickly turned to disappointment when she watched her father walk into one of the toughest saloons in Idaho City.

Ming Su rushed up to the window and looked in. She noticed Fong Yeo approaching three American men sitting around a square table that was obviously made of pine wood, probably from the local wood shop. The three men dressed alike but the one across from the empty chair was no doubt the leader or the boss. Fong Yeo stood behind the empty chair as he appeared to carry on a conversation with the man. With all the other people in the saloon engaged in conversation and laughter, Ming Su had no idea what was being said between Fong Yeo and the man. Fong Yeo reached into his pocket and pulled out what looked to be three or four bills of U.S. Currency before fanning them out and handing them to the apparent leader. The smile on Fong Yeo's face convinced Ming Su that he was paying off some kind of a debt. The apparent leader slowly stood up, never loosing eye contact with Fong Yeo. He reached out and quickly wrapped his gloved grip around Fong Yeo's long beard, pulling him to the point where their noses were almost touching. Ming Su could see the hostility in the man's face as he snarled something at Fong Yeo. She watched in fear as the man shoved her father away. Fong Yeo staggered backwards a few steps before colliding with a man sitting in another chair. With a frightened expression on her face she watched as Fong Yeo struggled to regain his balance before running towards the exit while the three men sitting at the table laughed out of control and spit beer, but she knew that there was nothing that she could do except to accept that her father had been in some kind of an awkward situation that she hoped was now behind him.

Fong Yeo wasted no time making his way to his next stop. It was just as suspected to Ming Su when she followed Fong Yeo to the Chinese Mercantile. She figured that Fong Yeo would purchase new clothes for himself perhaps new footwear, shirt and trousers. But she never gave it a second thought that Fong Yeo would purchase some used panning equipment, including a metal pan, shovel, and a stack of empty five pound sacks for carrying soil. She chuckled to herself. "I can't believe it, all he needed was some money to purchase some gear. If I have known that then I would have given it to him a long time ago. He may actually make something of himself now."

A little later when Fong Yeo exited the Chinese Mercantile he was approached by Ming Su. She cried out with a smile. "Fong Yeo, Fong Yeo, You purchase gear and supplies to look for gold?" Fong Yeo bobbed his head twice. "Yes Su, yes." He looked around cautiously. "I found a small bag of gold while I was cleaning horse mess. I paid a debt to mean American man I came here with and then I got panning gear. I am going to get my own gold now and return to my children in China as a rich man." Ming Su smiled and kissed her unaware father on the cheek before walking away with tears in her eyes.

Ming Su returned to the restaurant to speak with her best friend. "Oh no, Lanying. What have I done? I don't know how to feel. I want him to prosper but I don't want him to return to china to discover his children came to America."

"What are you talking about Su?" Ming Su explained her morning to Lanying."

"Su, I don't think that he will return to China. He would have to strike it really big with finding gold to have enough to make it worth it to return to China and even you said that he cannot see very well. I really think that he will be wasting his time at the river panning the sacks of soil because he would be blind to seeing any gold in the pan and perhaps get frustrated and give up."

"I cannot believe that you would be thinking that he would fail again."

"That's the word Su. "Again" He failed once and may even fail again."

"I just don't know how to feel. I don't want him to fail, I want him to succeed but I don't want him to waste a lot of the money that he makes to return to China for nothing. And to make things worse, I cannot tell him who I am."

"Then help him Hon." Lanying smiled at Ming Su. "You mean the rabbit hole?"

"Oh no, no, no. The rabbit hole is not the place for him. I will talk to Longwei. There are many prospectors who had left their own claims. Longwei will know who and where some of the claims are and then Hon can lead Fong Yeo to one of them. Perhaps he will find a little gold but not really enough to go home."

"Isn't that against the law?"

"It should be against the law that the prospectors came here and pushed the American Indians off their land so that they could hunt for gold. But some of the prospectors who own claims are from the East and more than likely will not return to Idaho City."

"I don't like the idea of breaking the law Lanying."

"Then don't. But make sure that Hon is very careful, like he has already been many, many times. Give Fong Yeo the chance that he needs. I think in time that you will discover that it was just a dream for the old man. Not everyone is meant to prosper."

Ming Su laid in bed thinking about the American Indians and how they were pushed off their land and how happy Flying Star and Smoke

Owl seemed on her journey a few years ago, especially since they impacted her life and decided that it was time to keep a promise to a native beauty and also to visit her brother. She wondered if the village would even still be there. Would Smoke Owl be there, or Lost Doe or most of all Flying Star, nevertheless in Ming Su's heart the one who she knew would most definitely be there was her brother Hai. She decided that the best bet would be to visit the sheriff in the morning and see if he would be able to find out the whereabouts of Smoke Owl and the Bruneau Shoshoni.

Ming Su explained everything to the sheriff about the Bruneau Shoshoni. He had no idea who Smoke Owl was, not to mention who the Bruneau Shoshoni was. However he was quite certain that U.S. Marshall James Alvord probably would since his duties would bring him into Oregon on occasion as he was expected to return to Idaho City from there within the next day or two.

It was around mid-afternoon when the sheriff and Marshall Alvord entered the front door of Kolinski's Restaurant. Their entrance seemed monumental, considering about a half of a dozen men dropped their utensils and headed for the exit. The two lawmen chuckled as if they expected a reaction from men running from the law. But their business wasn't to arrest fugitives, but to speak to Ming Su. As they sat the server took their order for coffee and a slice of cherry pie for the sheriff along with polite orders to summons Ming Su to join them.

Ming Su and Lanying made their way from the kitchen to accompany the two lawmen at their table. After introductions, Alvord quickly informed Ming Su of the Bruneau Shoshoni which he explained was also called the Snake Tribe because they were close to the Snake River. He also claimed to know Smoke Owl and Flying Star personally. However the rest of the news was to prove to be the most important. He explained to Ming Su as the sheriff and Lanying listened in. "I don't think that all the Bruneau Shoshoni are at the same location as they were back in 1863. With all the settlers and the Gold Rush in this part of the West, the government always seems to step in and sometimes causes more problems for the Native Indians than what they could ever imagine. They were pretty much forced to move but not too far. I do know where to find them. I will leave word with a colleague of mine in Boise at the Sheriff's office that you will be passing by within the next two weeks or so. If that will work? His name is Martin Eggers. He will escort you to the Bruneau Shoshoni for the three day journey from Boise." Lanying and Ming Su smiled at one another then thanked the Marshall before heading back to their duties.

21

Almost one week later a covered wagon, a team of four horses, an armed driver and an armed escort on a horse were chartered. Ming Su and Lanying took comfort in the horse drawn traveling home for the four day journey to the west end of the State of Idaho in search of Smoke Owl and the rest of the Bruneau Shoshoni.

Martin Eggers was not at all what Ming Su or Lanying expected. He was tall and stalky, dressed in worn out buck skin. He carried a pistol on each hip, a canteen over his shoulder and a rifle attached to his saddle on his big brown and black horse. He insisted on riding about a tenth of a mile ahead of the wagon.

On the forth day Ming Su recognized a particular clearing that would be familiar, right where Eggers stopped to wait for the wagon. It turned out that it was the camp where Smoke Owl rescued Ming Su from being abducted. The trees were just a little bigger and a little more full. She spotted the road where she followed Smoke Owl, Lost Doe and Flying Star back to the village on foot. She ordered the wagon driver to stay behind and to make camp. Lanying felt compelled to stay behind as well. Ming Su headed on the trail on foot with the armed escort and Eggers riding right behind her.

Barely fifteen minutes later a meadow came into view. There were not as many tee pees as she remembered. The fire pit was still in its place, deer and elk hides was hung drying then out of nowhere she heard. "Ming Su? is that you?" She turned to her right to witness an older Lost Doe approaching her. Lost Doe quickly set her basket down and charged toward Ming Su. Ming Su stood as tall as Lost Doe as they stood embraced in each other's arms, laughing and giggling. Lost Doe asked. "What are you doing here?" She chuckled. "Keeping a promise to Flying Star."

"Oh, I see. Flying Star lives in the other village at the Fort Hall Reservation. It's not far, let me get a horse and I will bring you."

"Wait!"

"What is it?" Ming Su looked in a particular direction and asked. "Can I see my brother Hai first?" Lost Doe nodded. "Yes, of course."

Ming Su asked Lost Doe and the two men to hang back as she visited her brother's grave. Eggers asked. "Su, should I go get Lanying and bring her back here?"

"Oh yes, please do. We will wait for you here."

Ming Su had about one hundred feet to walk before she reached Hai's grave. Fighting her tears back turned out to be much harder than she anticipated. She knelt as the base of the grave covered with stone. Her voice found a tenderness that had been lost for a long time. "My dear brother, Hai. I am now the age that you were when the mountain lion took you from me. I never realized how much that I really did miss you until I found myself kneeling at your feet. You should know that I did everything that we set out to do. I made it to Bannock Village which is now called Idaho City. I discovered a fortune in gold, I am one of the riches people in Idaho City and I also found father. He is doing okay. Tommy eventually made it there but betrayed me by trying to steal from me. He was not who we thought he was. The last I knew, he was in Boise." Quite a while had passed as Ming Su shared all kinds of news with her brother. She leaned forward, closed her eyes and kissed a gray stone. The silence around her was disturbed by the snorting of a horse that seemed much closer than where she left Lost Doe and the armed escort. She turned her head to look behind her. Her eyes opened wide as her face caught a surprised expression, forcing her to make her way to her feet and stepping towards a tall warrior sitting on a horse and a beautiful young native princess riding a white pony with a young boy sitting in front of her. There was no doubt in her mind that it was Smoke Owl, his daughter Flying Star and what appeared to be Flying

Star's son or younger brother. She stood and watched Flying Star climb down off her pony then help the boy down. Slowly they approached each other showing little emotion but a faint smile. Ming Su's eyes caught the boy's eyes as they got closer. Her mouth dropped open in amazement when she realized that the boy's eyes were like hers. She looked quickly at Smoke Owl in fear that he would present disappointment but a smile quickly grew on his face. His deep voice shouted out. "He is my grandson. He is Flying Star's son." Ming Su looked at Flying Star. Flying Star smiled and stated. "I named him Hai." Ming Su didn't know what to think. She shouted. "Hai was only sixteen. How could he be so sinful outside of marriage?" Flying Star rushed to Ming Su, but Ming Su stepped back with a disappointed expression. Flying Star extended her hands out. Reluctantly Ming Su took them into hers as she began to sob. Flying Star hugged Ming Su tightly and shook her head. "Hai was not the father." Ming Su looked confused. "He wasn't?" Flying Star let out a breath through her nose while shaking her head. "I was taken by the bad men not long after you left." She slowly turned her head to the ground. "There was a Chinese man with them. He forced himself on me, took my innocence from me and turned me into a mother and what little time that I knew Hai, I loved him a life time so is what I named my son. Ming Su hugged Flying Star again before they spun around dancing and laughing.

Ming Su noticed Smoke Owl walking towards her and stepped away from Flying Star. He smiled as he looked her up and down. Chuckling he said. "You don't have to look so high to speak to me now." Ming Su threw her arms around the warrior and rested her head against his chest. "It is good to see you Smoke Owl, I am sorry that it has been so long."

"Flying Star said that you would be back one day, I am glad that you kept your word." Suddenly Ming Su began to think that keeping her word was very important to her and to others but her thoughts were disturbed when she caught a glimpse of Lanying riding up on a horse being led by Eggers. She cried out as she tore away from Smoke Owl. "Oh! Oh! I need to introduce you all to someone special. This is my good friend Lanying. She took me in the afternoon that I arrived in Bannock Village that is now called Idaho City. We live together, we work together and we are best of friends so we travel together too. She wanted to meet you all. Eggers helped Lanying off the horse and stepped out of the way to allow her to meet Smoke Owl, Flying Star, Hai and Lost Doe. Through all the conversation and small talk Flying Star asked. "Have you seen Tommy?" Ming Su and Lanying looked at each other. Ming Su smiled and replied. "Yes we did. He came to Idaho City but didn't stay too long. I understand that he made his way back into Boise, but we don't know where he or Gordy is now." Smoke Owl whistled out loud and turned. Gordy was no longer young but proved that he still had many years left on him. He came running through the tall grass hopping over boulders and clumps of grass in his path. Ming Su cried out. "Gordy!" then dropped to her knees. For a middle aged dog the puppy in him had been rejuvenated when he recognized Ming Su. Smoke Owl wrapped his hand around Flying Star's shoulder and chuckled. "Six years and Gordy still remembers Ming Su."

"Yeah but, Tommy said that he got away from him while traveling to Idaho City."

"I guess it is quite possible but somehow, someway Gordy made his way back here."

"You will keep him I hope, He loves being here."

"Gordy will stay her with us, he is a great watchdog."

Three nights had quickly come and gone. Many stories were shared between Ming Su, Lanying and the Bruneau Shoshoni tribe. Nonetheless, Lanying had the opportunity to watch from afar as Ming Su shed tears, laughed, presented anger and sat quietly as she was able to spent time alone with her brother Hai, before they headed home. However Ming Su did have to keep her word one more time. She pulled Eggers aside. "Mr. Eggers, you worked out to be a great trustworthy man and I need one more favor from you."

"What is it Ming Su? Anything."

"I feel that it is important that my brother Hai and I keep our word to a Chinese man in San Francisco."

"You are not thinking about going to San Francisco are you Ming Su?" She shook her head and chuckled. "Oh, absolutely not. But Cheng is the owner of the Chinese Mercantile in San Francisco when we got to America. He gave Hai and me much supplies and an escort to get us on our way. Hai promised that if we ever find gold that we would pay Cheng back so I think that it is the responsible and respectful thing to do."

Okay, I understand that but what do I need to do for you little lady?"

"In this pouch is a small stack of money for Cheng and a smaller stack for our escort Wong Li. Do you know anybody trustworthy that will be going to San Francisco that can carry this to Cheng and Wong Li?"

"As a matter of fact I do. He goes to San Francisco in the Spring and in the Fall to transport Chinese goods to Idaho and Montana. I am sure that he knows who Cheng is. I will have him do what you ask as a personal favor for me."

"Oh, not for free, let me pay you and you can pay your friend."

"Ming Su you have already paid me more than enough. I don't want any more of your money and Van Tran will do it as a personal favor for me. But keep in mind that there is no guarantee that Cheng and Wong Li are even around anymore since the gold rush has died down. But I will make sure that Van Tran does his best to find them."

"If by chance your friend cannot find Cheng and Wong Li. Have your friend give the money to an orphanage for abandoned children or something like that anyways." Eggers smiled and said. "Absolutely Ming Su, absolutely."

"Thank you Mr. Eggers." Ming Su pulled on the man's arm for him to bend forward so she could place a kiss on his cheek.

22

Only certain people in Idaho City knew that Ming Su and Lanying had left on an excursion. The people who did know the details of their travel were instructed to keep their silence. One person who felt that he was neglected to be informed was Choy. Day after day he would visit Kolinski's Restaurant in hopes that Ming Su would be there working but day after day he would discover that she was still away.

Over the next two years the gold production almost seized to exist. With Choy arriving in Idaho City after the peak of the gold rush when over 20,000 minors populated the area, nobody took the young overly ambitious Chinese prospector very serious when he looked for work. Choy spoke clearer English and spoke of his rich father in Washington who discovered his fortune in gold and people had to question why Choy would arrive to seek his fortune in gold as the mountain was showing great signs of running dry. Chinese immigrants were known to be ambitious when it came to mining for gold but Choy was well mannered and educated which caused tension to the carefree, null mannered American prospectors. They looked at Choy as competition and had very little use for him. And with Choy's finances quickly diminishing, he lacked the equipment, supplies and manpower that he needed for a crew. Leaving him to settle for the bottom of the barrel grunt work as a laborer doing the worse of the worse kind of work and was also the first to be let go when the mountains failed to produce its precious metal. Nevertheless Choy's persistence and hard work did not remain unnoticed by a young Chinese woman who believed in him and accepted his hand in marriage around the time the Idaho City population had dropped to about 1,000 people. With Ming Su aware. Longwei made arrangements for Fong Yeo to ride in a wagon into Boise to find work and possibly a home.

Choy took employment under his wife, Ming Su at Kolinski's Restaurant, something that was unheard of in China and in America at that time. The restaurant was struggling and Ming Su had no choice but to sell off the equipment, dining tables and chairs to a Boise establishment. Choy turned out to be a great asset in preparing the merchandise for shipping so Ming Su could sell the building and property to a local investor.

The Chinese market was no better for Longwei. He too had to liquidate his merchandise before selling the building and property for a lot less than what he had ever dreamed that he would. Lanying married Longwei and moved to Boise, never to be heard from again.

In the middle Fall of 1871 Ming Su was with baby. Choy kept himself busy helping other businesses and residence pack and prepare to move on.

One night while Ming Su and Choy slept a cold rush of air traveled throughout the house, instantly waking up Choy. A pair of wool socks moved along the hallway floor into the front room, coming to a sudden stop. Choy discovered that the front door was open. He closed it then rushed back to the bedroom to fetch the scatter gun. However as he passed the front bedroom he noticed that the bed had been moved to the side, the rug folded over and a hidden door pulled up. He entered the room, looked behind the door and in the closet only to discover that he was alone. An eerie feeling struck him as he thought about Ming Su and their baby. He hustled to their bedroom to find his wife sleeping soundly. He closed the bedroom door enough to allow himself to retrieve the scatter gun. Slowly and quietly he made his way across the pine floor towards Lanying's former bedroom. He was quickly startled when he discovered a silhouette of a tall thin figure with a large brim hat and a long overcoat trying to open the window. Choy shouted. "Stop!" In a panic, the silhouette spun around and charged at Choy while gripping a hunting knife. Choy backed up quickly, slamming the butt of the scatter gun into the wall behind him, causing his finger to pull the trigger. With a bright flash and a loud explosion the silhouette stepped back before collapsing to the floor. In the state of shock Choy dropped the scatter gun as he noticed Ming Su rushing through the hallway. Choy stood in shock as Ming Su ran by him into Lanying's former bedroom to discover a body on the floor. She reached down to remove the hat from covering the man's face. Crying out. "Oh no! No! Not Tommy." Choy struggled for words but was unsuccessful as he thought he did something wrong. Ming Su whispered to her husband. "It's okay; it's not your fault. This is Tommy, He tried robbing us before too." Choy asked with concern. "You mean that young boy that traveled with you from San Francisco?" Ming Su looked back at Tommy and threw his hat at him on the floor as she cried out. "Why Tommy, why? Why did you have to try and take from me again? I mean what happened to the young sweet boy that traveled all those miles with Hai and me? " She stepped over to her husband and wrapped her arms around him. "I think that he would have killed me if you didn't kill him, and probably killed you and the baby too. We cannot leave him here and I don't think that the neighbors heard the gun shot. You will stay here. I'll get dressed and fetch the sheriff." Choy bent down and picked up his bride to carry her into their bed. She rolled away from him and curled up mimicking how she once lived in her mother's womb.

When Choy stepped outside it was apparent that the closest neighbor did hear the gun shot that echoed through the darkness. Choy explained to the curious neighbor what had happened and asked him to fetch the sheriff so he could tend to his bride.

It seemed like more than two hours had passed when the neighbor returned with the sheriff and one of his deputies. Once the sheriff determined that Tommy was by all means dead he ordered the deputy to gather up a couple men with a wagon to transport Tommy's body to Doctor Benton's office. The deputy shuffled for words with confusion. "Sheriff, Doctor Benton is no longer practicing in Idaho City, he sought better opportunity in Boise last week." The sheriff shook his head and snarled. "Dang, the gold is all gone and now the people are all gone too. Is there another doctor?"

"I don't think so sheriff, only Doctor Benoit."

"Nah! he's worthless. Why don't we do this then? Wrap him up in blankets and rope, put him in the shed beside the jail and we will make arrangements for him to be transported to Boise within the next day or two. But for now I need Ming Su and Choy to come by the jail house today and give their statements."

Ming Su's cry of pain coming down the hall caught the attention of all the men. They turned and looked at her. The deputy blurted out. "Oh no! It's the baby" The sheriff snarled. "What are you a doctor now?"

"No Sir, but that is how my wife acted when she lost our baby by miscarriage, we got to get her to a doctor." Choy rushed to his bride and helped her back to bed. The sheriff demanded. "Get a horse drawn coach of some sort with a heating stove. We got to get Ming Su to Boise."

The deputy became confused. "But sheriff, it is a nine hour journey on dry ground. What about Doctor Benoit in Placerville?"

"Not a chance deputy, Benoit is retired and a drunk. It is really our only option. Just make sure that there are four or better yet, six horses if they got em."

"Absolutely sheriff."

23

Ming Su laid in the hospital bed looking out the window at the lights that lit up the Boise night. She could hear the people enjoying their night life outside her window. Drinking whiskey, dancing to the music and laughing like the Americans had not a single worry in the world. Women's screams would carry from the brothel down the street but the occasional gunfire would quiet things down for a moment or two. Catching Ming Su's eye, an orange striped cat jumped up on the outside window sill of Ming Su's room. A smile grew on her face as she thought about the day when she and Hai did the impossible together as brother and little sister. She closed her eyes as she whimpered. "Things would have been so much different if you would have survived and made it to Idaho City with me. Would I have been abducted and discovered the rabbit hole? Would I have known Lanying and worked for Mr. Kolinski? Would Tommy still have tried to steal from me? Would father be a whole part of our lives? Would we have gone back to China as a rich family? I have so many questions that I just cannot answer but I know that you cannot answer them either. Sometimes I wonder if I should still go back to China, but I have nothing to go back to. I know that it was not your fault that the mountain lion took your life but missing you doesn't hurt any less." She wiped her eyes as she watched the door swing in with Choy grasping the handle. Choy asked. "Who are you talking to Ming Su?" She closed her eyes and lowered her head as she exhaled through her nose, then she whispered. "I was just thinking about how great of friends that you and Hai would have been if he was alive, and I just wonder if Tommy would still be alive too.

So much death since I left China... I never told anybody this, not even Hai." Ming Su paused for a moment then continued. "The day that we arrived in San Francisco and the workers on the big boat were throwing the old food and stuff overboard. I was watching two Chinese men arguing in the back of the boat. They started fighting. I blinked and the smaller man was no longer there. Sometimes I imagine the pain that he suffered from the big shark fish eating him alive. I don't think that anyone else saw what I saw but it was my first vast reality of nature taking human life." Ming Su held her hand out for Choy to take. Choy smiled and said. "I am so happy that you allowed me to ride in the stage coach that day. I mean if you wouldn't have then you may have just been a face that I would see from time to time in Idaho City until I moved on."

"You mean that you stayed for me?"

"You are the reason that I could not leave Idaho City and I tried harder and harder every day."

"The doctor said that I can still have babies, I want a little Hai someday and maybe a daughter too." Choy bent down and wrapped his arms around his grieving wife, he whispered. "I know that your heart will never fully heel. I am sure that mine too will remain in pieces over our baby but no matter what, I will always be your husband and you my wife." Ming Su replied. "I know." As tears ran down her face while they embraced.

That winter there was nothing to keep Ming Su busy. With less than a thousand people living in the old gold booming town of Idaho City. Depression set into Ming Su's heart. Her restaurant was gone, her best friend and mentor, Lanying was gone. She spent a lot of time lying in bed or covered up with a blanket as she sat in a rocker watching the snow fall from the night sky, not knowing if she should curse her fortune or embrace it, but one thing for sure. When she thought about the rabbit hole, returning to it was no longer an interest to her.

Choy sat on a fancy sofa with hand carved wood accents in the front room reading a book as the snow built up in the corner of the twelve little panes of glass in the window behind him. He kept the fireplace in the bedroom burning strong so Ming Su would be comfortable. The fireplace in the front room he left alone. He was content with an extra pair of wool socks, and a sweater to keep the chill away from his skin. A kettle made of metal sat on a metal wood stove in the kitchen keeping the imported Chinese tea hot for Choy to keep Ming Su's porcelain cup that sat on a matching porcelain saucer on the night stand filled.

Out the bedroom window Ming Su noticed four wolves taking down a young bull elk in the back yard that stretched deep into the forest. The howls of the alpha caught the attention of Choy who hustled in the bedroom to check on Ming Su. He stood behind Ming Su in her rocker watching the wolves tear into the flesh of the unfortunate young elk. Expressions on both of their faces were filled with unsettling amazement and fear as the fresh white snow turned red. Ming Su turned her head to look at Choy as a lost memory entered her mind and she chose to tell her husband of the last time she was abducted by the Murphy family. She spot lighted the howls that she heard while tramping through the deep snow, how she was in fear that wolves were pursuing her. It all came clear in those previous moments what would have come of her if the wolves had tracked her down.

Choy woke the next morning with the bright sun lighting up the back yard. He left his bride sleeping soundly as he slipped out of bed and made his way to the window to find that the white snow left a shape of a young bull elk. Just the snow covered antlers gave away what rested under the snow. Nevertheless out of the corner of his eye he noticed Ming Su tossing around under the warm covers. The fire had died down so he made it a priority to bring it back to life before preparing breakfast in the kitchen for Ming Su and himself.

Choy made it part of his and Ming Su's morning routine to get dressed up warm and take a walk down to the American mercantile. He was adamant about Ming Su getting fresh air and exercise everyday whether she wanted to or not. Some mornings she would be quiet without saying a single word, other mornings she showed excitement, talking so much that Choy couldn't even get a word in.

As usual Mr. Seymour was working behind the counter when he wasn't restocking supplies and food. Every morning there was a different sale on merchandise or supplies, but mostly food that Choy or Ming Su would prepare for dinner that night.

Little green buds began accumulating on the branches of the trees giving off the hint that spring has finally arrived and a cold winter was now in the past. The sun was high, with a mild temperature and an easy breeze blowing. Ming Su opened the front and back doors, and some of the windows to let the house air out as she began her Spring cleaning. Choy rolled up the rugs and hung them over a tight rope that ran between two trees for Ming Su to swing a looped branch at to beat the dirt and dust out. Choy spotted a little gray mouse racing along the baseboard of the front room. It hopped up on the bottom shelf of the book case that was built into the wall and ran behind the books. Choy whispered to himself. "You little scavenger, I got you trapped." As he pulled one of his boots off before kneeling down in front of the book case. One by one he removed the books, piling them up on the pine wood floor beside him. He became irritated when he removed the last book but there was no mouse to be found. However, he did notice a coin size hole that was drilled in the back of the shelf. He chuckled. "You think that you got away from me, you are so wrong you little scavenger." Slipping his finger into the hole, he tugged on the shelf. To his surprise the board pulled towards him and was easily removed. His heart jumped to his throat at his discovery. Quickly he returned the board before putting his boot back on his foot and rushing outside to speak to Ming Su. She was beating the last rug when Choy approached her. Looking at her with a concerned look he stated. "I think that it is time that you and I had a serious talk about our finances." Ming Su looked at him proudly. "What about our finances? Although I didn't make as much as I thought that I would selling off the restaurant and the equipment but we are pretty well to do."

"I understand that but that money is in the bank in Boise. I am just wondering about the money that is under the bottom book shelf?" Ming Su sighed and stated. "Lanying told me that I will forget how much money that I had."

"I don't understand Su."

"Come on Choy. Lanying and I owned Kolinski's Restaurant. You know what it all sold for; you also know how busy it was for years."

"Ming Su there is a lot more money under that shelf than what Kolinski's was sold for. I heard rumors that you were rich but I believed that your money was from the restaurant but now I feel like you didn't tell me everything."

"I just wanted to wait and see what was going to happen with you and me but now I suppose it is time to come completely clean."

"So what are you telling me Su?" Ming Su began moving and bouncing her head with a grin on her face before she stated. "I am one of the riches people that Idaho City ever knew."

"What do you mean?"

"Before I say anything more. You need to come with me for a walk in the woods."

"I don't want to go for a walk in the woods." Ming Su nodded and chuckled. "Yes you do, but don't worry I don't have any plans on killing you." Choy looked terrified. Ming Su chuckled. "You have nothing to worry about. Just don't hook one of the horses up to the buggy, we have a ways to go but we have to walk so you can understand my complete sacrifice, danger and risk that I took all the time. Day after day."

"This better be worth it Su."

"Just get ready so we can go, Bring along the scatter gun and a pistol."

"What! Is it that dangerous?"

"We are wasting time Choy."

The two set out on their journey into the forest barely speaking a word to one another. Ming Su set pace leaving it hard for Choy to keep up on the three and a half mile hike. When the boulder came into view Ming Su stopped and began to speak. "Remember the night that the wolves killed the elk outside our bedroom window?"

"Yes, I remember. Why?"

"I told you about the wolves that I thought were pursuing me."

"Yeah, I remember that too, but is there a point to all this?"

"Yes! I was able to hide in a place where they could not see me or even smell me in the heavy snow. See that big boulder?" She turned and pointed. "Yeah!"

"Come with me." As they walked towards the boulder Ming Su explained about the rabbit and where she discovered the rabbit had taken refuge too. When they reached the boulder, Choy followed Ming Su up alongside it and then behind it. Choy looked around and snarled. "It has all been dug up. It looks like it collapsed when the tree fell." The pine needles had fallen off their branches from the changing seasons and the rain, snow and hot sun.

"Exactly, my great husband." Ming Su took a few steps and moved the soil around to discover two pea size nuggets of gold that she turned and handed to Choy. His face instantly lit up. "You discovered gold here. This is the rabbit hole that I overheard Lanying mention to you. At the time it made no sense, now it does. You are rich."

"Yes, yes and yes. I just never had any intensions on returning here again but this is what I discovered that night but didn't know it until Lanying noticed the gold dust flickering in the fire light as it fell from my clothes. Suddenly Choy developed an angry tone. "So Lanying knew all about the gold too and I was never informed of it. Why?" Ming Su stepped alongside Choy, leaning on the boulder. "Try to understand Choy. I have seen thousands of men and women come to Idaho City seeking their fortune in gold but left with no more than aching, tired worn out bodies, no cash in their pockets, empty stomach and worse of all, on foot because they sold everything that they had just to live off of. I wanted you to walk with me out here today and walk back. You need to experience the sacrifice and danger that I experienced every single time that I came out here. I had to dress as a boy to fool the Murphy's and anybody else who was looking to sell me as a sex slave or worse. If anybody would have known that I was in the rabbit hole digging for gold then I for sure would have been dead. Sometimes my body ached so much that I could barely make it back to town. You can be angry at me all you want but it was a decision not to tell my husband whether it was you or someone else a long time before I ever met you." Choy slapped his hands together with a big excited smile upon his face. Ming Su's curiosity encouraged her to ask. "What's so funny?"

"Since we are married the money is now mine too then." Ming Su shook her head and asked. "Is that really how you feel Choy?"

"Yes, you are my wife, I am your husband." Ming Su nodded with a confident expression on her face. "Okay Choy, there is a lot of money at home and at the bank in Boise. Since I forgot about the money under the book shelf, you can have it all, all that money is yours." He chuckled. "That's wonderful Su."

"Just remember this Choy. When your money is gone, then your money is gone. If you spend it foolishly then it will go quickly and it will be all gone before you know it."

"I understand that Ming Su."

"Then what are your plans Choy? Move to Boise, Go back to Washington or live without having to work for the rest of our lives, as long as we are responsible with the money?"

"You are right Su. That money under the book shelf is yours, even though you forgot about it. I don't want to leave you and it's not because of the money. If you will agree to let me cut the limbs from the big dead pine tree and mine for gold some more here than I can do what I came to Idaho City for."

"I don't think that is a good idea Choy, I would rather give you the money."

"Su, Idaho City is almost a ghost town. Wouldn't it be nice to send my father a letter telling him that I have finally found gold?" Ming Su's attitude became evident to Choy. "This is all about your father being proud of you? He never even came to our wedding. You haven't seen or heard from him in years. He sent you out to fend for yourself instead of bringing you in and seeking more gold for the family empire." Choy sucked in a shallow breath. "Su, I want our family to be well off, if not rich. But what kind of man am I if I allow my wife to keep supporting me? This will allow me to find gold through my long hard work so I can support you and our children.

"I really don't like the idea of you mining the rabbit hole but if you must play the head role of our home then please be careful. But there is one more thing that I must show you."

"What is it?"

On their way back to town Ming Su wandered off the wagon road down another road that had grown even more over. Choy kept asking. "Where are we going?" But Ming Su kept her silence until they finally approached the stone foundation of the burned down cabin. Right away Choy noticed an upright piano in the corner of the cellar. "This is amazing Su. The fire didn't even destroy this piano." He began playing out of tune music." Ming Su sighed as she knelt down and pushed the leaves and pine needles to the side to reveal the five pound sacks of soil. "Forget about the piano, this is what I brought you here for." She explained to Choy what had to be done with them if he chose to. Together they counted seventeen sacks before they headed back.

Silence remained between the couple until they reached the familiar wagon road and Ming Su reached out, placing her hand into Choy's. "I love you very much Choy. I just ask you to please be very careful if you feel that you must scour for gold at the old rabbit hole."

"I will be careful Su. I promise." They walked a little further before Ming Su Chuckled. "I didn't know that you knew how to play the piano."

"I love the music that you make with the violin Su. I didn't want you to feel like you were not good enough with your music. I had to practice every day for an hour from the age of five until I was fourteen to learn discipline. My mother wanted me to be a musician in an American symphony. I haven't played in years but I am very good at it. I intimidated the children in school with my talent and skill."

"You didn't have to keep that from me Choy."

"Well let's just call it even for you not telling me about the rabbit hole or the money."

"Whatever the circumstances for either case we will just put it behind us... but I do want to get a piano now and maybe we can make some beautiful music together." Choy kissed Ming Su on the cheek and whispered. "I thought that we already made beautiful music together." Ming Su sighed with a smile. "I think that it's time that we thought about a family again before you become too distracted with the rabbit hole." Choy stopped in his tracks, instantly causing Ming Su to stop beside him. "That's what I am talking about Ming Su." Ming Su looked confused.

"Are we talking about making music or are we talking about making children?" Choy chuckled.

"Exactly my dear, Ming Su."

"Men, I will never understand them."

Choy didn't have to worry about purchasing mining equipment. The minors and prospectors left plenty behind, because they didn't want to travel with it and they couldn't sell it either. Ming Su ordered and had a piano delivered that she practiced on to help keep her from being worried on a daily basis at home wondering if her husband would return safely as he would hike to the rabbit hole and back, usually bringing gold back with him. Choy would sometimes be home for a week or two at a time before disappearing into the forest again.

When winter approached the couple would pass time together teaching each other how to play their musical instruments'. Choy was obviously a natural by the way he played and developed his skills playing the violin. However Ming Su was not so interested in spending so much time learning the piano, she rather listened to Choy make beautiful music.

Come the New Year, Ming Su's belly was much bigger than normal for a woman her size. Choy would chuckle as he watched his wife hobble around with her big belly. However he could never resist walking up behind her, wrapping his arms around her and kissing her cheek. When Choy wasn't chasing down his fortune in gold he waited on Ming Su hand and foot. Every night he prepared dinner, no matter how worn out he was from cutting and chopping wood for the fireplace and wood stove. He hired a live in house keeper that took over Lanying's bedroom. Sherry was a young American prostitute from Boise who wanted to get away from that lifestyle and live in the country. Choy paid her a weekly allowance and allowed her freedom within the house to care for Ming Su during her pregnancy and after child birth.

Doctor Benton traveled from Boise on a monthly basis to check on Ming Su and her pregnancy even through the winter months. Planning trips for when the wagon roads were packed down and melted enough to safely travel over. The middle of March was a big concern for Dr. Benton, Ming Su, Choy and Sherry. The big question was whether or not the wagon road would be clear enough for Dr. Benton to travel to Idaho City to bring the twins into the world around March 16th. Ming Su traveling to Boise was completely out of the question. It was nine hours on a clear day and clear roads. It could be more in the snow. Dr. Benton advised against it. It was pretty fortunate that snow fall after March 1st was minimal and Dr. Benton arrived the day before the twins were born.

At 1:17 in the afternoon on March 16th, a baby boy was born. Ming Su and Choy agreed to name him after her childhood protector and brother, Hai. Four minutes later a baby girl pushed through. It was agreed that she would take the name after Ming Su's beloved mother. Choy stood with great pride when he held his first born in his arms and when he looked into Yanyu's little brown eyes a tear of joy fell onto his daughter's cheek. He whispered. "You are as beautiful as your mother." Ming Su responded. "There is no doubt that Hai is as handsome as his father.

Fortunately for the family the snow was pretty much melted by the beginning of April. The roads were still wet from the melted snow, leaving it as mud. Therefore Choy waited until the third week of April to go to the rabbit hole. He was away for days at a time, leaving Ming Su and Sherry to care for the children. Choy took for granted that the wagon road was no longer traveled since the prospectors had moved on before winter. Perhaps he was confident or ignorant to have made permanent camp about one hundred yards before the rabbit hole. Never to realize, his fire brought curiosity to his camp by anyone passing by. He had no doubt that he was richer than his father and made that point clear to Ming Su on a frequent basis. Ming Su determined that she perhaps made a mistake as Choy became obsessed with the rabbit hole. Season after season Choy returned to the rabbit hole for more and more gold. The children watched for five years as their mother would beg and plea for Choy to not return to the forest. He let it to be known that he opened savings accounts for himself, Ming Su, Hai, Yanyu as well as a savings fund for Sherry once the children were eight. Leaving lifted eyebrows for the local criminal element.

A late summer morning Hai and Yanyu hid their father's boots so he could not make way to the forest. Choy knew that he put the boots in the closet by the front door but they were no longer there. Hai and Yanyu sat on the couch giggling as their father checked room after room but still coming up empty. He looked out the front door on the walkway but no luck. Ming Su sat in the rocker with a grin from the children being so amused with their panicking father. He finally snarled. "I need my boots now, I got to go." Ming Su began to chuckle. "Maybe the mouse is back and he will lead you to them." He looked at the bottom of the book case. "There they are. I wonder how they got there." The children quickly lost their humor as they watched their father slide the boots onto both feet. Yanyu slid off the couch and ran to Choy. "Please father, don't go." Needless to say, Choy returned no reply to his daughter. However, he looked at Ming Su and snarled. "I know that you put the children up to it, this is not a joke. I will be back in a few days." He stormed out the front door, slamming it after he exited. The children ran to the window to watch their father rush away. Ming Su sat in disbelief that her husband had spoken to her in such a manner in front of the children. She felt heartbroken as she retired to her bedroom.

A week had past and Choy neglected to return causing great concern for Ming Su, the children and Sherry. Ming Su waited two more days before approaching her neighbors. A senior couple, who was living out the rest of their lives in their home in Idaho City were the Hanson's. Mrs. Hanson stayed with Sherry and the children as Mr. Hanson carried Ming Su in his horse drawn wagon towards the rabbit hole. Ming Su was immediately struck with fear after discovering fresh horse and wagon tracks on the wagon road. Her first thoughts were of the Murphy family. She was certain that the tracks belonged to them. Mr. Hanson kept reassuring that despite what she thought, the wagon road was well traveled by minors and prospectors searching for gold, as well as hunters, trappers and fur traders. Unfortunately his suggestions were of no comfort to the frightened wife and mother. Mr. Hanson increased the speed of the horses and wagon but remained careful and cautious considering that he had never traveled on that particular wagon road.

When they arrived at the boulder it was evident that many men had been there on foot, horseback and in wagons. Ming Su asked. "How could I have been so stupid to have led my husband to this place?" They both stepped down from the wagon. Mr. Hanson followed Ming Su up the hill alongside the boulder. At that time she had no choice but to explain everything to the old man. The rabbit hole revealed evidence of careless digging with many boot prints but not of Choy's. Mr. Hanson suggested. "It is without doubt Ming Su that Choy will probably not be returning home and if we know what is better for us I believe that we should leave immediately. We have no idea when someone is returning and if they find us, we will be discovered many years from now as waste that came out of the tail end of a pack of wolves. I'm sorry Ming Su, but say your goodbyes here and now, and never, I mean never return here again."

Ming Su sat silent on the return ride home with her eyes puffy and pink from crying. She refused to let her children see her in such a devastated state so she sat and talked with Mr. Hanson on the wagon until she felt comfortable to enter the house. She explained to Mr. Hanson how Choy believed that Idaho City would make some kind of a comeback, attracting thousands of Minors and prospectors. She chuckled. "He could be so selfish and greedy. He was just trying to live up to what his father expected of him." She stared in Mr. Hanson's eyes and whispered. "We have more money that we know what to do with. I accidently discovered gold in the rabbit hole in 1863, not long after I arrived here from China. The pursuit of gold by my family has left devastation more than what all our money is really worth. I was abducted three times, another girl that I know was abducted but I was able to rescue her. My brother, our friend Tommy, our baby and my husband have all died for dream that I am cursed with." The two sat in silence as the evening breeze was closing in. Ming Su asked. "What am I going to tell our children? They are only five years old. They are not going to understand. I don't want to and I won't lie to them but I am afraid that the truth of their father's potential death would scar them worse than I was when my mother died... Was I wrong to come to America Mr. Hanson?"

"Ming Su, do not do that to yourself. You can't ever know. Things could have turned out better but they could have turned out a lot worse as well. Don't ever ask yourself that because when you do you eliminate every good thing that got you to this point in your life."

"That makes a lot of sense Mr. Hanson" Hanson chuckled. I have witnessed you for years. You earned the respect of all the business owners in Idaho City, the sheriff and even that old man that I watched you give food to over and over. Lanying taught you to be a well-mannered and respectable woman. You have two well-mannered children, a beautiful house and of course a wonderful neighbor to Mrs. Hanson and myself. What you have endured you are an exceptional survivor and a great conqueror. I am sure that everyone who knows you is proud to know you. I know that I am." Ming Su leaned towards Hanson and kissed him on the cheek before climbing down from the wagon. She looked at him. "Thank you Mr. Hanson. Give my best to your children." Hanson nodded and with his quick snap of the reins the wagon pulled away.

24

The children and Sherry knew right away when Ming Su walked through the door that something was not right. Ming Su had a hard time looking at her children as she made her way to the center of the sofa and sat down. Hai and Yanyu understood their mother's grief and took a place on the sofa on either side of her. Sherry turned and began to head into the other room when Ming Su whimpered. "You need to hear this too Sherry." Sherry stepped back to the rocker near the window and sat down awaiting the news.

As expected the children appeared to understand. Ming Su wrapped an arm around the shoulders of both her children to comfort them about their father's disappearance. Hai sat tall in his seat holding back the pain as Yanyu broke down crying. Sherry turned her head and stared out the window, trying to keep her composure in front of the children.

Another winter had come and gone. Ming Su sat up against the head board in bed, lost in thought with the only light coming from the embers in the fireplace. Sherry stepped in the room from the hallway, she whispered. "I have put the children to bed and tucked them in." Ming Su looked at her and nodded. "Will you sit with me for a moment Sherry?"

"Absolutely, Ming Su." Sherry sat on the edge of the bed. A moment or two passed before Ming Su spoke. "Sherry, living in this home without Choy, and the horrible memory of Tommy's death I have made a difficult decision. I cannot live in this home anymore. There are many great memories but the few horrible memories overtake the good memories. I will not live out my days or finish raising my children in this home or in this dying town. You are more than welcome to continue living with us if you choose, but in Boise. The children will eventually be turning eight years old in about two years. Nonetheless, I will not see you going back to that horrible life that you escaped from. I am sure that you are not aware of the savings fund that Choy had started for you at the bank but there is a substantial sum awaiting you when the children turn eight. I recommend that you become an entrepreneur or business owner. Needless to say, I could still use your help with the children if you choose to continue living with us."

"What if I just want to eventually find a rich tycoon of my own and marry him?"

"The savings fund is yours to do what you want to. But please use it wisely."

"I understand Ming Su and I actually hope that I could be a great inspiration to a younger woman one day that you are to me. You saved me from that beating by that horrible man that day and rescued me from a life that my mother had turned me out into. You gave me a home and a way to make an income. I want to honor you and Choy so there is never a hint of regret in your heart for everything that you did for me."

"Sherry, I don't think that you will let me or Choy down. I was given a chance too with Lanying and it proved to be a great thing for us both. I passed that on to you, and perhaps one day you will take in a needing young lady and help her out too." Sherry leaned over and kissed Ming Su on the cheek before getting up to exit the room. Ming Su cried out. "Will you please wake my children? I know that it is wrong for me to be so selfish but I do believe that they would find great comfort sleeping in bed with me tonight as I would having them sleeping with their mother." Sherry smiled. "Absolutely, Ming Su."

"Oh, and one more thing Sherry."

"Yes, what is it Ming Su?"

"My friends call me Su and I think of you as a friend." Sherry smiled. "I understand Su and thank you."

Mr. and Mrs. Hanson were eating lunch when a knock sounded from the front door. The couple looked at each other in concern before Mr. Hanson got up to walk through the living room. He pulled the door open to discover Ming Su standing there. "Hello Ming Su." He cried out. Her soft voice replied. "Hello Mr. Hanson. I don't mean to be a bother." Hanson shook his head. "You are not a bother Ming Su. Come on in. What can I do for you?" She followed Hanson into the kitchen and sat at the table. Mrs. Hanson served her a cup of tea. "Thank you Mrs. Hanson. But Mr. and Mrs. Hanson I have decided that it would be best that I traveled to Boise to purchase a home there." Mr. Hanson replied with concern. "Oh, I had no idea, are you planning on moving to Boise?"

"Yes, with the disappearance of my husband last year and Tommy being killed in this house I prefer to leave it behind me. I think that it would be best for the children too. But we are all going to travel to Boise. Would you be so kind as to keep an eye on the house for me? I would be happy to compensate you for it."

"We would be happy to but we don't want your money. Just be safe."

Ming Su sent a telegram to Boise requesting an armed escort and a stagecoach to carry herself, the children and Sherry to Boise along with all the money and gold that Ming Su knew of that Choy had hidden within the walls of the home.

A few days later a stagecoach arrived with an armed escort as scheduled. The former deputy stood guard with his scatter gun in hand as the armed escort riders carried and loaded up a heavy wooden chest with about eighty pounds of gold hid under a fake bottom. And other luggage containing clothing with stacks of bills folded in between the individual garments.

Hai caused a little bit of a fuss when the stagecoach driver denied him permission to ride alongside him due to safety issues. However Hai did find comfort and amusement kneeling on the floor with his head out the window watching the forest pass by. Yanyu sat across from her mother mimicking Ming Su's proper posture as a lady.

The bank manager agreed to stay late to allow Ming Su to make a substantial deposit of cash and gold, she also made arrangements for the gold to be converted into cash. Nonetheless she had an appointment set up for the next day with a bank representative to view upscale homes in the suburbia areas of Boise. The second house they viewed was two stories tall with attic space that was a finished loft as well as three bedrooms and a den upstairs on the second floor and a master bedroom and a guest bedroom on the first floor, a large living room in the front of the house, with a sizable kitchen in the rear of the house, a spiral type stair case. All the wood was stained and not painted, a fireplace in the living room, wood stove in the den on the second floor, a patio on the first and second floors on the front of the house. The exterior painted a light brown with white trim, a small barn and stables to house four horses on two acres of grassy property. Ming Su and the children felt that even though it had an extra bedroom that it would still fit them all perfect. So Ming Su made arrangements to move forward with the purchase.

25

Boise offered better opportunity for Ming Su and Sherry to meet new people and proved to be evident when Sherry met a reporter for the Idaho Statesman. Joseph P. Sheridan, a graduate from the University of Washington in Seattle who moved to Boise seeking a life in a growing city, the second son of a fisherman and the first to spread his wings to leave the nest. However, Sherry decided to follow Ming Su's example and not inform Joseph of the savings fund that Choy had created for her. She also decided not to give him too much information about her later teenage years. When he asked about her parents she kept to the truth. Her father abandoned her and her mother when she was eight and her mother moved on when Sherry came of age as an adult.

The 4th of July celebration caused a spooked horse to run frantic through the down town area as Ming Su was walking that afternoon. Unaware of the horse running up behind her, Ming Su was knocked off her feet, slamming her side into the wheel of a wagon. She was promptly transported to the home and medical office of Dr. Mo Juang. He determined that two of her ribs were not broken but fractured. He recommended that she stayed in bed as much as possible for four weeks. In the evening as he made his rounds he would stop by and check on Ming Su. Dr. Mo Juang was an American Chinese descent who was a successful doctor that had taken an interest in Ming Su. He began bringing her flowers and other gifts to courtship her and eventually won her heart. But before she could move forward she still had unfinished business that she needed to attend to before the early fall began to get too cold. Her and her fiancée Mo Juang traveled to Idaho City to sell the house to an American couple who had been renting it but had also inherited a substantial amount of money and decided to purchase Ming Su's house as well as other real estate in Idaho City. Not long after they returned to Boise they got married.

The night before the wedding Ming Su called her children into the living room. They were both ten years old and she felt that she needed to take the time and see how her children felt about Mo. She didn't know whether to be surprised or not when Hai and Yanyu were in acceptance of Mo becoming their stepfather. Ming Su had a couple things that she need to settle with her children. Come bedtime she sat on the edge of Yanyu's bed as Yanyu sat on the pine wood stool like every other night Ming Su slowly brushed her daughter's hair as they carried on conversation that brought interest to each other. Yanyu asked her mother what was wrong when Ming Su stopped brushing her long black hair. Ming Su replied. "I know that you never had the opportunity to know either one of your grandparents. But as I have told you in the past, my mother used to brush my hair every night before bed and on one particular night. Not long before her death she gave me this necklace." Ming Su passed a thin silver chained necklace from her own neck that a star pendant of sparkling silver hung from, over Yanyu's head as she watched the North Star drop just inches below her chin just before her mother fastened the clasp. "My mother told me that no matter where I am the North Star never moves. Now I want you to have it."

"Thank You, mother. I will wear it with honor... Wait a minute, you are not going to die are you? I need you mother. Hai needs you too." Ming Su chuckle. "No my young daughter. I was almost ten when my mother gave me the necklace so I felt it was appropriate to give it to you now that you are ten." Yanyu smiled. "Will you tell me what grandmother was like?" Ming Su chuckled. "Your grandmother looked a lot like I do now. She was quiet, not necessarily shy. Perhaps just afraid to be who she was because of tradition. In China a woman has no place to speak. She honors her husband whether she believes in him or not, but she was so beautiful. Anyone could tell that your grandfather was so in love with her. And creative, your grandmother was so creative. She could draw and paint beautiful pieces of artwork. Her sewing skills were amazing. She died of a sickness that slowly took her life." A knock on the door caught Ming Su's and Yanyu's attention. Hai stepped into the room. "I didn't mean to be over hearing your conversation but what was Uncle Hai like?" Ming Su just laughed. Hai walked across the pine wood floor and sat on the edge of the bed next to his mother as she began to speak. "Your Uncle Hai was a crazy one but not in a bad way.' Ming Su smiled and closed her eyes as she remembered her brother. "He was always doing funny things to make me laugh but he knew when to be serious. He protected me. He was six years older than I and the best brother that a young girl could ever ask for. And he was smart. Father showed him once how to hunt and fish and he was so natural at it. He knew what directions; North, South, East or West was just by looking at the sun or the stars. He could tell that it was going to rain just by looking at the leave on a tree and the smell in the air. You don't know this Hai, but there is another boy who is actually a man now that was also named after your Uncle Hai."

"There is? He must have been well liked and respected."

"That he was. I know that you heard me speak of Flying Star, the beautiful Native Indian girl."

"Yes. Uncle Hai was in love with her."

"And she him. When I was sixteen and I returned to the village to see Flying Star, Her father Smoke Owl and the old Chinese woman that they called Lost Doe, I learned that Flying Star had a young son. "Yanyu perked up and asked.
Mother Uncle Hai didn't..."

"Oh no no no, Yanyu. Flying Star was also abducted by the bad men to be sold into slavery or prostitution but was able to escape with some other girls but not before a Chinese man had his way with her by taking her innocence and planting a seed in her womb."

"You mean a baby?"

"Yes, I mean a baby. Flying Star loved your Uncle Hai and she was devastated almost as much as I when he was killed so she honored him by giving her fatherless baby that was conceived through an abusive sin his name. Which reminds me, I have something for you too Hai. Stay here with your sister, I shall return quickly."

Moments later Ming Su returned. She handed her son Hai a hunting knife with a hard wood handle and leather sheath that was scratched up and worn but still had many years left on it. "This was your Uncle Hai's. I would think he would feel that if anybody should own it now that it should be his nephew that also carries his name. " Hai reached out, taking the knife from his mother and slipping his belt through the loop on the sheath before refastening his belt.

Ming Su decided to purchase another restaurant to keep her busy since her new husband had a growing practice. She decided to call the restaurant Kolinski's as it was in Idaho City and serve the same dishes.

It wasn't long after the grand opening of Kolinski's that many of the former residence of Idaho City connected the name "Kolinski's" with the Kolinski's in Idaho City. The familiar customers began to frequent Kolinski's once again. The image of Kolinski's signage formed a familiarity to the memory of an older Chinese man. His beard was still long and scruffy, his body still thin and fragile but his clothes were more American.

Ming Su noticed the familiar old face peering through the window. She sighed with a smile of relief and immediately brought a bowl of soup, two bread rolls and a cup of tea out to him. The estranged father and daughter carried on a conversation as if they were always in each other's lives. Fong Yeo spoke of his journey from China many, many years before. "I was so devastated when my wife had passed on. We were making plans to come to America as a family during the California gold rush but she got too sick to travel. I knew that I was going to lose her and our children would be without a mother too. I was so grief stricken over Yanyu's death that I could no longer focus on my obligations and commitments in China, not even my own children. I was so ashamed of myself that I couldn't even look at them. I had no more honor. My heart was weak and almost to the point of being dead. I sold everything of value that we had in the home that barely paid for a ticket to cross the ocean to America. There was no way that I could bring my children. But I knew that I taught my son Hai well to take care of his sister Ming Su. Sometimes I try to visualize what they look like now that they are all grown up. I mean that I cannot see much with my bad eye sight as it is. I wonder what kind of life that they are now living though. Are they married? Are they happy? Are they rich or poor? I just don't know and I know that I will never know. It was a long five weeks on the junk that brought me to America. There was never enough food to eat aboard the vessel so many nights I went without eating... When I got to America, everyone was so mean and rude. I was attacked and robbed of my only money by American youngsters. I was without nothing in San Francisco for over a month until the owner of the Chinese Mercantile, Cheng I think his name was introduced me to an American prospect, Mr. Esposito that was traveling to Bannock City with other men. It was not a good idea. Those men were very cruel, especially Mr. Esposito. He had no conscience and no remorse for what evil he would do. I saw him kill a man an old man with a dog because the old man would not sell him his rifle. Mr. Esposito was a bad man. I was told by one of the other men in Idaho City that he traveled with that Mr. Esposito was shot by another prospector over a claim of land. I suppose that it was all for the best... Su, my search for gold was the biggest failure that one could ever imagine. I did get lucky one morning though. I found a small sack of gold. You must remember that day when you wouldn't take my money so I paid for the young Chinese family's breakfast."

"Absolutely, I do remember that day. How much gold did you find?"

"A little over four pounds. I paid off Mr. Esposito right away and bought some panning gear but it just didn't pan out for me. I guess that I just wasn't meant to be rich... I remember one night I was sitting and staring up at the moon. An eerie feeling come upon me as if someone who loved me was staring at the moon at that exact moment. Perhaps it was my daughter Ming Su, She likes the beautiful things that nature provides us to see. My heart just ached but was also full of joy and I felt this peace come over me." Ming Su's eyes filled with tears as she reflected on a similar moment not long after she left San Francisco and her heart ached with pain of regret. She stood up and stated. "I must get back to my duties in the restaurant. Enjoy your lunch and come back for dinner."

The winters in Boise did not have a snow accumulation like Idaho City but the temperature still got very cold at times. Ming Su had the old man followed to an abandoned covered wagon in a vacant field. There was also a formation of stones forming a circle to conceal a fire with log sections that were more than likely used as seats around the fire pit. On the days that the old man didn't show up at the restaurant, Ming Su had a dinner brought to him by an employee on his way home from work. Ming Su persuaded her husband to check on the old man about once a month. He never asked why and she never offered any information about the old man. Mo knew that his wife was in the habit of feeding the old man and that was enough to satisfy his curiosity.

After about a two week freeze Mo arrived home and informed Ming Su that he had to administer medication of potential pneumonia to the old man. If he hadn't then the old man would have suffered a slow painful death.

Ming Su had turned thirty eight earlier- that year when her teenage son walked into the living room. "Mother, the old Chinese man did not eat the soup from yesterday. It is ice cold in the bowl sitting on the log. I think that he is quickly fading fast by the sickness that set into his chest." Ming Su thought about how the old military blankets inside the old man's run down abandoned covered wagon would prove to be his place of death if he did not receive medical attention soon. A tear ran down her cheek as her heart filled her throat. Moments passed while she silently sat in her finely hand carved chair with the cushions covered with a beige soft plush material. She stared out the window watching the wind blow the tree branches around. She could feel deep inside that another long, cold coming in from the mountains had finally taken its toll on the old man and he was not going to last much longer in his condition. Her thoughts were disturbed by the sound of her son's boot heels as he walked toward the rooms exit. She said in a soft tone. "My son, please stand before me." Instantly Hai thought that he was in trouble as he dropped his head and walked over to stand in front of his mother. She said to him. "Have the old Chinese man brought to our home and place him comfortably in the empty warm bed in the spare bedroom down stairs. We shall care for him."

"Mother, we don't know this man, he is just a beggar." Ming Su wiped her eyes with a linen cloth and blew her nose. "Understand my son, I know him better than you think."

"How do you know him mother?"

"I used to feed him in Idaho City too but it does not matter at this point Hai, just do what I ask.

"Mother I don't think that it is a good idea to bring that man into our home, he could be dangerous." Ming Su raised her voice, shocking her son considering that she is usually soft spoken. "Do as I ask Hai."

"Yes mother." Less than a moment later Yanyu walked into the living room. "Are you okay mother?" Ming Su looked at her daughter with a fake smile. "Yes Yanyu, I will be fine. Please sit. I have something that I must share with you." Yanyu walked up behind a wooden rocking chair, wrapping her fingers around the two outside pillars, lifting and maneuvering it over by her mother. She then sat and asked. "What is it Mother?" Ming Su let out a sigh through her nose as she tried to smile. "As you know I have traveled a great distance from my homeland to Idaho City. My journey was often stressful and tiring. I never knew from day to day if I would be abducted or dead come the next day. Many times I wish that your uncle and I had never left China and endured the suffering and turmoil that we had. Despite my arrival and settling in Idaho City it turned out to be a great blessing to have seen what I have and to have experienced what I had through my journey. It was hard on me as a young lady to want to accept the death of your Uncle Hai, my brother. I don't think that I had ever fully recovered from his death at such a young age for him and myself. He had such a great personality, he was loving and caring and as a brother he would do almost anything for me as he protected me from any and all danger. My mother died when I was less than ten years old. Our father gave up hope without her and I understand how he felt since your father had not returned to us in many years. There is something that I need to show you."

"What is it Mother?" Suddenly the outside door swung open. The cold blew into the house. Hai quickly entered, followed by a Chinese man on either side of Fong Yeo as they held him up. Ming Su struggled to keep her composure at the mere sight of her dying father. He walked with what little strength that he had. They followed Hai across the living room and into the spare bedroom and laid the Fong Yeo on the fresh white linen sheets. Ming Su instructed Hai to bring her chair into the room and set it by the window." Hai could not understand why his mother was so concerned about the old man who had nothing but the dirty clothes that reeked of body odor and campfire smoke but with a shrug of his shoulders he honored his mother's request.

Ming Su thanked the two Chinese men and asked that they leave as Hai placed the chair in front of the window. Ming Su said to Yanyu. "Please fetch me a bowl of soup broth with no meat of vegetables and Hai I need you to gather a set of warm trousers and a shirt from your wardrobe."

"You are going to give him my clothes mother?" Quickly Ming Su became irritated. "Do as I tell you without question. Why must you keep questioning my authority?"

"Yes Mother." Hai replied.

Ming Su closed the door behind her children and walked over to stand beside her father. He turned his head and looked up at her with his squinty eyes. He fumbled to say his first words to her. "Su? I have seen you many times, you have given me money to help me survive, you have sent food from your restaurant to feed me here and in Idaho City and now you bring me into your home. Why is it you do this? You owe me nothing. I am just a worthless old man who has nothing and nobody. You should just let me die in peace." Ming Su's eyes filled with tears as she struggled to maintain a straight face." She asked. "You are from a small town on the coast of China, are you not?"

"Yes I am." At that point Yanyu opened the bedroom door and entered with a warm bowl of soup broth and a silver spoon followed by Hai with a clean set of clothes. Ming Su took the bowl from her daughter and began to feed the broth to Fong Yeo. After a couple spoons full of broth Fong Yeo shook his head and said. "No more." Yanyu took the bowl from her mother and stepped back a step. Fong Yeo looked at Ming Su and said. "You remind me so much of my deceased wife of many years ago, Sing. We had two beautiful children together but I became stricken with the idea of becoming rich here in America." He began to sob. "I selfishly left my children behind to discover gold on my own and I never discovered gold and I never saw my children again." Yanyu stepped closer to her mother's side. She asked. "Mother?" Fong Yeo's eyes opened wide as he focus on the young woman. He sobbed as he said. "And you look so much like my precious Ming Su." Ming Su knelt down on the pine floor. Hai's mouth dropped in disbelief. He asked. "Who is this old man Mother?" Ming Su took the back of Fong Yeo's hand into hers and then placed something into his palm. Quickly Hai sighed as tears filled his eyes, wrapping his arm around Yanyu and pulling her closer to him. The children could not speak as Fong Yeo looked down at his hand to find a worn out, aged wooden horse. The old man took a quick deep breath and looked into Ming Su's tear filled eyes. "Where did you get this? I carved this for my daughter from Golden Larch. It was my gift to her when she turned ten." Ming Su just stared in his tired eyes. He asked as he choked. "Why are you torturing me?" Yanyu knelt down beside her mother and put her palm on the far side of Fong Yeo's face to softly pull it toward her. He looked into her eyes as she smiled. "Fong Yeo..." She closed her eyes, forcing tears to run down her cheeks. After reopening her eyes she whispered. "Grandfather, my mother... My mother is your daughter, Ming Su..." Fong Yeo slowly turned his head looking at Ming Su. A smile slowly developed on his face, his eyes filled with tears. Ming Su could no longer hide the truth any longer or keep her composure. She slowly wrapped her arm around her father and embraced him close. Hai's head dropped as he stepped forward and knelt down on the other side of his mother and placed his hand on her shoulder before placing his other hand on his grandfather's forearm. Fong Yeo looked at Hai. Ming Su whispered to him. "This is your first grandson Father, his name is Hai, just like my brother and your son. The old man began to cough and choke. Then he asked. "Where… Where is my son?" Ming Su looked at the crack in a pine plank within the wall and stated. "He was killed by a mountain lion Father, he was killed protecting me. He tried to keep me safe but met his demise by the spirit of the big cat." Fong Yeo let out a couple more coughs and asked. "What do you mean the spirit of the big cat?"

"Hai told me the story that you told him about the tiger and its worth. Hai and I killed the mighty tiger to sell for the money to pay our passage on the junk to come to America."

"I didn't know that. I am sorry for what I did. Not a day went by that I did not live through regret and even hatred for my selfishness and greed that was nothing more than a dream."

"Father, you must rest." Ming Su stood up, her children followed suit. Hai and Yanyu wrapped their arms around their mother and embraced her tight. Hai whispered "I understand now mother." Fong Yeo made a grunt sound catching the attention of his daughter and his grandchildren. They turned and looked down at the frail man lying on the white linen sheets. He reached his hand up. Ming Su placed hers into his before he lightly tugged on hers, encouraging her to bend down and place her ear close to his lips. He whispered. "Forgive me Ming Su." His head fell back and to the side as his eyes closed and his chest fell, forcing out his last breath. Ming Su's face turned to a frown as the tears fell like waterfalls from her eyes. She said. "I do Father, I always had. I have missed you and I love you."Yanyu and Hai embraced each other as the tears fell from their eyes.

A moment later as Ming Su felt obligated considering that the old man was her father. She told Hai to let the Sheriff know about his grandfather. He quickly embraced his mother then turned and left the room. Yanyu closed the door behind him and stood by the door. Ming

Su sat on the edge of the bed alongside her father, taking his lifeless hand into hers and whispering with pain in her tone. "I believe that you can still hear me Father. Please forgive me. It was my own bitterness and scarring that kept us apart all these years. I caused you to miss out on the welcoming of your grandchildren Hai and Yanyu. Yanyu is such a Beijing Jade. She is so much like her mother and Hai is so much like the man that I named him after.

In his middle 80's, Ming Su's father was buried in one of the biggest burial plots at the local cemetery in Idaho City. Many Chinese locals paid their respects after hearing about who he was, the father of a young traveler who became a Restaurant owner and the grandfather of Yanyu and Hai. Others showed anger toward Ming Su for waiting so long for her to recognize the old man for who he was, her father.

A couple days had passed after the burial of Fong Yeo. Hai and Yanyu developed a disconcerting attitude towards their mother. However, Ming Su was not the type of parent to allow such a negative sentiments from her children. She called Hai and Yanyu into the living room to sit in the light of the glowing embers of the fireplace. With Hai being the oldest by merely minutes he was the one always in charge of the two. Ming Su asked him. "What is this tension and disrespect that I am feeling from both of you?" Hai looked at Yanyu as she looked back at him. He then looked at his mother and snarled. "Mother Yanyu and I are feeling a little bit upset."

"Not at me. Did I do something wrong?"

"The truth is mother. For years Yanyu and I had brought food to Grandfather Fong Yeo. We treated him as a stranger as if we were better than him or he was not good enough for us because it was how you taught us to present ourselves to even our grandfather, your father who had the same blood running through his veins as you, Yanyu and I."

"Children, there is so much that you just don't know. Your grandfather, my father abandoned your Uncle Hai and myself, leaving us to fend for ourselves. Your Uncle Hai was only sixteen and I had just turned ten. We lived in a one room building that was about the size of one of the horse stables out back. Hai and I would have died in China of starvation if your crazy Uncle Hai didn't come up with the idea to kill the tiger on the mountain."

"Kill the tiger on the mountain. What are you talking about mother?" Ming Su chuckled. "I suppose it is time."

"Time for what?" Ming Su stood up and headed towards her bedroom. She reached inside her dresser drawer and pulled her necklace with the tiger claw on it out before re-entering the living room and handing it to Hai. "Try to understand children that it cost a lot of money to come to America. It cost a lot of money to purchase the supplies to travel from San Francisco to Idaho City. We knew Idaho City as Bannock Village but learned that it was actually Bannock City that was renamed Idaho City. Fong Yeo talked about the gold in Bannock City all the time, even when your grandmother was still alive but after she died Hai and I knew that father was going to come to America but we also thought that he was going to bring us with him. He left cowardly in the middle of the night without us knowing." Yanyu asked. "Do you still see him as a coward mother?" Ming Su slowly nodded many times. "Yes I do. I am not trying to be a hero but he would have died a long time ago if I didn't make sure that he ate and got shelter in Idaho City." Hai was getting aggravated. "Can you just tell us about the tiger mother?" Ming Su chuckled. "Your Uncle Hai came up with a crazy, I mean very crazy idea that your grandfather filled his head with. And I have no idea how I let him talk me into it. But we had to walk deep into the forest before it was even light outside. Once the mountain mist began to lift and the other animals were awake and looking for something to eat. Hai had me run down a trail that made a big circle back where he was. I had to yell and make noise to attract the tiger. When I attracted him, I knew it. I could feel the weight of the big cat as his huge paws pounded the ground while it chased me." Yanyu asked. "Where you scared?"

"Scared? That is not the word that I would use to describe how I felt. Terrified was more like it. I was running and running. Tears were running from my eyes because I thought I was going to be the tiger's breakfast. Your Uncle Hai instructed me to climb over the fallen tree and duck down on the other side and wait." Hai asked. "Wait? Wait for what?"

"I ducked down on the other side and waited for the tiger to jump over the fallen tree. Your Uncle Hai had planted a bunch of wooden spikes sticking up from the ground. I was never so terrified when I felt the weight of the tiger push down on the fallen tree but when it jumped it landed on two wooden spikes that pierced its body, almost instantly it died. I was so mad at your Uncle Hai but he said that it was the fastest way to make a large sum of money to be able to come to America on the junk. Yanyu asked. "Mother, what is a junk?"

"Oh, a junk is a Chinese word for ship or vessel that carries people across the ocean to America. It is like a big, big boat... So your Uncle Hai sold the tiger to a local shop owner for a lot of money. It was dark by the time that we got home and there was still so much to do, especially for your Uncle Hai. But the next day our long journey had just begun. We traveled many miles on foot. I had to cut my hair and dress like a boy so I wouldn't be abducted by the bad men that I called them but they wanted to take me and sell me into slavery." Hai asked. "So that is where the tiger claw came from on your necklace?"

"Yes, we kept two tiger claws and I made two necklaces, one for me and the other for your Uncle Hai."

"Mother, I heard you mention the spirit of the big cat to father. What exactly does that mean?"

"An elder Chinese woman that the Native Indians call Lost Doe presented an explanation for your Uncle Hai's death."

"Oh, I get it. Uncle Hai killed one big cat and its spirit entered another big cat like to avenge the tiger?"

"Something like that, but I don't believe in that stuff. It was just bad timing and a perfect opportunity for the mountain lion... When I got to Idaho City I eventually recognized your grandfather but I kept my distance. I was too hurt and disappointed because it was apparent that he failed altogether and if I hadn't come to America then he would have never seen me again or never had the chance to meet you two. I admit that I was wrong to not let you get to know him but you didn't know him, he would have come into our home and made it his. He could be sneaky and I believe that he would have searched the house for money. Try to understand that he was a traditional Chinese man that knew nothing but poverty. Us three have much of the American culture within us. I had to protect our family and our fortune. One day all my money will be split up between my two children, the house and the restaurant will also become yours but I believe if my father was in our life, we wouldn't have what we do today."

"Couldn't you have just given him some money and not let him into your home?"

"Lanying and I talked about that and decided to plant one thousand dollars in gold nuggets for him to find. We witnessed him finding it and he spent it the way that he saw fit."

The three of them sat in silence for a few moments. "Please understand that I loved my father but I wanted better for you than I ever had. I had to protect what I found otherwise you wouldn't live like you do now. Fong Yeo would have destroyed that."

Ming Su instructed. "Hai, I would like you to ride over to the Northwest Stage Line and see if we can reserve a stage for three days, going to and coming back from Idaho City." Yanyu responded. "Mother that is such a long ride to Idaho City and then back two days later. We just got back from Grandfather's burial."

"I know that it is a long ride Yanyu, but I feel that you and Hai should accompany me to the rabbit hole." Hai began to panic. "Mother that is where father came up missing, he just disappeared. Someone probably killed him. I don't want to die and I don't want you or Yanyu to die either."

"My son, Idaho City is a dead town now. There is barely one hundred people there. We already know that one of the hotels are still in operation. Armed escorts are usually on call and I will hire two and Mo will come with us too." Hai let out a long, loud sigh. "Okay mother, okay. I'll be back."

26

The Armed escorts rode their horses as Ming Su felt that it was adamant that her children and husband accompanied her on foot as Choy once did to understand what she endured each and every time that she traveled to the rabbit hole. Ming Su also made it clear that she would not tolerate any complaining or negative attitudes concerning the long walk or the purpose of being there. The wagon road that led to the rabbit hole looked as if it had not been traveled in years. It was evident by the tall dead grass that sprouted up in the previous years where the wagon wheels once rolled. Smaller trees had lost their rooting and fell across the road. Removal was quite easy for Hai, Mo and the two armed escorts. Nonetheless to the native wildlife they were considered intruders, a threat, possibly even predators. Squirrels and chipmunks shook their tails and carried on with a continuous annoying squeaks that echoed for what seemed like miles. The deer that was once fearless of the Idaho City inhabitants took to the deep forest almost at the instant sight of Ming Su and her party.

The walk was long and tedious. Three different conversations had sprung within the travelers. Ming Su and Mo led the expedition exchanging conversation about economics and medicine. The twins passed time by talking about the other kids at their school and the upcoming events that they were planning on participating in. The two armed escorts were obvious longtime friends who developed a trustworthy kinship between the two. There was a strong understanding that at any time, either or the two would proudly lay down his life for the other if their experience as sharp shooters had failed them.

Like anyone else they had first names that were not mentioned by either. One called the other McNerry. McNerry referred to his friend as Preacher. Preacher was by no means his name but his title from a life as a man who preached from the pulpit on Sundays until outlaws raped and killed his wife and robbed his two children of their lives as well.

Without warning Ming Su came to an abrupt stop. Her head dropped as she began to weep. Without hesitation her children rushed to her as Mo tried to comfort her just the same. Preacher took in a deep breath then said. "That boulder there is what you seek, is it not?" Ming Su looked at him and nodded her head. "Yes it is Preacher. I am having a hard time believing that such a beautiful place had been completely destroyed by the greedy and selfish people looking for their last chance to discover their fortune in gold." Yanyu asked. "Mother, no disrespect but isn't that what you did?"

"Absolutely not, my daughter. The last time that I mined here, I left no evidence that I had been here. I considered the beauty of nature. Look up on the hill. The vegetation had once been burned perhaps by lightning or an ember from somebodies tobacco. But what gave your father and I so much life looks like nothing less than death now." Hai stated. "Mother there are little saplings breaking the surface of the ground. Grass is making its way towards the sun. It will not always look like this. I promise that it will once again be the beautiful place with life." Ming Su stepped over to Hai and held his chin in the palm of her hand. "You are such a wise young man my son. Thank you!" Mo let out a breath through his nose. "If you would like dear, we can take those burlap bags on the ground and fill them with the empty whiskey bottles, broken tools, and the other debris that was left behind." Ming Su smiled as she nodded, encouraging everyone to gather the waste.

Hai discovered a rusty shovel that was left behind. He picked it up and slammed the blade into the ground. Mo took notice and began to cheer Hai on, and then Yanyu shared in the chanting. But when Hai's effort only revealed stones, pebbles, dead broken tree roots along with broken glass from whiskey bottles. Mo chuckled. "I need to find another shovel." Hai and Mo laughed and carried on as they dug for gold.

Yanyu grouched. "You're wasting your time, you are not going to find anymore gold." Suddenly Ming Su yelled. "Stop!" Instantly Mo and Hai stood up straight and looked at Ming Su. "Hai, Mo stop! I was obsessed with the money that came from countless of hours of digging up gold here. Your father Choy became even more obsessed with the gold that the soil produced. I will not allow you to dig another blade full of soil and watch either of you become another greedy and selfish gold seeker as your father and I. As horrible as it may seem, it will be a blessing to me, you and the future generations of our family that none of us shall ever, I mean ever return to this place again to seek gold. I chased down my father's dream. My loving brother died for me. My father died with more regret than a person should have to suffer. He died of shame, pity, worthlessness and alone." Hai replied. "Mother he didn't die alone, we were all there." Ming Su gave her son a look that put so much fear in his heart that he hoped that he would never see again. "I am sorry mother." Mo was afraid to look at his bride. Instead he stepped over to Hai and removed the shovel from his grasp before placing both shovels on the ground and picking up another whiskey bottle.

Not a word was said for a few moments as they tidied up the area. Suddenly Yanyu noticed a sparkle reflecting the sun and reached down to use her finger as to roll the remainder of it from beneath the soil, leaving her excited to have discovered a gold nugget about the size of a small grape. Her eyes stayed glued to the morsel of precious metal as she sat on a boulder to study every detail of it. However, nobody seemed to notice for a moment or two until Hai asked with a tone. "Are you planning on helping or are you going to just sit there and look at your fingers?" Yanyu twisted her body and held the pricey chunk of soft metal between her finger and thumb. Hai smiled and cried out." Yanyu found a piece of gold." Ming Su stood up straight and stared at her daughter's find with no expression on her face. Yanyu looked back as her smile slowly disappeared then looked at McNerry and Preacher who seemed to show excitement of her discovery. She looked at her brother's expressionless face and then at Mo who looked away. She nodded her head a few times as a big smile filled her face and stated.

"You know what mother? You are right. There is no reason for us to be here after today and I promise that we will never return to seek gold." Yanyu walked towards McNerry and Preacher and handed McNerry the precious nugget while stating. "Split this between you two, you were never here, neither were we." Ming Su smiled as she approached her daughter wrapping her arm around her. McNerry began to act panicked. "I don't want to be cursed." Preacher chuckled. "Partner, you are not going to be cursed. Consider it a bonus for our services or a gift from God, either way half of it is mine." The group shared in laughter.

The group finished gathering the odds and ends that were left by others, Hai asked. "Mother, how many times do you think that you came out to the rabbit hole?" Ming Su replied. "I think about fifteen to twenty-five times a year for about five or six years, I never thought about keeping track."

"Was there ever a time that you came all the way out her but didn't find any gold?"

"Hai, it wasn't like going fishing or hunting, it was more of an absolute than a chance. Every single time that I came out here I returned with gold, it may have only been a pound but most of the time three or four pounds and a couple times five to seven pounds."

"Wow mother that was a lot of gold."

"That it was Hai, that it was... The other thing was that I was always more careful and cautious heading back to town than I was coming out. I always had to deceive everyone into thinking that I was a boy first of all but other than that. Perhaps I was paranoid to feel this way but if I was to be abducted again and then searched. Any gold that I was carrying may have been discovered then I would be forced to explain where I got it. Therefore I usually carried the gold nuggets in my water canteen. I figured that it was the better and safest place if it was going to be on my person. There was also the issue of transporting five pound sacks of soil that I would leave inside the old stone foundation of a burned down cabin that would later be gathered up by Mr. Pfeiffer and transported down to the river."

"You mean that pastor man?"

"Yes, Pastor Jim Pfeiffer secretly worked for me panning for gold from the many, many five pound sacks of soil that I hid inside the old stone foundation. For his hard work I gave him 25% of the money from the exchange that the gold brought in from all the five pound sacks of soil, and believe me. He made out like a bandit in the night... Oh yeah! There was one other time that I came out here and returned with nothing but a headache."

"A headache?"

"Yes, I can't even think of her name though, but it will come to me. Oh yes, Nuying. She was the daughter of the Chinese Mercantile clerk that wanted to be my friend and the ignorant little girl followed me all the way out here."

"Then she found out about the rabbit hole?"

"Oh no, no, no. I knew that she was following me all along... Come on, I want to show you all something." The group followed Ming Su a little deeper into the forest, past the clearing that was well grown over with grass and other vegetation. Further up the wagon road, around the bend then she stopped. She explained to the group about the incident that Nuying forced her into. She pointed to the tree up on the left that she hid behind then pointed to the old rotted wagon that was upside down, lying against a tree. "I look back and it's hard to believe that it has been over twenty years since that day."

"What happened to that Jacob Murphy guy? Did he die from his injury?"

"No I didn't kill him and we were both lucky that I didn't. He may be dead by now but the last time that I saw him was a couple years later. He didn't act like he had all his horses pulling the stagecoach." She chuckled. "Try to understand that it is hard for me to have any sympathy for him or his family. Just think about what would have happened if I didn't escape from him, his brother and mother that day. You children wouldn't be my children. But then again perhaps the rabbit hole would still be just that, a rabbit hole. A person can go crazy thinking about what could have, would have or should have been... But looking back I wouldn't have it any other way... Maybe one day I will write a book but for now let's go home."

27

Years passed by for Ming Su. Her black hair found gray, her smooth skin was no longer smooth. Her body became frailer as her walk was slower. For a grandmother she couldn't have been more proud of her grandson when he decided to take up arms with the United States Government to fight in the Great War. Jian was a well-educated eighteen year old man in May of 1917 who was also very much in love with a local young woman whose father had found fortune panning for gold North of Idaho City. Sadie, like any other American born Chinese child grew to understand her culture and language but also learned the American culture and language as well.

Thirteen weeks of basic training earned Jian a one week leave before being deployed to France. However Jian felt that he had no time to waste. He returned home to Boise to spend 3 days with Sadie and his family. As many soldiers would, Jian asked Sadie to accept his hand in marriage and on his last day of his visit Sadie married Jian. The wedding was quick and small. Ming Su and Jian's mother Yanyu did not have a lot of time to plan the wedding but Sadie and Jian could not ask for more.

The stage coach was reserved for Jian and three other young men that were leaving Boise to go to France. A crowd stood around the stagecoach as the four young men expressed their goodbyes. Jian hugged and kissed his mother before bowing before his father then shaking his hand. He turned to his grandmother, Ming Su and held her tight a she fought to keep her composure. But last and definitely not least he stepped up to his new young bride. The sweet taste of her lips pressed against his had tasted like the sweet cherries that Sadie liked to eat. The scent of her perfume was nothing less than the best for her new husband to remember. The stagecoach driver hollered "Daylight is wasting, we must go." Jian's father opened the door to the stagecoach to allow the young soldiers to enter. Jian was the last since he could not let go of his young bride. He stood before his father and saluted him as an American soldier. Then turned and blew three kisses, one to his mother, second to his grandmother and the last and longest to his bride. He laughed and walked around his father who was still holding the door and then climbed up beside the driver of the stagecoach as he smiled at his grandmother, remembering a story that she once told him about his great Uncle Hai. Jian stood tall holding his hands on both sides of his mouth and yelled. "France, ready or not, here we come, yahoooo!" With a snap of the reins and a whistle, the team of six horses found their footing and pulled the stagecoach with ease down the dirt road. Jian turned and waved to his family as the other men hung their heads and arms out the windows waving back. In those moments Ming Su chuckled when she saw the craziness of her brother Hai riding away on the stagecoach. Sadie, Yanyu and Ming Su stood and watched until the cloud of dust settled back down to the ground and the stagecoach was out of view.

At the age of 84, Ming Su passed away of natural causes sleeping sound in her bed with an old hand carved wooden horse in her grasp, a fancy necklace around her neck with a tiger claw as its charm and her iconic smirk on her face. She was survived by two children, seven grands children and nine great grandchildren. Her last wish was to be buried in a marked grave on the hill above a boulder in the forest of Idaho City.

Perhaps if you are ever in Idaho City, Idaho and by some chance you are hiking on the right wagon road. Just maybe you will stumble upon a three foot tall stone monument at the top of a hill, right above the boulder that Ming Su chose to call the rabbit hole.

THE END

INSPIRATION

THE INSPIRATION TO WRITING MING SU, A DAUGHTER'S JOURNEY

I would like to thank you for reading Ming Su. It was a great pleasure writing this story. I am an artist of many mediums. I have found inspiration by things that I have seen, heard or even smelt. Inspiration may even come from something that I saw on television and even in a dream. But never in a million years would I think that my inspiration would come from a report that my youngest daughter made me aware of at bedtime the night before it was due. I knew that in less than eight hours I had to get up to go to work. However, like most dads I wanted my 13 year old daughter to be successful in school and everything else that she did so she would be successful out in life.

I admit, I was a little bit unsettled and grumpy from the long day and one more still to come, since it was Thursday night. Needless to say, I grabbed my laptop because I knew that I could type faster than my daughter. I asked Andria what she wanted to write about. She explained to me that it had to be a story of something that could have happened in Idaho City, Idaho, where we lived at the time, but somewhere in history. She already had a character in mind, a young Chinese girl who discovers gold during the Gold Rush in 1863. In about three hours we had created a mini story that Andria called "Ming Su". I was so impressed by the story that daughter and father put together with a little help from mom and I decided that I would like to take Ming Su to the next level and expand on the story more in depth and detail as my second published novel. Nonetheless, I got started, but I didn't rush it. My daughter had her own teenage interests, she had little interest in co-writing Ming Su but her personality, character and the person that she is, inspired me along the way. Although Ming Su is purely fictional, she exists in my heart greatly. I laughed with her. I felt her pain and her fears. I understood her triumphs and her failures. And a lot of her character I wrote based on my daughter Andria. If you can't tell, I am a proud dad. However, there is nothing I would change about Ming Su's character or personality. Therefor I cannot take credit for the Ming Su's character, or personality but I am so proud to dedicate this novel, Ming Su, A Father's Journey to my daughter, Andria Lee.

-DISCLAIMER-

ALL CHARACTERS, PLACES AND EVENTS IN THIS NOVEL. EVEN THOSE BASED ON REAL PEOPLE AND/OR REAL PLACES ARE ENTIRELY FICTIONAL. ANY RESEMBLANCE OR SIMILARITIES TO ANY PERSON, PLACE OR EVENT, WHETHER EXISTING AT ONE TIME OR ANOTHER, LIVING OR DEAD IS ENTIRELY COINCIDENTAL.

Also by Danel / Dan Lee, look for HIGHWAY DISCIPLE where you purchase or order books.

Inspired by True Experiences:

Take a ride on this inspirational journey from hopelessness to redemption with the Outlaw Motorcycle Club Member, Lenny Richardson. Through a series of life-threatening events that transpired on his motorcycle journey from Phoenix, Arizona, to Treasure Valley, Idaho. A traveling minister helped Lenny discover a way to put his dreadful life and sinful past behind him and to rethink his destiny by using his motorcycle as a tool to disciple to the rest of the world. But positive changes in his life would not come without resistance from the outlaw club Lost Rabbles, law enforcement, and the new people that he meets, and not even his faith in Jesus would be able to stop the grave threat that continued to pursue him... Dan Lee

www.ingramcontent.com/pod-product-compliance
Lightning Source LLC
LaVergne TN
LVHW041702060526
838201LV00043B/535